TWAYNE'S WORLD AUTHORS SERIES

A Survey of the World's Literature

THE NETHERLANDS

Egbert Krispyn, University of Georgia

EDITOR

Daniel Heinsius

TWAS 477

Daniel Heinsius
ca. 1645

by Jacob van der Merck
Amsterdam University

DANIEL HEINSIUS

By BAERBEL BECKER-CANTARINO

University of Texas

TWAYNE PUBLISHERS

A DIVISION OF G. K. HALL & CO., BOSTON

Library of Congress Cataloging in Publication Data

Becker-Cantarino, Bärbel.
  Daniel Heinsius.

  (Twayne's world authors series ; TWAS 477 :
The Netherlands)
  Bibliography: p. 171–76
  Includes index.
  1. Heinsius, Daniel, 1580–1655—Criticism
and interpretation.
PT5659.H46Z58   801'.95'0924   77-26238
ISBN 0-8057-6318-X

Contents

About the Author

Baerbel Becker-Cantarino is presently Associate Professor of German at the University of Texas at Austin. Her edition of Daniel Heinsius' *Nederduytsche Poemata* (1616) is appearing as No. 31 of the *Nachdrucke Deutscher Literatur des 17. Jahrhunderts* (Berne: Lang, 1978). She has published articles on Martin Opitz, Neo-Latin poetry and on other aspects of seventeenth and eighteenth-century German and comparative literature, which have appeared in, among other journals, the *Zeitschrift für deutsche Philologie, Deutsche Vierteljahrsschrift, Jahrbuch des Freien Deutschen Hochstifts, Daphnis, Colloquia Germanica, The German Quarterly* and in the *Revista Hispánica Moderna.*

Preface

Humanist and classical scholar, poet and literary critic, professor and librarian, Daniel Heinsius, one of the foremost men of letters of his time, experienced his most productive years on the eve of the Golden Age of Dutch literature. Today his scholarly and literary works are often mentioned but little known, primarily because many of his finest achievements are in Latin, unavailable in suitable editions, and because of his participation in the Synod of Dort and his quarrel with Salmasius. This may explain why my study is the first devoted to his major literary works. A comprehensive presentation of all his publications would by far exceed the concise format of this series, and specialized articles can deal with some works of lesser interest. Moreover, Heinsius' *Nederduytsche Poemata* (1616) will become available in an edition prepared simultaneously with this monograph.

My study proceeds from a description within the literary tradition and the age to a critical analysis and interpretation of Heinsius' Dutch and Latin poetry, dramas, and work on tragedy. While his Dutch poetry has been considered mostly from the point of view of bibliographical detail and its reception, and while his Latin poetry has remained almost untouched since Georg Ellinger's work, I hope to bring together his Dutch and Latin works and give special attention to their literary significance. In contrast to the lively and fruitful discussion of *De tragoediae constitutione* by Paul R. Sellin and J. H. Meter, the Latin dramas and *De contemptu mortis* have previously been relatively ignored. Due to the formal limitations imposed by this series, a study of Heinsius' extensive prose work, orations, invectives, philological and theological writings could not be included here.

My research on Daniel Heinsius would not have been possible without the discovery that the Humanities Research Center of The University of Texas at Austin contained in its Parson's Collection some two thousand volumes of Netherlandic publications from around 1550 to 1650 including nearly all of Heinsius' Latin works. I am grateful for financial support from the University Research Institute of The University of Texas; for the kind cooperation of Kathleen Blow and Elaine Albin of the library at Austin, and the librarians at Leiden, Wolfenbüttel and Göttingen, and for the help of Christina Ahrendt and Jeanne Redrow Willson in preparing the manuscript.

My sincere thanks go to my colleagues George Schulz-Behrend and Vicente Cantarino and to Professor Paul R. Sellin of the University of California, Los Angeles, for their assistance, advice, and encouragement.

BAERBEL BECKER-CANTARINO

University of Texas

Chronology

1604   Janus Dousa dies.

1605   Is appointed Professor Extraordinarius of Greek.

1606   *Spiegel vande doorluchtige vrouwen* (Mirror of Illustrious
        Women) published under his pseudonym; *Poematum nova
        editio* appears.

1607   Is appointed university librarian upon Scaliger's recom-
        mendation.

1609   Scaliger dies, Heinsius holds funeral oration.

1609–   Twelve Years' Truce with Spain.
1621

1610   Becomes secretary of the Academic Senate.

1611   Edition of Aristotle's *Poetics* of 1610 appears with treatise on
        tragedy appended; revised in 1643 as *De tragoediae con-
        stitutione* (On Plot in Tragedy).

1612   Treatise on satire, *De satyra Horatiana*, is published with his
        annotated Horace edition of 1610. Is appointed Professor of
        History and Politics, most prestigious chair at Leiden outside
        of theology.

1613   His Greek poetry and the important 4th revised edition of his
        Latin poetry appears; new emblem series "Het ambacht van
        Cupido" (The Trades of Cupid) is published under his
        pseudonym.

1616   *Nederduytsche Poemata* (Dutch Poems) published by Petrus
        Scriverius, containing *Lof-sanck van Bacchus* (Bacchus
        Hymn); *Lof-sanck van Jesus Christus* (Christ Hymn) appears
        separately later that year.

1617   Is appointed Historiographer Royal to Gustavus Adolphus;
        marries Ermgard Rutgers.

1618   Terence edition, with an essay on Plautus and Terence.

1618–   Serves as secretary of the Lay Commissioners at the Synod of
1619   Dort (November-May).

1619   Oldenbarnevelt is executed.

1620   Son Nicolaas, later a distinguished latinist, is born; *Acta* of
        the Synod of Dort, prepared by Heinsius, are published.

1621   *De contemptu mortis* (On Contempt of Death) and the 6th
        and most important revision of his Latin poetry is published;
        joint edition with Scriverius of Seneca's tragedies with notes;
        edition of Aristotle's *Politics*.

1625   Sudden death of his brother-in-law Janus Rutgers, Swedish
        ambassador to the Dutch Republic; Prince Maurice dies.

1627 Is appointed historiographer of the Province of Holland and West-Friesland by the university to prevent him from accepting an invitation to Stockholm; publishes *Aristarchus sacer*, annotated edition of Nonnus' paraphrase of St. John's Gospel, and the letters of Scaliger.

1629 Publishes the famous Elzevier Horace (with the final version of *De satyra*) and the works of Ovid.

1631 Claudius Salmasius receives a privileged appointment at Leiden (until 1650); beginning of constant animosities between Salmasius and Heinsius.

1632 Verse drama *Herodes infanticida* (Herod, Child Murderer) and a panegyric for Gustavus Adolphus upon his death.

1636 Edition of Erasmus' *Colloquia;* publishes *Epistola* in response to De Balzac's criticism of the Herod drama.

1639 Publishes textual commentary to the entire New Testament, *Sacrarum exercitationum ad Novum Testamentum,* considered by Heinsius his most important scholarly contribution.

1648 Peace of Münster is signed between Spain and the Dutch Republic; Heinsius receives temporary dispensation from teaching which he never resumes.

1649 Final edition of Latin and Greek poetry prepared by son Nicolaas.

1650 Last edition of Dutch poetry.

1653 Is relieved of his position as Keeper of the Library.

1654 Is replaced as secretary of the Senate due to illness.

1655 Dies on February 26.

CHAPTER 1

Life and Letters at Leiden

W HEN Daniel Heinsius was born, the seventeen provinces called the Low Countries were engaged in their fight for independence from Spain. The struggle against the Spanish attempt to incorporate the Netherlands securely into its empire had been heightened by religious differences; for the northern provinces were mostly protestant. The Heinsius family was uprooted by the political and religious turmoil. Daniel Heinsius was born on June 9, 1580[1] in the short-lived Calvinist Republic of Ghent, the son of Flemish protestants, who both came from well-to-do and distinguished families. His father was clerk to the Council of Flanders. On his mother's side, his uncle and godfather Daniel Burchgrave was close to the Prince of Orange and influential in Dutch politics as the secretary to the earl of Leicester from 1586 to 1588 during the English intervention for the Dutch Republic, after which he followed the earl to England.[2]

In September 1584 the Spanish army under Alessandro Farnese, the nephew of Philip II and governor of the Netherlands since 1578, advanced through Flanders and Brabant in order to return the rebel provinces to Spanish rule, and Ghent surrendered. In 1583 the Heinsius family had already moved to the North to relatives in Zeeland, then they went to England (Dover and London) for a few months, from there to Rijswijk near The Hague, and in 1588 to Vlissingen which had been surrendered to the British as security for payment of the expenses of Leicester's military expedition. Many Flemish protestants fled to the North before the Spanish forces; they were mostly educated and well-to-do, energetic and capable people who quickly gained influential positions. Their strong patriotic, anti-Spanish and anti-Catholic feelings helped shape the developments in the Dutch Republic in the North. Because they were supporters of Leicester and favored military reprisals against the

South, they were increasingly distrusted after Leicester's departure and were removed from important offices. Heinsius never mentioned the political activities of his family after 1588 but always referred to himself as the exile from Ghent who was driven from his native city by unfortunate circumstances. Any bitterness, however, over this fate gave way to gratefulness for his new homeland in the North.[3]

After receiving his basic education at the Latin School at Vlissingen, Heinsius was sent in 1596 to study law at Franeker Academy, where Descartes was later to study. Franeker was then only a young school of little reputation with mostly orthodox Calvinist teachers, but here he went to school with sons of other Flemish refugees. He developed an interest in classical literature, spending more time on Greek, Latin, and the writing of Latin verses than on the study of law. In 1598 he matriculated at the University of Leiden, where he was fascinated above all by classical studies, ancient philosophy, and theology. But he disliked law. His father, who had long ago destined him for the legal profession, recalled him. However, probably because of the interest shown in him by the great scholar Joseph Scaliger,[4] his father finally acknowledged Daniel's exceptional talent for classical languages; and in October 1600 Daniel was allowed to return to Leiden where he was to spend the rest of his life and achieve international fame as one of the outstanding classical scholars of his age.

The University of Leiden had been founded in 1575 by the estates of Holland and Zeeland only a few months after the triumphal relief of Leiden from the long siege by the Spanish.[5] By 1600 it had already acquired a faculty of international reputation and was soon to become the leading protestant university in Europe. Calvinism had always encouraged education; and because of the tradition of humanistic learning and practical toleration, the university curators (three trustees appointed by the estates of Holland and four annually appointed burgomasters of Leiden) were able to attract famous scholars. Among them were the neo-Stoic philosopher Justus Lipsius in 1579; the literary critic, famous classicist, and Neo-Latin poet from France, Joseph Justus Scaliger in 1592; and later the French Huguenot philologist Salmasius in 1631. Under Scaliger classical scholarship was emancipated from the domination of philosophy; Lipsius' lectures on Tacitus were instrumental in making history into a respected subject. Furthermore, the subjects of the old *trivium* (grammar, rhetoric, dialectic) evolved from an ancillary position as the first required course in the Faculty of Arts into independent disciplines. Although divinity was the most important faculty, it never dominated humanistic learning and scholarship. In contrast to her Catholic rival Louvain University, the University of Leiden appointed professors and accepted students requiring only that they obey university statutes.[6] Foreign students constituted from one third to one half of the enrollment (about 440 annually between 1635 and 1650) during the first half of the seventeenth century, with the largest number coming from Germany, England, France, and Scandinavia. Many of them became scholars, and by reason of their birth and ability they were destined to play important roles in their own countries after having encountered the considerable freedom, prosperity, and learning in the Dutch Republic. It was freedom that attracted students and professors to Holland, as Salmasius admitted: "Surtout la liberté. Nostre France n'est plus France pour ce subject."[7]

During this period of intellectual and physical growth of the University of Leiden, Daniel Heinsius established himself as a scholar, outstanding teacher, and poet. His career as a classical scholar began in 1600 with an edition of Silius Italicus; and numerous editions, commentaries, and Latin translations of Greek texts were to follow including among other authors Aristotle, Hesiod, Horace, Maximus Tyrius, Ovid, Seneca, Terence, Theocritus, and Vergil.[8] Heinsius' command of Latin and Greek, and his knowledge of classical literature had immediately attracted the attention of the Flemish professor of classics, Bonaventura Vulcanius,[9] and even more important of Joseph Scaliger, whose favorite disciple he was to become. His attractive personality, elegant speech and appearance, and brilliant intellectual talents quickly gained Heinsius the friendship and admiration of Scaliger, "whom he visited daily reading to him whatever he had written, and who listened with great pleasure."[10] Thus Heinsius entered the circle of outstanding young men who had gathered around Scaliger: among them Petrus Scriverius, poet and historian, who later edited Heinsius' Dutch poems; Janus Rutgers, later a Swedish ambassador and Heinsius' brother-in-law; and the child prodigy, poet, jurist, and scholar, Hugo Grotius. Heinsius soon established himself as a patriotic and scholarly writer. He gained the admiration of the nobleman-poet, Janus Dousa, who had defended Leiden during the Spanish siege, had become a founder and was then a curator of the university; and of the diplomat-poet Marnix van St. Aldegonde, the last burgomaster of Antwerp before it fell to the Spanish. In 1602 Heinsius published *Auriacus*, a Senecan tragedy in Latin verses dealing with the assassination of William the Silent in 1584. It was publicly performed in the Leiden city hall to wide acclaim by his learned contemporaries and influenced the development of Neo-Latin and Dutch tragedy. His first collection of Latin poetry appeared in 1603 and underwent extensive revisions and additions in 1606, 1610, 1613, and 1617 before its most important edition in 1621, of which the final revision prepared by his son Nicolaas appeared in 1649.

With this abundance of highly acclaimed scholarly and literary publications it was small wonder that Heinsius advanced quickly in his university career although he never acquired an official academic degree. Upon Dousa's recommendation, he was granted the permission to lecture in 1602. In the philosophical auditorium he delivered a public lecture on Horace with such success that, though still a student, he was awarded a fee for it. In May of 1603 he received the appointment of Extraordinary Professor of Poetry (Greek and Latin). Many students attended his classes because he was an exciting lecturer and a stimulating teacher. He was kept busy giving as many as one public lecture and three private readings a day, covering such authors as Aristophanes, Hesiod, and Callimachus, which were not widely studied at the time. That same year, since the plague was raging in Leiden and the appointment of the controversial theologian Jacob Arminius as professor of theology had caused some unrest, Heinsius deliberated seriously on whether to accept an invitation to Paris proposed by the French Ambassador. Though the eminent scholar Isaac Casaubon encouraged him, Scaliger's advice and a substantial raise in salary made him stay in Leiden.

The prominence of the University of Leiden and the scholarly productivity of Heinsius would not have reached such heights without the printing industry in the Dutch Republic. An almost complete freedom from censorship for authors and printers resulted in a flourishing book trade in Holland whose production was mostly sold in other countries. In Leiden alone there were sixty-one presses recorded between 1600 and 1624. They printed primarily books for scholars and the learned reading public, and often their texts were more accurate and on better quality paper with superior type than elsewhere. Heinsius became especially closely associated with two famous presses in Leiden. The Officina Plantiniana, a branch of the Antwerp office, was the official university press owned by Flemish-born Franciscus Raphelengius,[11] in whose house Heinsius lived intermittently from 1600 to about 1608. Scaliger's works printed in the Netherlands appeared mostly at Plantin's in Leiden; Heinsius' first scholarly works and many later ones appeared there until it closed in 1619.

The most important Dutch printing house was the Elzevier Press at Leiden which had its shop in the university square.[12] Founded by refugees from Antwerp, the press maintained strong business relations with the South. Besides the typographical artistry which they had perfected in the first half of the seventeenth century, their introduction of inexpensive scholarly editions in a pocket size (duodecimo) with clear type and quality paper represented an important innovation in the book trade because this allowed the educated to afford, carry, and read with ease the majority of books. Heinsius was closely associated with the Elzeviers throughout his academic career, advising them on publications, writing introductions (many unsigned) to numerous classical editions, and publishing most of his Latin works with them.

In 1605 the curators lauded his excellence and industry and promoted him to Extraordinary Professor of Greek with a comfortable salary; upon Scaliger's recommendation he received the position of university librarian in 1607 which he held until 1653. He substantially increased the Leiden collections during the next decade, also repeatedly revising the catalogue—in 1612, 1623, and 1640. But after 1620 he seems to have encountered increasing opposition from the curators which, together with his active scholarly life, led to reduced effectiveness as a librarian in later years.[13] Soon Heinsius was asked to help Vulcanius, the blind and aging professor of Greek, in his duties as secretary to the Senate; he himself had become a voting member and officially the secretary by 1610. For the next forty years the "luminary of the illustrious Leiden Academy" was to serve the university in these distinguished positions.

Upon Scaliger's death in 1609 it was Daniel Heinsius who held the official funeral oration and who was appointed as the literary executor of Scaliger's manuscripts. Shortly before his death Scaliger asked Heinsius to select some books from his famous library for himself. The bulk of the library was willed to the university and the rest auctioned off. Heinsius was also to edit unfinished works by Scaliger,[14] which meant renewed intensive philological activity. He had turned to Aristotle and the study of tragedy, in 1611 a Seneca edition and his treatise *De tragoediae constitutione* (On Plot in Tragedy), which he appended to his edition of Aristotle's *Poetics*, appeared. In 1612 his observations on satire, *De satyra Horatiana*, introduced his earlier annotated Horace edition of 1610. In recognition of Heinsius' international reputation as a prolific classical scholar, the university promoted him to the prestigious chair of Professor of Politics and History later in 1612.

Besides his demanding work as professor, librarian, and secretary to the academic Senate, besides his scholarly and literary publications, Heinsius found time to write poetry in Dutch, a playful pastime which nevertheless produced some remarkable poems in a period when the vernacular language was rated second to Latin, the language of learning. Under the pseudonym Theocritus à Ganda (Theocritus from Ghent, Theocritus being the Greek name for Hebrew Daniel and also referring to the Greek poet of pastoral verses during the third century B.C.), Heinsius had written Dutch poems for a collection of love emblems as early as 1601. Several enlarged editions and reprints followed. Not until 1616 did Heinsius' friend and colleague Petrus Scriverius collect and edit these and his other Dutch verses as *Nederduytsche Poemata*, a sizable volume which provided a model literary language, imagery, and topics for the poets in Holland and Germany at the beginning of the seventeenth century.

Heinsius' brilliant career was paralleled by the consolidation and growing prosperity of the Dutch Republic. By 1596 *de facto* recognition of Dutch independence had come from France and England. Under the military leadership of Maurice, William the Silent's second son, the old territories north of the Rhine and Meuse rivers were firmly in the hands of the Dutch who had resigned themselves to the fact that the South remained Catholic. Meanwhile their easy access to the sea had brought the Dutch maritime superiority and the leading role in world trade, as was evident from their unequaled economic development. In 1609 Oldenbarnevelt, grand pensionary of Holland and the political leader of the republic, at last concluded the Twelve Year's Truce with Spain, a period during which domestic religious conflicts shook the young republic.

Heinsius was to witness this theological confrontation with politi-

cal dimensions at the Synod of Dort. Insisting on an orthodox interpretation of the Calvinist dogma of predestination, Franciscus
Gomarus, a professor at Leiden from 1594 to 1611, had attacked the
views of his colleague Jacobus Arminius (at Leiden from 1603 to
1609) who had taken a moderate stand on predestination. This
gradually forced the entire church, which as yet represented only a
minority of the Dutch population, to take sides. When mediation by
the estates of Holland, many of which did not belong to the Calvinist
Church, failed, they supported the more tolerant Arminian minority. In 1610, the Arminians addressed a "remonstrance," an appeal
for help to the estates of Holland after which they were called
Remonstrants, while the Gomarists were referred to as Counter-
Remonstrants. By 1617 Prince Maurice openly supported the Gomarists although he was not really interested in the theological is-
sue. The majority of the States General and Amsterdam followed
him while Oldenbarnevelt and the majority of the estates of Holland
supported the Remonstrants. A national synod convened at Dort
from November 1618 to May 1619 and as expected condemned the
Arminian doctrine. The political confrontation ended with the arrest
of the Arminian leaders: Hugo Grotius was sentenced to a long
prison term but escaped through his wife's cunning in 1623. Oldenbarnevelt was executed in May of 1619, while other leading Remonstrants found refuge in Antwerp; Maurice remained in control
until his death in 1625. Internal strife again became secondary to the
struggle with Spain in 1621 when the truce ended and the Thirty
Years' War in Germany complicated the situation on the continent.

During the decade of the controversy of the Remonstrants, religious and political problems assumed a greater importance for
Heinsius than before. An adherent of the orthodox, Gomarist
dogma, he had deplored as early as 1603 the appointment of Arminius to the faculty of Leiden although he remained a good friend
of Hugo Grotius and other Arminians until the Synod of Dort. In
1617 his marriage to Ermgard Rutgers, the niece of Hugo Muys van
Holy, Prince Maurice's favorite, aligned him with a powerful Orangist family and outspoken opponents of the Arminians and Oldenbarnevelt. He accepted the post of secretary to the Lay Commissioners
at the Synod of Dort, the gathering of leading theologians from the
Reformed Church of Europe, which had been called by the States
General. Almost as many foreign delegates as Dutch ones—all
orthodox—participated with full voting rights. Eighteen Lay Com-

missioners were appointed by the States General to carry out the orders of the states. Heinsius' duties consisted in translation and explanation of pertinent transactions under discussion and communicating decisions to, and mediating between, the commissioners and eminent theologians from abroad. Most important, he revised the synodal articles and produced the definitive versions of the resolutions in the spring of 1619 after the close of the synod. With his versatility in languages and administrative matters Heinsius carried out his duties, which were secretarial rather than policy-making, with great ability. He adhered to his orthodox convictions, although he was accused of having deserted his Remonstrant friends such as Hugo Grotius when their political fortunes were shattered.[15]

During these years Heinsius turned away from the love poetry of his youth to philosophical, religious, and scholarly topics. A renewed interest in Stoic philosophy with an eminently Christian outlook is evident in his funeral oration for professor of medicine Reinerus Bontius in 1623 and in his finest didactic poem, *De contemptu mortis* (On Contempt of Death), of 1621. In a biting satire *Cras credo, hodie nihil* (I'll Believe You Tomorrow, Not Today), also of 1621, he derided his Remonstrant detractors and in 1622 a popular prose encomium *Laus asini* (Praise of the Ass) followed. The next fifteen years he devoted primarily to the study of the New Testament. In 1627 he brought out a large edition with commentary of Nonnus' paraphrase of the Gospel according to St. John, entitled *Aristarchus sacer*, in which Heinsius considered Nonnus as a poet and as interpreter of John. Soon afterwards he began to work on a textual commentary of the entire New Testament, a line-by-line philological (not theological) explication including the Semitic texts, the Septuagint, ancient commentaries, and patristic literature; this work finally appeared in 1639 in a folio volume of around 650 pages as *Sacrarum exercitationum ad Novum Testamentum* (Sacred Annotations on the New Testament).[16]

His marriage in 1617 had brought him into a close, but frustrating, relationship with the Swedish crown. His brother-in-law, Janus Rutgers, had been appointed to the Swedish Council of State in 1614 and served on diplomatic missions for Sweden in the Dutch Republic. Heinsius was appointed Court Historian to Gustavus Adolphus; but since he never received access to official documents he was not able to write the official history; nor did he receive his promised salary or any other stipend. Rutgers' unexpected death in 1625 brought Heinsius into embarrassing difficulties: As the sole heir to his brother-in-law, he loyally turned over the confidential diplomatic papers to the next Swedish ambassador, assumed the expenses for the state funeral, maintained the Swedish embassy for six weeks, and even performed some diplomatic duties. He was never remunerated for these services, nor were Rutgers' sizable loans to Swedish merchants and nobles ever repaid in spite of constant promises and numerous petitions by Heinsius and later by his son Nicolaas. In 1627 Heinsius seems to have seriously considered an invitation to go to Sweden; the curators of the university compensated him with an appointment as official historiographer of Holland and West-Friesland and a salary increase to make up for the Swedish promises. Yet as late as 1649 he toyed with the idea of accepting an invitation to teach at Stockholm proffered by Queen Christina, for whom his gifted son Nicolaas worked as librarian of rare manuscripts from 1649 to 1655.[17]

In 1631 the famous French philologist, Claudius Salmasius (1588–1653), accepted a privileged position at Leiden as the successor to the chair Scaliger had held. Exempted from teaching, he was placed in rank and salary above all other scholars. A continuous bitter animosity developed between him and Heinsius, who seems to have opposed the appointment, partly due to Salmasius' egocentric vanity and quarrelsomeness and Heinsius' irreconcilably hurt pride and ambition.[18] Polemics between scholars were the order of the day, but the aging Heinsius was mostly on the defensive, watching his life's work viciously destroyed by his opponent; posterity, too, often sided with Salmasius. One of the many and often trifling issues in this controversy was Heinsius' last creative work, the Latin tragedy *Herodes infanticida* (Herod, Child Murderer) of 1632. This influential and widely read work had been severely criticized by Salmasius' Paris friend, De Balzac, who ridiculed its mixture of Christian and pagan elements. But the theological or philological disputes of Heinsius' later years yielded no intellectual results, serving mostly as an outlet for the querulous predisposition of the scholars involved.

Besides this bitter and lengthy quarrel, recurring illnesses overshadowed Heinsius' last years and impeded his activities and publications which virtually ceased after 1647 when he was excused from teaching. His wife had died in 1633 and his only sister had then taken care of the household until her death in 1646. His daughter (born in 1623) was married to the jurist Goesius; his son Nicolaas became a distinguished Latin scholar and poet who had many friends all over Europe and traveled constantly. Heinsius' last work, a panegyric on the peace between Philip IV and the Dutch, celebrated the final recognition of the Dutch Republic at the Peace of Münster in 1648. Thereafter his health, mind, and appearance deteriorated drastically. Towards the end of 1654 Heinsius was confined to bed without hope for recovery, and he died on February 25, 1656. The greater part of Heinsius' private library, the catalogue of which contained over four thousand volumes, was publicly auctioned off later that year. In the funeral oration his colleague and successor as librarian, Antonius Thysius, praised Heinsius' "genius in teaching, an unbelievable eloquence and sparkling ardour in oratory,"[19] while the scholarly world deplored the loss of one of the outstanding writers of the century.

CHAPTER 2

The Nederduytsche Poemata

I *Renaissance Poetry in the Netherlands*

T HE publication of Daniel Heinsius' collection of Dutch poetry
in 1616 was a genuine landmark for the literature of the
Netherlands. Martin Opitz, his admiring disciple, praised the poet
for using his mother tongue and thus reviving "Germanic" poetry:

> Die Teutsche Poesy war gantz vnd gar verlohren,
> . . . . Wir redten gut Latein,
> Und wollte keiner nicht für Teutsch gescholten sein.
> . . . . Ihr habt sie recht verlacht,
> Vnd vnsre Muttersprach in jhren werth gebracht.[1]

(German poetry had completely perished, . . . we spoke Latin well and
nobody wanted to be called a German. . . . You laughed at them rightly and
restored the esteem for our native tongue.)

Leiden, which had become the citadel of humanist scholarship and
thought by the turn of the century because of Scaliger, was now
regarded as an important center of poetry in the vernacular because
of Heinsius. Exaggerated as Opitz' praise may seem, there was
substance to his view. With the Dutch verses of the Swan from
Ghent, as Heinsius was often called, Renaissance poetry had received a decisively new stimulus in the Netherlands.

The transition from medieval to Renaissance poetry[2] was more a
break in tradition in the Germanic lands than in the Romance countries because it involved a complete change of verse rhythm: a
change from poetry based on the principle of stress to syllabic verse.
In the sixteenth century a distinction was made between *Rhetorica*
and *Poësie*. The former referred to the *rederijker* verse used by the
poets of the Chambers of Rhetoric, which was mostly a long four-
beat line with an indefinite number of unstressed syllables, then

somewhat shortened after about 1550. *Poësie* was written in the new meters taken over from France, from Ronsard and other poets of the *Pléiade;* they were the alexandrine and *vers commun* with a strong tendency towards the regular alternation of stressed and unstressed syllables of the iambic meter.

Two geographically separated groups of poets existed. In the South there were the painter-poet Lucas de Heere (1534–1584) who introduced poetic forms of the Renaissance into Dutch literature in his *Den Hof en Boomgaard der Poësien* (The Garden and Orchard of Poetry, 1565); the fervent Calvinist and critic of the Roman Catholic Church, Marnix van St. Aldegonde (1540–1598), who like De Heere translated from the Psalms; and Jan van der Noot (1539–ca. 1595) from Antwerp who abandoned the *rederijker* manner and based the rhythmical pattern of his verse on Ronsard and the poetry of the *Pléiade*. The southern group was dispersed by the onset of the war and the persecutions under the Duke of Alba. In the North a group had formed around Janus Dousa (Johan van der Does, 1545–1604). Here Renaissance poetry, written mostly for friends and fellow poets and circulated in manuscript form, was developed during the patriotic movement by Dousa's group which was later to lay the foundation for the Dutch poetry of the Golden Age.

Janus Dousa the Elder, the famous Latin poet, historian, and governor of the university, had gone to Paris in 1564 after studying at Louvain and Douai; he became a pupil of Dorat, was acquainted with Ronsard, and with other poets of the *Pléiade* and with one of the foremost Neo-Latin poets, George Buchanan, an emigrant from Scotland. After successfully defending Leiden against the Spanish siege in 1574, Dousa played a key role in the establishment of Leiden University. He visited England frequently, in 1585 on diplomatic business, and in turn in 1586 Sir Philip Sidney came to Holland accompanying Leicester.[3] After his appointment to the supreme court, Dousa moved to The Hague in 1593. At one time or another his circle included such eminent scholars as Justus Lipsius, Dominicus Baudius, Janus Gruterus, and poets like the Leiden Town Secretary Jan van Hout (1542–1609) and Hendrik Laurenszoon Spiegel (1549–1612) whose *Hertspieghel* (Mirror of the Heart, completed ca. 1600 and published only in 1614) employed alexandrines with an iambic character. During the last quarter of the sixteenth century a vast amount of poetry in Dutch was written by Van Hout and Dousa, though only very little has survived: religious poetry and verses in classical forms as well as translations from Petrarch and Horace and from the Dutch Neo-Latin poet Janus Secundus and others. Most of these efforts existed only in manuscript form. They were circulated among friends or entered in an *album amicorum* (poesy album), and some appeared together with other works, as did four poems by Van Hout and Gruterus that were published with the Dutch translation of 1584 of Lipsius' famous treatise *De Constantia*.

Two poems, a poetic exchange between Dousa and Heinsius, are another example of such verses. Dousa's poem "Aen Daniel Heins, eerst gekomen sijnde om te studeren tot Leyden" (To Daniel Heinsius, When He First Came to Leiden to Study) must have been written around 1600 but only appeared in print together with Heinsius' homage to Dousa in the collection *Den Bloemhof* (The Flowergarden) of 1608. After the fashion of the time Dousa explained Heinsius' name as characterizing its owner:

> O Heyns die van den Heynst dijn naem voert, door wiens hoef
> Ontsprongen is geweest uyt 't grasig Helicone
> De Caballijnsche vloet . . .[4]

(Heinsius who takes his name from the horse through whose hoof the horse-stream sprang up at the grassy Helicon . . .)

This equation of "Heyns" (Heinsius' Dutch name) with "heynst" (horse, i.e., the winged Pegasus of the Muses, who with a blow of his hoof caused the Muses' fountain Hippocrene to spring from Mount Helicon) is often used to allude to Heinsius. The title page of the *Nederduytsche Poemata* in the lower left-hand corner shows the winged Pegasus taking off from Mount Helicon, a pictorial representation of the poet Heinsius.

Heinsius' reply "Aen Ioncker Ian van der Does, Heere van Noortwijck" is a graceful homage to Dousa and to the rebirth of poetry in the Netherlands through his circle: Poets have falsely maintained that Apollo was born on Delos. Heinsius affirms that, though he was born near the ocean, he speaks Dutch:

> Ick wil voortaen met recht Boeoten laeten vaeren
> Met al den Grieckschen pracht, en Pindaro zijn snaeren
> Gaen senden, als ick sie, dat hy, die onsen geest
> En onse konste stiert, van Hollandt is geweest. (64)

(Henceforth I will rightly leave Boeotia with all its Greek splendor and return the lyre to Pindar, since I see that he who rules our spirit and our art is from Holland.)

Heinsius goes on to describe the ocean, the lonely beach, and concludes with the arrival of Venus and Cupid, an allegory for the advent of Renaissance love poetry in Dousa's circle. He then bids antiquity farewell:

> Anacreon vaert wel, vaert wel voortaen Athenen,
> En ghy Romeynen oock. ick wil my van u spenen.
>   Als Delos by ons is, en Phoebus van dit landt,
>   Soo wil ick u voortaen niet nemen in de handt. (66)

(Farewell Anacreon, farewell now Athens, and you too, Romans. I will wean myself from you. Since Delos is right here and Apollo from this country, I will henceforth not take you in my hand.)

Dousa is celebrated as Apollo, the patron of the arts; ancient Greece has now come to the Netherlands. The allegory is very much in keeping with the pictorial taste of the time: Apollo with laurel wreath and lyre is the crowning figure on the title page of *Neder-duytsche Poemata*. It is also an homage to Dousa's role in the foundation of Leiden University and its development. At the opening ceremonies in 1575 an elaborate procession was held during which the nine Muses and Neptune arrived in a boat symbolizing the arrival of the arts and letters. An engraving of the event was displayed in the library. Heinsius has transformed the references to classical mythology into a fable about the rebirth of poetry in Holland, narrated with descriptive allusions to his patron and country. He successfully blended the classical tradition with a modern endeavor toward the re-creation of poetry in his native tongue summing up the essence of his efforts and expectations at the beginning of the seventeenth century—to be superbly realized in subsequent decades.

After the turn of the century, numerous collections of songs were printed in which the new Renaissance love poetry was represented. A significant volume of such lyrics was *Den Bloemhof van de Neder-lantsche Ieught* (The Flowergarden of Dutch Youth, 1608 and 1610) abounding in translations and adaptations from Ronsard, Du Bellay, and Du Bartas. Heinsius and some major poets of Dutch Golden

Age literature, such as Hooft and Bredero, contributed poems to the collection; many other verses were modeled on Heinsius' Latin elegies and his Dutch alexandrines, while the songs and sonnets bear resemblance to those of Hooft. Heinsius was well acquainted with Hooft, the patrician from Amsterdam, who after his journey to Italy wrote the pastoral play *Granida* (1605), and was a student in Leiden in 1606. He published his first collection of accomplished love poems with the *Emblemata amatoria* (Love Emblems, 1611). Bredero, who like Hooft was a member of the Amsterdam Chamber *De Eglantier* (The Eglantine), wrote perhaps less refined, but more spontaneous, poems which were published in a collection only after his death in 1618. It was during this early phase of Golden Age literature in the Netherlands, from about 1600 to 1616, that Heinsius wrote his efforts in the vernacular to be gathered in the *Nederduytsche Poemata*.

II   Nederduytsche Poemata: *Editions, Scriverius' Preface, Arrangement*

About 1600 Heinsius began to write verses in Dutch along with his much more voluminous production of Latin and Greek poetry. His first collection of love emblems[5] of 1601 contained, besides an eight-line poem for each emblem, a long introductory poem "To the Maiden of Holland"; in the enlarged edition of around 1607 his "Elegy or Lament at Night" and "Cupid's Mortuary" were added, and the 1613 edition also contained the "Wedding Song" and "The Death of Adonis."

It was through the initiative of Heinsius' close friend, the Leiden scholar and poet Petrus Scriverius (1576–1660), that the collected Dutch poems, including his love emblems, appeared early in 1616[6] in a stately, illustrated volume in quarto format published, not in Leiden, but by Willem Jansz in Amsterdam. In this volume the dedication to the patron of the arts, Jacob van Dyck, and a lengthy poem by Scriverius are followed by Dutch poems (pp. 3–66), the two series "The Trades of Cupid" and "Love Emblems" (pp. 68–92), with the separately titled and paginated "Bacchus Hymn" concluding the volume. In 1616 a second edition came out with the same title page, some corrections (distinction of the two emblem series), and changes in Scriverius' annotations to the Bacchus hymn; the collection was issued again in 1618 (dated 1616 on the title page) and reprinted in 1621 (dated 1618 on the title page) with three

further editions in 1621 and 1622. Obviously there was a great
demand for Heinsius' Dutch poetry between 1616 and 1622; yet
there was only one later edition—in 1650.

Scriverius dedicated the *Nederduytsche Poemata* to Jacob van
Dyck, a wealthy advocate in the service of the Swedish king and a
patron of the arts, who held literary gatherings in his residence at
The Hague[7] where Heinsius read his "Hymn to Jesus Christ" on
New Year's Day 1616. Scriverius' introductions (a prose preface and
a poem) are important because of the plea for Dutch, his mother
tongue. Together with Heinsius' reply to Scriverius (prefaced to the
Bacchus hymn) they provide lively testimony of contemporary literary activities and tastes in Leiden and the Netherlands. In a concise
argument taking its examples from antiquity and the Romance literatures, Scriverius pleads for the importance of a national Dutch
literature in the Dutch language, very much in accordance with
national sentiment during the consolidation of the young Dutch
nation. He takes his point of departure from Horace who, having
placed too much importance on Greek as did his contemporaries,
was visited by Romulus in a dream and reminded of his Roman
heritage.[8] Scriverius chides his compatriots for likewise following
the Greeks and Romans and neglecting their own language. Then he
points to the recent creation of national Romance literatures in Italy,
France, and Spain as examples for the Dutch. He names the great
Renaissance authors whose influence is present at the beginning of
Dutch Renaissance literature: Petrarch, Poliziano, Sannazaro, Ronsard, and Du Bartas. No Spaniard is referred to by name, and
England is not even mentioned. Scriverius chides the Dutch who
"alone are ungrateful to their own language" (6) and consider it
only good enough for the uneducated. He comments that in their
native language poets, in the beginning even the French, made
mistakes in word accent *(toon)* and meter *(maate);* a good poet must
be divine and full of inspiration, learned and well versed in Latin
and Greek. Scriverius thus rephrased the concept of the Renaissance poet, of the *poeta divinus* and *doctus* who possesses the *furor
poeticus.*

In his poem Scriverius turns to the present state of Dutch literature with his famous remarks on the crude and unrefined *rederij-
kers;* but Amsterdam is an exception:

> V neem ick alleen uyt, ô constich Amsterdam!
> Op uw toonelen heeft die konst, die was verloren,

> Haer adem weer geschept. by u is zy herboren
> Het Hooft dat steeckt ghy op. ick sie uyt uw maras
> Yet rijsen in de locht: ick sie een nieu Parnas. (14–15)

(You alone are an exception, o ingenious Amsterdam! On your stages art which had perished has again taken breath, with you it is reborn. You stick your head up again [or: Hooft has revived you]. I see from your marshes something rising into the air: I see a new Parnassus.)

The reference to the poet and dramatist Hooft is an acknowledgment of his rising talent, although Heinsius was then still regarded as the greater and more important poet and as his teacher. Leiden is the "Athens of the North." In spite of a tendency to cling to the heritage of antiquity, the struggle to surpass it is a major drive. Scriverius in his exhortation to the Dutch to look at their own talents rather than to foreign ones also recognizes Bredero. His plea for the use of the native language arises concurrently with the awakening nationalism, with the recognition of one's own cultural heritage and worth; Scriverius does not criticize classical studies and literatures but signals growing independence from the models of antiquity, a prominent theme in the Renaissance of the North. Even if the preface falls somewhat short of what has been called a "program of a national renaissance,"[9] it is certainly a timely recognition of the beginnings of a new era of vernacular literature in the Netherlands, in which the poetry of Heinsius, in part through Scriverius' edition, opened up new horizons.

We must assume that the twenty-nine Dutch poems were arranged by the editor Scriverius. They are not a mere miscellany, but grouped according to theme and poetic style. Three poems with a patriotic theme—the verses on Admiral Heemskerck, on Ostend, and on Leiden—open the collection very much in keeping with Scriverius' emphasis on the renaissance of national Dutch letters. Heinsius' early poems, "To the Maiden of Holland" (ca. 1601), the "Foreword to the Illustrious Women" (1606), and some others from that early date, have been put at the end. The early work was probably regarded as somewhat inferior, just as Heinsius relegated his early elegies ever farther toward the end of his Latin poetry volume in subsequent editions.

Love, the major theme in the entire collection, is introduced with the fourth poem addressed to Rossa, the girl in his early Latin elegies, and is followed by seven short strophic poems. The ex-

change with Anna Roemer Visscher,[10] three poems altogether, precedes three adaptations from Theocritus. The exchange with Dousa,
with its programmatic lines, concludes the volume. The collection is
a pleasant array, including some engravings and a decorative initial
for each poem, in which groups of thematically related poems alternate and achieve a variety of poetic styles within this homogeneous
and original collection of Dutch Renaissance poetry.[10a] We shall
discuss the significant poems from the major groups in the *Nederduytsche Poemata*.

III   *The Elegies*

The close relationship between Heinsius' Dutch and Latin love
poems is most evident in the elegies.[11] Heinsius introduces the
Dutch readers to the girl of his Latin elegies in "To the Reader, to
Inform Him About His Girl Called Rossa in His Latin Poems." In a
series of Petrarchist metaphors extending over eighteen lines he
praises the features of the girl under whose gentle tyranny he has
become a slave. She is the source of inspiration for his work.

> Ia sonder yemandt meer beneven u te achten,
> Stort ick in uwen schoot het merch van mijn gedachten,
>   Het beeldt van mijn gemoet: gelijck ick altijdt ben
>   In 't midden van den brandt getrocken met de pen. (14)

(Without looking at anyone except you I thrust into your lap the innermost
of my thoughts, the picture of my mind: as I am always drawn by the pen in
the middle of the fire.)

Love is the subject of his poetry, the girl his Muse whom he implores: "Goddess, look at this song . . . look at this work" (14). She
has quenched his thirst before—a reference to his Latin elegies
where Rossa appears as the patron Muse and Heinsius begs her to
smile at him, that is to say, at his work again. Similar in theme to the
introductory elegy of his Latin work, the poem may well be regarded as programmatic for his collection, as an introduction of his
Dutch love poetry to his audience.

The "Elegie" (pp. 20–25) is one of the longest and most important
poems in the collection, its theme being the poet's entreaty to his
beloved. Approaching the "princess of the Dutch cities" (Leiden)
the poet is not interested in the buildings, nor in its university, but
only in a girl. Should he not find response, he will set sail to un-

known lands ready to die; but he implores the girl to listen to what
could be his last words and conjures up a death fantasy at his grave.
Reproaching the girl for being the cause of his death, the poet
proceeds to invective in a long series of addresses, which climax in
the rhetorical question "who do you think I am?" This the poet
answers himself by "pouring out his heart." It is expecially the
second half of the poem in which the author states his own position
as a poet that raises the "Elegie" above other more conventional
love poems. After praising the Stoic who meets his fate with steadfastness, the wise man who is master of his years and not afraid of
death, Heinsius invites the girl to climb the mountain (Parnassus)
with him. He knows the way since from early childhood he has
explored these paths with the Greeks and the Romans:

> [Ick hebbe] . . . . ten lesten opgedaen
> Den ongebaende padt daer Nederlandt mach gaen,
> Soo datse van nu voort met Phoebi susters danssen
> Op't hoogste van den berch, niet passend' op de Franssen. (24)

(I have at last opened the untrodden path where the Netherlands may go,
so that they henceforth dance with Apollo's sisters on top of the hill without paying attention to the French.)

Here Heinsius sees himself as the first national poet breaking away
from French models, leading the Dutch to the wellspring of poetry.
In a trancelike state he revels in the inspiration gained from this
spring so that his work "naer de Goden rieckt, en naer den hemel
smaeckt" (smells of gods and tastes of heaven, 25).

The "Elegie," which appeared for the first time in the *Nederduytsche Poemata*, is one of Heinsius' most important Dutch poems.
Several indications point to a rather late date of composition some-
time after 1613. It was not included in the enlarged emblem series
of that year. Its length, narrative content, and certain passages, such
as the poet's frenzy and inspiration, make it akin to the Bacchus
hymn; didactic and moral observations on the poet as a Stoic point to
parallels from the 1613 Latin *Poemata*. In this "Elegie" Heinsius
uses a Petrarchist theme, the poet's entreaty to his beloved, en-
riched by an array of traditional motifs from lyrical and reflective
poetry and expanded into a poetic narrative by imaginative scenes.
The poet's search begins with his metaphorical arrival in the city, a
realistic Dutch picture. It is continued in a metaphorical voyage and

the vividly imagined scene at his graveside. The second half starts
with a renewed plea heightened to a denunciation of the girl, which
is then reversed into a defense of his own position. Another imaginary scene, the journey to Mount Parnassus, concludes the poem.
The paradox of the independent poet as a servant to the girl is
elaborated upon several times, transforming this Petrarchist motif of
self-pity into one of self-irony apparent in such descriptions of himself as "van licchaem niet te groot, maer groot genoech van herten"
(25) (of small stature, but of a large enough heart).

The reflective lines in the central section contain commonplaces
from contemporary Neo-Stoicism, later a major theme in Heinsius'
didactic poem *De contemptu mortis* (On Contempt of Death), and
from humanist concepts. The poet does not want to belong to the
"gemeene volck" (22) (common people), an echo of the ubiquitous
Horatian "Odi profanum vulgus et arceo" (I hate the masses and stay
away from them) *topos* of Renaissance poetry. Instead Heinsius
points to his independent spirit, his disinterest in a political career
(in the anticourtly tradition), his contentment with what he has, his
abdication of riches and wordly goods, his equanimity toward fate.[14]
He hopes to find immortality through poetry. The entreaty to the
girl is at the same time a quest for poetic fulfillment. The "Elegie,"
then, embodies Heinsius' search for inspiration, for poetry itself.
That he finds it in Leiden clearly opens the way for Dutch poetry.
The impetuous plea, the exuberant poetic journey to Mount Parnassus, counterbalanced by the more ponderous Stoic statement of his
own position, make this Dutch poem an equal of the more mature
Latin verses of 1613, in which similar motifs are prominent.[12]

IV   *Verses with a Motto*

A group of seven love poems were conceived by Heinsius each to
illustrate a Petrarchist line,[13] all but the last motto are in Latin, and
that one is in French. The first poem returns to the theme of the
Latin Rossa elegy: The motif of the poet-lover as slave is elaborated
upon under the oxymoron "Dominae servitium libertatis summa
est" (service to the lady is the height of liberty). In this song with ten
four-line stanzas, the poet invites those who envy or hate him to
look at his prized possession, the girl for whom he gladly gave up his
freedom. The short line, a basically trochaic verse with four stressed
syllables, allows only an uncomplicated syntax; each two verses form
a sentence following each other in a straightforward way to the end

so that this poem has the rhythm and simplicity of a song. The use of images from the Petrarchist tradition (the doors of coral, the lover a slave, love is honey) and the lines completely regular in the alternation of stressed and unstressed syllables, show the poem to be closely modeled on the song in the Romance languages.

In the other six poems of this group Heinsius uses the rhymed alexandrine couplet, his favorite meter, which he employs in the majority of his verses and in the closely related emblems series. "Dominae praesentia vitae fructus est" (the presence of the lady is the fruit of life) tells of the poet's longing for his girl:

> Deur regen en deur windt gekomen hier tot Leyden,
> Hebb' ick naer u gevraecht u arme martelaer,
> Sieck sijnd' om uwent wil. Ick hebbe moeten beyden
> Van u te spreken aen, en ben gegaen van daer
> Ellendich sonder hoop, vol pijn, vol smert, vol lijden,
> vol droefheyt in de geest, vol jammerlick verdriet. (16)

(Through rain and wind I have come here to Leiden and have asked for you, as your poor martyr sick because of you. I had to wait to address you and I left in misery, without hope, full of pain, of sorrow, of suffering, of gloom in my heart, full of miserable dejection.)

The anticipation of the waiting lover is stated in clear, melodious language; the alternately rhyming male and female lines add to the musicality of the verse. The accumulation of expressions for his dejection—a frequent stylistic feature in Neo-Latin poetry—increases the intensity of the lament and is further enhanced by the repeated sense of rejection in the following lines culminating in "Ick ben bedroeft, ick queel" (I am miserable, tortured), and the poem concludes with an epigrammatic antitheses:

> Want om by u te sijn ses dagen kan ick wachten,
> Maer om u niet 'te sien, twee dagen is te veel. (16)

(For to be with you I can wait six days, but not to be with you, two days are too much.)

The absence of mythological or traditional metaphors sets this poem apart from the others in the group in which mostly Petrarchist concepts are elaborated.

These seven love poems show Heinsius' superb mastery of this tradition. The verses share a circular structure: A seemingly contradictory motto is explained in a realistic situation, which serves as a fitting example for the sententious heading which is then repeated at the end of the poem. Almost all poems are addressed to the beloved or an object representing her; many are written in the first person, enhancing the immediacy and realism of the scene. A melodious language and an uncomplicated sentence structure—generally a series of short statements or questions spanning only a line or a half-line with parallel parts reiterating or expanding the statement—is accompanied by a simplicity of imagery and content. These poems closely resemble the lines Heinsius wrote for his emblem series, especially those of "Het ambacht van Cupido" (The Trades of Cupid, 1613); in fact, the picture illustrating the poem "Tout amant estropiat" (19) showing a lover tortured by Cupid appears with only slight variations in emblem books: in Vaenius' *Amorum emblemata* (Love Emblems, 1608) and the *Thronus Cupidinis* (Cupid's Throne, ca. 1618) illustrating the pains of love. Here, as in his emblematic verses, Heinsius unriddles the often enigmatic and at times farfetched conceit; the choice of sententious Latin mottoes, akin to proverbial expressions though based on Petrarchist concepts, already indicates the shift towards realistic explanation.

V *Translations and Adaptations*

Heinsius' commentary on Theocritus[14] meant more for him than a product of philological scholarship. The study of, and lectures on, Theocritus and the Greek poets introduced him to some of the finest lyrical poetry of antiquity. His interest in the significance of individual phrases and in poetic style and form, evident from the notes in his commentary, went beyond the time-honored philological practice of amending a corrupt text which dominated the treatment of classical literature at that time. The 1606 edition of his Latin poetry already contained a section "Verses translated from the Greek" in which the bucolic and epigrammatic poems of Theocritus were rendered into Latin in such a way "that verse corresponded to verse."[15] In this there was a Latin translation of Idyll XII, "Aites," which he rendered into Dutch, probably modeling it after the Latin and calling it an "Oversettinge" (translation). Noting the lyrical quality of the poem in his Theocritus commentary, Heinsius gave a very faithful and at the same time remarkably fluent and melodious translation. "Aites" is a poet's monologue expressing his love toward a boy who returns after two days' absence. In a series of images the delight at the reunion is shown, and the poet wishes that the love may be mutual and perpetual and win them fame in future ages. The example of Diocles, who gave his life for his friend and in whose honor boys competed in an annual kissing contest at his grave, concludes the poem. The unrestrained passion in the first half contrasts strangely with the display of learning in the second half, and it has been suggested that Theocritus was writing at least partly in jest.[16] Heinsius strove for an accurate rendering of the Greek text, though he occasionally substituted a more familiar expression[17] and played down the presentation of two male lovers—the Dutch version addressed "mijn liefste kindt" (my dear child) rather than the "boy" as did the Greek and Heinsius' Latin versions—perhaps because this did not fit in with the other love poems. His fluent and melodious rendering attests to his mastery of the Dutch language.

Two other poems were taken from Theocritus. "Adonis doet" (The Death of Adonis) published in 1613, is a translation of Idyll XXX, now no longer ascribed to Theocritus; it concerns Venus' grief over Adonis who was slain by a boar. Venus has the animal tied, and the boar confesses that it was the passion aroused by Adonis' beauty that made him kill Adonis with his "passionate teeth." Venus is moved, has him untied, and the boar becomes her constant companion: "En brand' in vier zijn tanden af,/ Die hy de schult van't soenen gaf" (41) (And in the fire he burned his teeth which he blamed for his kisses). Thus Heinsius' exact translation of Theocritus' poem, in which he uses only one extra syllable and follows the Greek syntax line for line, ends with an interpretative rendition of the somewhat obscure Greek: "Having approached the fire, the boar kept burning his loves." Heinsius brings the poem to a logical conclusion: the boar's teeth, the cause for his passion, are consumed by Venus' fire, by the heat of love.

The iambic line with four stresses is likewise used in "Cupido Honich-dief" (Cupid, the Honey-Thief, 1613). The short poem, in which the initial situation is more elaborate than in its model, Theocritus' Idyll XIX, is similar in structure to verses Heinsius wrote for a Latin motto. While plundering the beehive, Cupid is surprised by a small bee's sting, but his mother asks "sijt ghy groot/ Die yeder brengt in sulcken noot?" (42) (are you big that you bring everybody into such distress?). This epigrammatic ending fits in

well with the Anacreontic playful poem, the genre that Heinsius
favored in his emblematic verses. Here Heinsius condenses the final
lines to make the point (in the Greek Cupid is explicitly compared
with the bees) while expanding the descriptive beginning. This and
the Adonis poem represent stages of deliberate reshaping of the
contents from a classical model, no longer a translation, but not yet
an independent creation.

Such a new creation in the Anacreontic manner is "Het sterf-huys
van Cupido" (Cupid's Mortuary) published about 1607. It is based
on the paradoxical idea that Cupid dies from falling into his own fire.
An invitation is issued to the gods to purchase his belongings. The
good bargains are described with playful irony as the effects of love.
Heinsius transfers Cupid to Holland where the sale of the household
goods of the deceased is a regular event in bourgeois society. Classical mythology is curiously blended with everyday life in this poem
with the strophic pattern (five stanzas of eight trochaic lines each) of
a song. Its appearance with the emblem series in about 1607 make it
one of the earlier Dutch poems. It also indicates that the above
renditions from Theocritus belong in the same period. Thus Heinsius' study and apprenticeship of Theocritus came during the forma-
tive phase of his Dutch and Latin poetry.

The "Pastorael" published in 1613 is a song written in the bucolic
manner of Theocritus. The shepherd Corydon's lament over his
unrequited love is the setting in Vergil's second eclogue. This type
of pastoral song became a favorite vehicle for autobiographical remarks by the Renaissance poet; Heinsius transfers the pastoral setting to his homeland, "close to the waters of the Rhine" (26). Corydon, the shepherd-poet, has been in love with Phyllis for two years.
He had met her at a wedding and upon returning to Leiden became
lovesick on seeing only her picture before him. He goes to The
Hague to distract himself, and asks for medical advice, but all is in
vain. Phyllis does not return his love. Although he is of small stature, his name and song are well known in the Netherlands and from
Noordwijk (Dousa's estate) to England. The story line here must be
referring to Hugo Grotius' wedding in 1608 at which Heinsius fell
in love with a girl and courted her with verses until she married
another man in 1609; this would indicate that the "Pastorael" was
written around 1609–1610.[18]

The poem is long, consisting of thirty six-line stanzas in a trochaic
rhythm; it is appealing because of the fluent and melodious rhythm

and the personal perspective. His defense of his own person is an expression of Heinsius' assertiveness and involvement. Mythological references have been integrated into a Dutch setting, the Netherlands furnishing a bucolic background. This device and the simplicity of the language enhance the directness of the poem, a quality which is much more difficult to achieve in the Latin elegies on a similar theme. The translation of Theocritus' Idyll XII and the modified adaptation in "Adonis doet" and "Cupido Honich-dief," lead now to the poems "Pastorael" and "Het sterfhuys van Cupido" representing original poetic re-creations in the bucolic and Anacreontic tradition.

VI *Wedding Poems*

The contemporary custom of presenting a bride and groom with a poem which was usually recited or sung at their wedding banquet produced a flood of such verses. Besides Heinsius' Latin epithalamia, there are only two such Dutch poems—there must have been many more—included in the *Nederduytsche Poemata*.[19] The poems share the same structure; a story, fable, or simile introduces the love and wedding theme. Then the poet turns to the actual occasion and addresses first the groom, then the bride, and concludes with remarks about the wedding night and the union.

The "Bruylof-liedt" (Wedding Song, first published in 1611) with its subtle irony, its fantasy, and vivacity points to the early period of Heinsius' Dutch poetry. The poet sets out to describe Jupiter's palace in the sky where the gods assembled before love was known. Then Jupiter paints a wonderful picture of Cupid poisoning all the gods with a sweet fever which then spreads over all the earth. Turning to the groom, the poet describes the fever in detail and assures him that the pain will now turn into enjoyment. He concludes with appropriate remarks to the bridesmaids and the bride about the wedding night. The mythological fable freely and imaginatively elaborates the traditional setting. However, Heinsius dwells on the groom's desires, and a much more sensuous poem results than in his Latin verses. With its combination of creative mythological narrative and realistic description of the anticipation of the union the poem greatly influenced subsequent epithalamia.

The "Troudicht. Ter eeren van Daniel de Burchgrave, met Anna Oosterlincks" (Wedding Poem) which was written for his cousin's Leiden wedding in 1603 and first published as the opening poem in the collection *Den Bloemhof* in 1608.[20] Much less sensuous and more reflective than the "Bruylof-liedt," the poem consists of an explicitly nautical simile which is applied to the groom. First the picture of sailors returning after a successful voyage is drawn. They enter the harbor and fold their sails. Then the nautical picture is explained in detail: The raging sea is life, the wind is love, the stars are the beloved's eyes showing the way, the rudder intellect, the anchor is speech, etc. The poet wishes the groom a good passage, a place to anchor, and a propitious end to his journey and in conclusion wishes that "his own boat" (52) be remembered. The nautical metaphor is carried through the entire poem and explained with reference to the particular situation, since such a metaphor was a ubiquitous one.[21] In the Christian tradition life was a perilous voyage, heaven the safe port; in the classical tradition elaborated by the Petrarchists, the stormy voyage meant the pains and uncertainties of love, as Heinsius had depicted them in emblem 17 of "Het ambacht van Cupido." In using the port metaphor for the wedding Heinsius has merged the two traditions. This "Troudicht" with its reflective mood centering around the desirability of the marriage, though written in 1603, is closely akin to "Op zijn eygen Bruyloft. Ex persona sponsi" (1617) in which Heinsius praises his wife—and the married woman in general—as the fulfillment of his life. The virtues of bourgeois family life have superseded playful courtship. Here is a final farewell to his love poetry as well as to his poetry written in Dutch. This is an autobiographical poem and programmatic in that it signals Heinsius' almost exclusive preoccupation with religious writings after 1617.

VII   *Patriotic Poems*

The importance of Heinsius' three reflective poems on patriotic themes is evident from their position at the beginning of the *Neder-duytsche Poemata* in 1616. The laudatory verses "On the Death and Great Victory of the Brave Hero, Admiral Jacob Heemskerck Buried in Amsterdam" open the collection; they are a tribute to Jacob van Heemskerck (1567–1607) who was famous for his voyage to the East Indies to protect Dutch trade interests and for an expedition to the Arctic. In 1607 he led a Dutch fleet to attack the Spanish coast and was killed in the Straits of Gibraltar in what was to be the last major battle before the truce of 1609. Heemskerck was felled by the second shot from an enemy ship while standing on deck in full armor with his sword drawn. His death was actually concealed from his men until victory was complete, but in the contemporary patriotic versions the death was said to have spurred the Dutch to win the battle in spite of the fact that they were greatly outnumbered by the enemy. Heemskerck was buried in Amsterdam with great honors on June 8, 1607, and an engraving of his tombstone is placed before the Heinsius poem opening the *Nederduytsche Poemata*. The tombstone carries a Latin homage to Heemskerck's accomplishments and Hooft's famous couplet above the picture of the sea battle at Gibraltar in 1607:

> Heemskerck die dwars door 't ys en 't yser dorste streven,
> Liet d'eer aen't land, hier 't lyf, voor Gibraltar het leven. (2)

(Heemskerck who dared to go through ice and iron, left honor to his country, here his body and at Gibraltar his life.)

Heinsius' poem, probably written at the time of the funeral, pays homage to Heemskerck and celebrates the Dutch victory. It opens with an address to the grave in which lies the famous hero who is now "sitting next to Jupiter." But the tone of the funeral poem changes with Heinsius' vivid description of the hero's greatest accomplishment, the victorious sea battle. Heinsius passes over his death quickly and elevates him to the realm of heroes from where he follows the remainder of the fierce battle described with vivid theatrical detail. Heemskerck sees his men carrying out his orders; he sees a hail of bullets crossing the waters, the ocean turning red, the ships burning. A courageous sailor pursues a Spaniard to Hades so fiercely that even Charon, the ferryman in the Lower World, flees. Hell is less to be feared than the rage of a Dutch patriot, who is like a lion attacking a sheep or an eagle holding his prey in his talons:

> Marane neemt ons wech ons landen daer wy leven,
> Wy sullen sonder vrees ons in de zee begeven:
> > Daer nu de schepen gaen, daer sullen wij tot spijt
> > Van uwen trotsen moet sijn even wel bevrijt. (6)

(Spaniards, take away the land we live in, and we shall move fearlessly into the sea: where now the boats sail, there we shall in spite of your haughtiness be really free.)

The challenge to the sea power of the Spanish echoes from Heinsius' lines. The Dutch are born for freedom. The hero Heemskerck is now in a happier place; he has died for his people.

In this reflective poem the fate of the individual is linked to the collective experience of his people. It is a patriotic, propagandistic poem; but the technique of poetic variation breaks the monotony of pathos often found in such a poem. The initial theme, the praise of the hero, is concentrated in a short survey of his deed, while the main body of the poem consists of a theatrical description of the sea battle. This is followed by a general statement concerning its significance for the Dutch. The concluding eight verses return again to the initial theme, the importance of the hero's death for his country. Heinsius uses the basic structure of a laudatory poem and expands it to embrace the collective experience of the Dutch, thus transforming it into a patriotic poem. Instead of constant praise of an individual issued in an elevated tone, he retains a direct approach vividly describing the actions and the historical event which make this man a hero. It is the narrative of the battle with the individual acts of bravery that lends interest to the poem. Taking the perspective of Heemskerck witnessing the continuation of the battle from above, Heinsius gives an immediate, vivid account alternating between description (the armor, the bloody ocean) and action (the taking of the flag, the Dutch sailor pursuing a Spaniard). The poet is presenting history like a "living picture" so popular in the theater of the time. Homage to the patriot is integrated into its wider significance for his country. The poem is the expression of an important contemporary feeling shortly before the truce with Spain.

"Op het belech van Oostende" (On the Siege of Ostend) is a more concise and somewhat earlier poem written in conjunction, or in competition, with Hugo Grotius. After a three-year siege and the loss of around ten thousand men on both sides, the city of Ostend surrendered to the Spanish on September 22, 1604. When Grotius published a Latin poem anonymously in which he let the besieged city speak ("Ostenda loquitur"), it immediately became famous and was even ascribed to the revered Joseph Scaliger.[22] After a short lament about the trials endured by the city culminating in the cruelty of the Spaniards, Grotius' poem ends with an epigrammatic statement about the meaningless victory:

> Fortuna quid haeres?
> Qua mercede tenes mixtos in sanguine manes?

> Quis tumulos moriens hos occupet hoste perempto,
> Quaeritur, et sterili tantum de pulvere pugna est.

(Why do you linger, Fate? What reward do you promise the souls spattered with blood? Who while dying will occupy these graves after the enemy is slain is the question; the battle rages only over barren ground.)

The Heinsius poem likewise ponders the meaning of the victory, but it is not a mere translation of "Ostenda loquitur" as has been assumed.[23] For Heinsius the battlefield is "a small stage" (tooneel); he describes in greater detail than Grotius, using more exaggeration and extremes, the sufferings in this siege and the brave resistance of the inhabitants. His epigrammatic ending reveals the essence of a Spanish victory in which nothing has been won:

> Waer wilt de vyandt sijn? wat heeft hy toch begonnen?
> Oostenden is hy quijt, al heeft hy't al gewonnen.
>   De menschen staen int sandt, hoe dat het komt of gaet,
>   De Stadt is lange wech, de Spanjaert komt te laet. (13)

(Where does the enemy want to be? What has he begun? He lost Ostend, although he won it. Men build on sand, whatever may happen, the city is long since lost, the Spaniard comes too late.)

The antithesis between destruction and conquest in this futile victory has been extended over four lines starting with a rhetorical question and ending with the climax "the enemy has come too late."

The Heinsius poem contains ideas and phrases reminiscent of Grotius as well as a similarity in structure and an arrangement in three major parts with an epigrammatic ending. The first four lines of Grotius and eight of Heinsius describe the siege; the following section of the same length for both poems portrays the resistance of the Dutch; the final three lines of Grotius and four of Heinsius present the futility of the victory. The longer, more visual, and explicit description is characteristic of Heinsius' Dutch verses even in comparison with his own Latin poetry. But for Grotius the siege is an example of the indifferent fate of war: "Fortuna quid haeres?" (why do you linger, Fortuna?) is the central question and the battle rages over "barren ground," an indirect accusation of the senseless devastation of war. The Heinsius poem exhibits patriotism in its celebration of the brave resistance of Ostend and the Dutch and its questioning of the meaning of the victory as a positive gain for the Spanish. In Heinsius the optimism and joy over a national victory is clearly audible, while the early Grotius poem already shows his more reserved view of war.[24]

The *Nederduytsche Poemata* would not have been complete without a poem for Leiden: It is the longest one and resembles the hymns in structure and tone since it is likewise a laudatory poem. Written for Jan Orlers' famous history of Leiden which appeared in 1614, it is a tribute to Heinsius' adopted hometown as a center of learning in the newly victorious and flourishing Dutch nation. Heinsius' patriotic poems followed in the tradition of Marnix van St. Aldegonde and Dousa's Latin odes on Leiden rather than in the popular tradition of religious and patriotic songs such as those in the *Geuzenliedboek*[25] of 1601. Patriotic themes occur in only a few of Heinsius' early Latin elegies, while they are much more pronounced in Hugo Grotius' Latin poetry. Using the regular iambic meter of the alexandrine couplet, Heinsius was one of the first poets in the seventeenth century to lend support to the fight for independence and freedom in his *native Dutch* tongue. He was followed by Vondel who regarded his play *Pascha* (Passover, 1612), an allegory of the redemption of mankind, as a parallel to Holland's liberation. Later there appeared such collections as Adriaen Valerius' *Nederlandtsche Gedenck-clanck* (Dutch Memorial Songs, written 1622–24, published posthumously in 1626) and Jacobus Revius' *Over-IJsselsche Sangen en Dichten* (Songs and Poems from the Upper Ijssel, 1630).

Thus Heinsius' patriotic poems, though only three in number, occupy a special place. Their fluency and vivacity overcame the abstract reflection of previous patriotic Latin verses. Although Heinsius' work incorporated ancient mythology, his classical metaphors are integrated into a very realistic, though exaggerated, description of actual events such as the sea battle or the siege which approach stylistic features of the Baroque. The shift from an abstract address to a person or object, from laudatory sentiment to a real situation, such as the battle as Heemskerck views it from above, enlivens the poems and takes them out of the confining pathos, the lofty level of speech found in laudatory verses.

VIII   Lof-sanck van Bacchus *(Bacchus Hymn)*

Because of its form and contents the *Lof-sanck van Bacchus,*

Heinsius' last major secular poem in Dutch, was set apart from the main body of the *Nederduytsche Poemata*. It was printed with a separate title page and introduction and placed at the end of the collection. Heinsius' preface is addressed to Scriverius and dated "the evening before Lent 1614" making January-February of that year the likely time of composition for the poem. As a homage to the god of wine Heinsius' poem belongs in the long tradition of hymns to Bacchus dating back to classical antiquity.[26] In the prefatory open letter [27] to his friend and editor Scriverius, Heinsius refers to this tradition, mentioning the *Dionysiaca* of Nonnus, [28] the Neo-Latin poems of Flaminius, Marullus, Muretus, Julius Caesar Scaliger, and his French model Ronsard: "But while writing I found that Ronsard said much but has left out even more" (102), Heinsius states. The Dutch poem is meant to show that his native language is likewise suited to a rendering of the classical myth in poetic form; moreover, with his erudition as a classical scholar he will allude to much that was omitted or glossed over by Ronsard.[29] Heinsius' poem follows closely the Latin hymn and the encomium as developed especially by the Renaissance authors he mentions, whose works were translated into the vernacular by Ronsard from whom Heinsius took stylistic and structural details.

The choice of subject matter is elaborately defended in the prefatory letter. The use of mythological material, the major source for fable, imagination, and metaphors in Neo-Latin and Renaissance literature, is discussed at length in reference to this Dutch hymn to Bacchus. Heinsius begins with a criticism of the use of mythology in antiquity: "When reading the works left to us by the Heathens I find nothing more strange than the great blindness in which they persisted: it went so far that they ascribed their faults to heaven and worshipped their sins. Against this folly not only the great men of Christianity have fought, such as the Church fathers, but also the wise Socrates and Euripides . . ." (99). The people of antiquity, Heinsius maintains, ascribed their own human follies to the gods they venerated; this was criticized by the Christians, but also by antiquity's great philosopher, Socrates, and his spiritual disciple, Euripides. The Greeks even seemed to admit secretly that the peoples without a god were wiser than they, who worshipped such foolish deities. But for the poets of antiquity, as well as for the Renaissance authors, the gods are simply an allegory for a certain concept: "With the name of Vulcanus, Bacchus, Venus, and the like the poets meant to characterize only fire, wine, love, and their powers good and evil, their application and abuse" (101). For Heinsius the mythology of antiquity embraced philosophical insight into the world, into life and death. Such insight was concealed in the plots of fables, in the actions of the gods: "Almost the entire wisdom and philosophy, which Aristotle then had wanted to reform, is hidden under these [mythological] names" (101). This, Heinsius continues, was especially the case with the Bacchus myth which he then traces through the ages.

Heinsius, to be sure, wanted to explain the significance of mythology to his orthodox religious readers, especially the Calvinists of the Netherlands; he did, of course, not believe in these heathen deities. The hymn was a learned jest written for the carnival, a witty celebration of wine, and at the same time a *poetic* version in Dutch of an ancient myth. Heinsius' defense of classical mythology must also be viewed in the context of the literary conventions of his day. In the literary program of the *Pléiade*, mythology—a fable covering truth with a veil of mystery—had become an essential part of poetry.[30] Ronsard's hymns (published 1554–56) freely fused Christian concepts and classical myths (e.g., in the "Hymne de la Mort"); in essence these hymns represent an animism of the universe. During the ensuing religious wars in France the demand for a Christian literature was soon made. After attacks upon himself and his circle, Ronsard resorted to allegorization; Du Bellay and especially Du Bartas presented Christian themes in which classical mythology was branded as folly, blindness, and lies. After about 1570 religious poetry became extremely important in France, and toward the end of the sixteenth century the superiority and necessity of Christian subject matter was presented in the poetics, as in Vauquelin de la Fresnaye's *L'Art Poétique* (Published in 1605). Heinsius defended the classical tradition of the humanist poets against the shallow allegorization of mythology and against the changing literary taste which now preferred religious and biblical subject matter and rejected ancient myths as products of a heathen age.

The poem *Lof-sanck van Bacchus* is framed in a reference to its purpose as an entertainment for Mardi Gras:

> Wat kan men beter doen des avonts voor de Vasten,
> Als dat men Bacchus prijst in 't midden van zijn gasten
> Aen eenen goeden dis?   (1–3)

(What better can one do on the evening before Lent than praise Bacchus among the guests at a good table?)

And Heinsius ends the poem as he is ready to go to the celebration at the "good table" in his friend Scriverius' house. Into this contemporary frame, which is almost identical with Ronsard's lines, the long hymn to Bacchus is placed, following in content and structure the tradition of the Neo-Latin encomiastic poem.

The second half of the proem (5–10) more succinctly outlines the subject matter, the god's power and his many names. Following an arrangement similar to Ronsard's and to that of the mythological handbooks of the Renaissance, Heinsius presents the story of Bacchus' birth (11–20), national origin and rearing (21–44), his names (45–53), personal attributes (54–93), his love life (94–134). With a reference to the god's immortality contrasted with human misery in death (135–142), Heinsius opens a transition that presents the second major topic (143–224): what the god represents, namely, wine (the story of the ram); the joys derived from it; an antidote for the hangover (cabbage); and wine as a comfort in the miseries of this life.

The next major section (225–460) refers to several mythological stories further expounding the beneficial effects of wine: Bacchus winning over Ceres (the goddess of grain from which beer is produced); Ariadne in her grief over Theseus' infidelity being comforted by the arrival of Bacchus and his train; Bacchus helping Vulcanus to regain favor with Jupiter and proving to be the god's strongest defender against the Giants, a reward for which he is placed at the head of Jove's table creating the custom of toasting. A tribute to Bacchus' strength culminates in a procession with the god in his chariot drawn by two panthers and followed by a swarm of maenads and allegorical figures (461–476).

The last major section of the hymn (477–608) deals with the reverence for wine by great men of antiquity (Cato, Socrates, the Scythes) and the effect of wine on men, especially as an inspiration for the poets (Pindar, Homer, Anacreon) but even on learned men like Cadmus. Having prepared the way with these classical personalities for the picture of a wine-inspired poet-scholar, Heinsius concludes his hymn by imagining himself in an ecstatic frenzy as a follower of Bacchus who prefers sweet, divine oblivion to the miseries of this world (609–664).

The hymn is certainly a product of Heinsius' learning, his thorough knowledge and wide reading of classical and Renaissance authors, especially in the field of mythology. Important parallels, references, and explanations were given in Scriverius' notes appended to the poem. In the manner of the Alexandrian school such annotations were common practice for classical philologists and represented almost the only type of criticism and interpretation of literary works, especially for those in Latin. While such notes elevated this poem in the vernacular to the status of a classical work, they also were a tribute to Heinsius' erudition, much of which would have gone unrecognized and unappreciated by the nonhumanist Dutch-reading public. In spite of all the scholarly references, Heinsius has managed to present a fluent and lively narrative, forging the mythological stories and more general psychological observations on the use and effect of wine into a well-structured, integrated work. The technique of individual involvement sustains the poem: The personal frame, the poet writing this poem before leaving for the Mardi Gras celebration, is continued in the frequent use of "I," in his reactions to, and observations about, the effect of wine by which he imagines himself in the end to be subdued.

An address to Bacchus is used throughout the poem, keeping the immediacy between the poet and the deity who is repeatedly called "father." The close relationship of mythological figures to human life manifests itself in the lively presentation of mythological narratives such as Ariadne's story. This section closely follows Ovid's *Heroids,* but the story is retold by Heinsius with concrete and visual detail and further enhanced by the twelve engravings designed by David Vinckboons which accompany the poem. The myth has thus received a realistic, psychological interpretation which has been integrated into the poetic rendition.

The many details for which Heinsius is indebted to Ronsard's hymn range from almost literal renditions of phrases and verses to paraphrases of longer passages, especially in the proem, the conclusion, and the procession of Bacchus. Traditional thematic similarities occur frequently, since Heinsius is dealing with the same aspects and details of the Bacchus myth but by means of a different arrangement and structure. At times he ironically answers or corrects a Ronsardian line: for instance, when he replies to Ronsard's humorous, self-confessed confusion about the god's birthplace:

> Ick meyne dat ghy sijt geboren aen den Rijn.
> Van daer komt 't edel nat naer Dordrecht afgevaren

> Dat Nederlant verheucht: daer waren uw' autaren,
> Daer is noch uwen naem. (24–27)

(I think you were born on the Rhine. From there the noble liquid which the Netherlands enjoy is brought to Dort. Your altars were there, your name is still there [a reference to the town Bacharach as derived from Bacchus].)

Heinsius attempts to connect the myth with the sphere familiar to him and to the reader, but Ronsard also had alluded to "his Loire"[31] in another connection. Ronsard's long list of names which fills several lines (231–236) is a feature already present in the Bacchus hymn of the *Greek Anthology,* which consists almost entirely of names, and in the *Orphic Hymns.*[32] Heinsius has extended Ronsard's catalogue of names over ten lines (631–41) in the manner of the hymn from the *Greek Anthology* by adding a series of expressive Dutch paraphrases, such as "Tong-binder" (tongue-binder), "Hert-vanger" (heart-snatcher), and "waggel-voet" (wiggle-foot). These ironic names sum up essential aspects of the god while also making up part of the final ecstatic prayer in which the poet pictures himself by the end of the poem as under the god's influence.

Heinsius adapts many topics from Ronsard, extending and transforming them; but his essential innovations lie in the poetic and realistic description of the effect of wine. A poetic addition is the lively narrative of the Ariadne myth: the story of the forsaken lover comforted by Bacchus and fixed in the heavens as a constellation. This realistically contrived addition presents a coherent narrative describing the poet's inspiration by wine which is heightened to frenzy in the last third of the hymn. The passage in Ronsard is interrupted by mythological references and allegorical observations, while in Heinsius it pictures an inspired poet who finds himself engulfed in Bacchus' swarm for the final, theatrical climax to the poem. Ronsard's hymn fluctuates between irony and pathos, Heinsius' between realistic humor and ecstasy.

The subject matter of the hymn has contributed to the assumption that Heinsius loved to drink and had a drinking problem in his later life,[33] which in turn is used to account for his lack of original poetic production after about 1621. It has also been called an expression of Heinsius' "Dionysian love of life," of the unreconciled dualism for him between sensuality and spirituality[34] which supposedly manifested itself in the abrupt juxtaposition of the Bacchus and Christ hymns. To be sure, Heinsius' almost exclusive interest in religious questions after about 1617 is a major development in his life and will be discussed in relation to the Christ hymn. But whether the Bacchus and Christ hymns really represent unreconciled duality of the flesh and the spirit is another question. Subtitled "Waer in 't gebruyck ende misbruyck vande Wijn beschreven wort" (wherein the use and misuse of wine is described), the Bacchus hymn belongs first and foremost to the literary tradition of the learned encomium, a prose treatise or poem in ironic praise of an unpraiseworthy yet common subject, a popular genre with the humanists since Erasmus' *In Praise of Folly*. Just as Erasmus' work is not an apology for foolishness, but does contain many serious observations in ironic garb, the *Lof-sanck van Bacchus* is not a glorification of drinking, or the life of the flesh. Rather it is a humorous self-portrait of the poet-scholar himself in search of inspiration, and a poetic rendition of the Dionysian myth. It is at the same time a learned reflective poem in which the didacticism is clothed in encomiastic form, a worldly subject is treated in a humanist manner.

IX   Lof-sanck van Iesus Christus *(Christ Hymn)*

On New Year's Day 1616 Heinsius read the *Lof-sanck van Iesus Christus* to his friend Jacob van Dyck, patron of literature and the arts. It was published later in 1616 and from 1621 it preceded the body of the *Nederduytsche Poemata*. Containing 804 verses, the poem is considerably longer than its formal predecessor, the hymn to Bacchus. Four prefatory compositions are an important initiation for the reader into the significance of this religious poem: Heinsius' long prose preface addressed to Jacob van Dyck is followed by a short poem to the same patron and by Scriverius' verse dedication to Heinsius. Then a short prose passage explains "Contents and Usefulness of the Hymn." In the prose preface Heinsius takes his point of departure from David, the singer of the Old Testament—in the Bacchus hymn it was Horace—who for Heinsius is the first to proclaim the advent of Christ. The songs of the Old Testament mean Christ, just as the events are prefigurations of Christ. The Psalms are hymns; Christ is God on earth, God's revelation to this world. From these basic theological assumptions that echo the typological interpretation of the Old Testament, Heinsius proceeds to the historical tradition of hymns to Christ created by the early Christian authors whom he wants to follow with his poem.

In the short subsequent poem Heinsius explains that the hymn marks a departure from his former favorite topic as a poet: love.

De vruchten van de jeucht, de soetheyt van het minnen,
Een rechte toovery, van ons en onse sinnen,
   Is nu met ons geweest. Ick late Venus gaen,
   En met het blinde kint zijn blinde wercken staen.
Den hemel eyst het zijn. die selve sal verdwijnen,
Wanneer den Heer en Vorst als rechter sal verschijnen,
   Beschreven in dit liet. (199)

(The fruits of youth, the sweetness of love, a real delusion of us and our senses, have now left us. I let Venus go and with the blind child I leave the blind works behind. Heaven demands its part. It shall disappear when the Lord and Prince appears as judge described in this song.)

The poem signals the end of "his youth" and marks the beginning of the new, religious phase in Heinsius' poetic and scholarly work. Such a farewell to the poetry of his youth and to secular topics, though it may well have been personally motivated by his marriage (1617) and historically motivated by the pervasive theological dispute among Gomarists and Arminians, also had literary models. Ronsard in his famous sonnet "Au milieu de la guerre" ("Sonnets pour Hélène," II, 26) also bade farewell to the love of his youth in the midst of civil war; love then appeared to Ronsard as folly, fury, aberration. To Heinsius, Venus and "her blind works" now likewise seem a "deception of ourselves and of our senses." He has outgrown and exhausted the conventional love poetry in the Petrarchist manner. Now he feels the story of Christ the Redeemer presented in poetic garb is the highest service the poet can render to his readership, or as Heinsius' prefatory statement puts it: "In this life the highest joy for those souls who hunger for righteousness and their salvation is the perpetual and constant contemplation of the Lord Jesus Christ . . . such consolation is presented by the author in this hymn" (203). This is not a sudden change of heart for the sake of convenience, but the fruition of a gradual development noticeable from the beginning in the reflective, mostly Stoic passages in the poetic work of this religious scholar-poet who after about 1616 dedicated as much of his scholarly and creative activities as possible to the "true understanding and grasp of God's will . . . the real knowledge of and service to God's Word, that is to say, Jesus Christ" (204).

   The *Lof-sanck van Iesus Christus* is a carefully structured hymn.

The introductory section (1–40) deals with Jesus' divinity and eternity, his union with God in essence, but his separateness as a person. The first four verses, a paraphrase of the initial lines of the Gospel of St. John (which in turn are a paraphrase of the beginning of Genesis), serve as an introduction to the first section, presenting its theme in a condensed form. Christ was with God during the Creation; he is the shepherd of the world, "the Father's right hand" (8). This assertion is directed against heretical Arianism which had maintained that Jesus was the product or offspring of the Father, making Him in essence a demigod. Christ, Heinsius affirms, "was dan het begin van allerhande saecken,/ En was in het begin" (9–10) (was the beginning of all things, and was in the beginning). Christ, the visual manifestation of God, is the true light; he was not a product of the Creation and though he is God's son become man, he is divine himself. Christ embodies all of God's wisdom. A rhetorical question—how can man grasp the incomprehensible Trinity?—concludes the passage with a reference to the inseparable and equally incomprehensible sun and its rays. A transitional passage (41–48) using a nautical metaphor further elaborates the idea that the poet is trying to explain things which are rationally beyond the reach of mortals. The second major section (49–140), an introduction to the main body of the poem, deals with the story of the Old Testament: the fall of men from paradise into sin, the promise of the Savior, God's pact with Israel and His support of the Chosen People. The events of the Old Testament are seen as a prophecy of Christ's advent. The divine predetermination of the world and man's fate is the basis of the hymn and of Heinsius' Calvinist faith. The main body of the poem (141–580) tells the story of Christ's life on earth. In verses 141–462 the annunciation, birth, and baptism of Jesus are vividly described coupled with a long hymnic welcome to the Child. A comparatively short passage about Jesus' preaching and miracles (463–496) is followed by his death and resurrection (497–580). With Jesus' promise of redemption for mankind Heinsius has returned to the inexplicable Trinity, the theme of the introduction. The final section (581–804) contains a song of praise to Christ summing up numerous qualities and names of Jesus based on the metaphorical language of the New Testament (581–676); a timely prayer for mankind (677–700); a lament over man's defiance, hatred, quarrels, and envies (701–739); and a final prayer of thanksgiving for man's salvation (740–804).

The hymn is an expression of a deeply religious man who is

searching for the essence of the Christian faith and God. This is revealed as he tries to put into poetic words the inexplicable Trinity in the first part of his hymn. Heinsius' Calvinist faith makes itself felt in his firm belief in mankind's predestination for grace, but he avoids narrow dogmatic phrasing. Christ and the New Testament are at the center of this faith: His is a personal God, in contrast to the Stoic Lipsius' seemingly impersonal deity which is perceived as representing the divine order of the universe.

Heinsius' presentation of Christ is based on the writings of the Church fathers and the early Christians. His interest in the Church fathers, while omitting more recent theologians, is shared by such famous Dutch contemporaries as Grotius and Vondel and reflects the beginnings of the ecumenical trend of the time especially in the Low Countries. To them a return to the early Christian Church meant a return to true Christianity before it became corrupted by the practices of later centuries. This was the common ground for all denominations and here there remained some hope of overcoming the dogmatic differences created by the Reformation. Grotius' didactic poem *Bewijs van den waren Godsdienst* (In Defense of True Religion) written in 1619 during his captivity at Loevestein,[35] represented one outstanding attempt of the irenic movement advocating peace among all warring factions of Christianity and a return to the truth of the early Christian Church. Grotius' poem culminates in a plea to *all* Christians to recognize their common God and His Truth.

Heinsius' hymn, on the other hand, aims to express his personal Calvinist belief by means of a poetic yet scholarly praise of God, leaving theological disputes aside. It is not a piece of Gomarist propaganda but an attempt to breach the two factions of Calvinism. Scriverius, who unlike Heinsius leaned toward the Arminians, wrote the annotations to the *Lof-sanck van Iesus Christus*. These are even more extensive than the poem itself and they attest to Heinsius' thorough knowledge and skillful use of theological writings. They serve as further explication of, and instruction in, religious matters for the interested lay reader; at the same time they elevate this piece of poetry to the rank of a scholarly work by illuminating its profound, erudite frame.

The hymn itself, however, is not dominated by rationality, scholarship or partiality for orthodox Calvinism, but permeated by an unshakable faith. Whatever man cannot understand about God, Heinsius maintains, will be revealed to him in paradise, and he warns of fruitless theological disputes:

> Die verder willen gaen, die moeten onder blijven,
> Niet doende gants den dach dan twisten ende kijven,
> Doorgronden uwen raet, en soecken sonder end',
> Het gene dat noch haer, noch ander is bekent.   (717–20)

(Those who want to go farther [in their search to understand God] must err, passing their days with dispute and quarrel, investigating your wise plan and endlessly searching for what neither they nor others can know.)

This is clearly a message to the clashing factions of the Remonstrants and Counter-Remonstrants on the eve of the Synod of Dort. Heinsius' lifelong motto "Quantum est, quod nescimus" (how little we know) is also his underlying theme, expressed in the reverence for God's wisdom, which cannot be grasped by man's intellect.

The goal in this religious poem is to render in a poetic, metaphorical presentation the mysterious truth of God's existence. The incomprehensible can only be expressed in paradoxical terms; Heinsius' language circles around the mystery in full awareness that the divine message can only be grasped in a rhetorical paradox—for instance, in a paraphrase of the Trinity and the Father-Son relationship:

> De Vader was het al. de Soon was al in allen:
> Des Vaders eygen beelt, des Vaders welgevallen.
>   God self, en eewig God, als God. maer niet te min
>   De Vader gaf de Soon, als Vader, zijn begin:
> Wt hem, maer niet naer hem. Waer souden wy wat halen
> Om dit te meten af? Siet aen de klare stralen,
>   De stralen van de Son. zy sijn noch voor noch naer,
>   Maer met, en uyt de Son.   (33–40)

(The Father was one and all. The Son was all in all: the Father's own image, the Father's joy. God himself, an eternal God, a God. But still the Father gave to the Son, as a father, his beginnings: from Him, but not after Him. Where can we take a comparison from? Look at the bright rays, the rays of the sun. They are neither before nor after, but with and out of the sun.)

Far from being empty rhetoric these lines were carefully selected from the scriptures of the Church fathers, as Scriverius' commentary explains, in order to express the mystery in their own paradoxical terms. Antithesis, paradox, and oxymoron are deliberate and

functional major stylistic features of the hymn. Similes visualize
religious concepts. But they are short and kept within biblical
metaphorical language, such as the angels as an army (273–76) or
Mary likened to the morning star, the sun to a rose (329–36), the
resurrection to the eruption of a volcano (553–58). Rather than frequent or long similes, the highly metaphorical passages alternate
with vividly depicted individual scenes such as the annunciation to
Mary (141–66), Mary and Joseph in Bethlehem (210–12), and the
description of the events at Jesus' death (516–52). Parallelism, variation, and repetition of phrases and concepts occur frequently. In the
hymnlike reception of Christ the line "welcome great child" is reit-
erated six times in a passage of eighty-five verses (377–462); the
birth of Christ is presented in ever new variation on this same
theme. Rhetorical questions lead up to a prayer for the redemption
of mankind. All these stylistic devices, an extension of the poetic
style of Heinsius' earlier efforts in Dutch, contribute to an elevated
tone which matches the religious content of the poem.

The Christian contents of *Lof-sanck van Iesus Christus* called for a
clarification of Heinsius' stand on pagan mythology. As an appendix
Scriverius added "Notes on certain worldly histories, words, and
ways of speech used in this hymn" (320–29) in which he cites the use
of classical mythology in St. Augustine, Ambrose, and the Vulgate,
and shows "that the Holy Ghost condemned the teachings of the
heathens, but not their words" (320). Scriverius reiterates the distinction of *res* (subject matter) and *verba* (words, style) from the
rhetorical tradition and at the same time draws the line for the use of
ancient mythology. The subject matter is Christian, the formal
tradition is classical. This delineation has a long history and corresponds to Luther's stand on the use of classical learning.[36] Luther
fully recognized the qualities of a humanistic education which was to
provide the linguistic and stylistic, that is, the formal training.
Logic, rhetoric, and poetics taught young people eloquence in
speaking, writing, and preaching; but the contents, the subject matter of all learning, were the teachings of the Christian faith. In
contrast to the Bacchus hymn the subject matter of the Christ poem
calls for a clear distinction between pagan gods and Christ in the
poem itself (215ff). In a rhetorical paradox Heinsius laments that
Christ comes too late, the world is full of gods already and divided
up among them. He denounces the heathen gods of the Greeks,
Romans, Persians, and Egyptians equating them to the Golden Calf

of the Old Testament, to the work of the devil. Christ has conquered the heathen deities which can merely serve to illustrate the dark lower world, as at Christ's death (540–53), and can symbolize the devil's realm. Heinsius continues to employ mythological names and references though sparingly; but his content is eminently Christian. The use of ancient mythology in a work with a Christian content was to be the main point of the criticism some twenty years later by De Balzac of Heinsius' biblical drama *Herodes infanticida* (Herod, Child Murderer).[37]

The hymn has been regarded as Heinsius' major poetic achievement in the Dutch language;[38] its beauty was praised by the contempories as in Bredero's preface to his play *De Spaanschen Brabander* (The Spaniard from Brabant, 1618). Heinsius is considered to be a pioneer of Calvinist poetry in the Netherlands, as his hymn ushered in an era of religious poetry and it was hardly accidental that in 1616 Zacharias Heyns' important translation of Du Bartas' *La Sepmaine ou Création du Monde* (The Week, Or Creation of the World, 1579) appeared.[39] In the same year Vondel, who was influenced in his early works by Du Bartas, translated parts of *La Sepmaine*. Heinsius greatly admired this religious work which is a lengthy hymn on the Creation and, in its sequels of 1584 and 1591, a hymn on the Old Testament, rather than an epic. The *Lof-sanck van Iesus Christus* is akin in spirit and execution to the work of the French Huguenot. Heinsius had left Ronsard for Du Bartas. In the fervent religious discussion which climaxed at the Synod of Dort in 1618, Heinsius voiced the protestant individual's faith which centered around the teachings of Christ. The neo-classical form of the hymn had been filled with a protestant religious content. The playful forms and themes of Renaissance love poetry, to which most of Heinsius' Dutch verses from 1600 to 1615 belonged, were superseded by a reflective poem on a religious theme which Heinsius himself as well as his contemporaries, such as the German poet Martin Opitz, viewed as his crowning poetic achievement.

CHAPTER 3

Love Emblems

I *The Vogue of Love Emblems in the Netherlands*

SINCE the sixteenth century the combination of allegorical pictures *(pictura)* accompanied by mottoes *(inscriptio)* and expo-
sitions in verse or a prose commentary *(subscriptio)* were called
emblems.[1] Usually picture and words complemented and illustrated
each other. Drawn from the medieval allegory and bestiary,
emblem books developed as a pictorial literary genre in Italy and
became popular throughout Western Europe in the seventeenth
century. The age of ceremony, pomp, and spectacles took special
delight in visual pleasures; the combination of didactic and sensual
elements in the emblem was akin to the spirit of the age. Since the
emblem was closely related to the poetic image, it became an important artistic device in the Baroque age, when the use of similes,
metaphors, and conceits was considered essential for the pictorial
literary style.

Alciati's *Emblematum liber* (1531) already contained some love
emblems; and several conceits of the Petrarchan love lyric were
crystallized in Maurice Scève's *Délie* (1554); yet the vogue of amatory emblem books started in the Netherlands with the appearance
of the slender, anonymous volume *Quaeris quid sit amor* (You ask
what love is . . . ?) in 1601.[2] This collection was repeatedly reprinted
and later supplied with different texts and engravings; it was also
widely imitated and plagiarized. In about 1607 its third edition was
published entitled *Emblemata amatoria: iam demum emendata*
(Love Emblems: Now enlarged),[3] since then the title commonly
used for Heinsius' love emblems. The "enlargement" merely consisted of the addition of two more Dutch love poems. An entirely
new series of twenty-four emblems entitled "Het ambacht van
Cupido" was included in the 1613 Leiden edition: *Afbeeldingen van*

55

Minne. Emblemata amatoria. Emblemes d'amour. Op een nieu over-
sien ende verbetert door Theocritum a Ganda (Love Emblems . . .
Newly revised and Enlarged by Theocritus à Ganda). The trilingual
title, the Latin distichs by Petrus Scriverius, and the French quatrain added to each emblem point to a large printing for a reading
public in the Netherlands, France, and Germany.

Heinsius' success was duplicated by a series of distinguished
emblem books from the Low Countries, all exclusively devoted to
the theme of love. Otto van Veen, one of the foremost painters and
engravers of his time in the Low Countries and a teacher of Rubens,
first published an emblem book illustrating Horace, then the very
popular *Amorum emblemata* (Love Emblems, 1608), appearing in
Antwerp simultaneously in four polyglot versions. In this as in
Heinsius' work, Cupid pursues love in all possible forms; Van Veen
used several of Heinsius' ideas, while Heinsius in 1613 incorporated
some of Van Veen's. In 1611 Hooft issued the *Emblemata Amatoria.*
Afbeeldinghen van Minne. Emblemes d'Amour, a series of thirty
love emblems with inscriptions and couplets in Latin, Dutch, and
French, followed by a collection of his songs and sonnets.[4] The
pictorial series is framed by allegorical presentations of Venus and,
like Heinsius' emblems, it is introduced by a Dutch poem "A Preface to Youth;" in most of the emblems Cupid presents the ways of
love. In 1618 the anonymous *Thronus Cupidinis* (Cupid's Throne)
was in its second printing,[5] containing many emblems derived from
Otto Vaenius' (van Veen) *Amorum emblemata*. Besides poems by
Bredero, Vondel, Roemer Visscher,[6] Heinsius, Marot, and Ronsard, it has some pictures similar to those in the *Nederduytsche*
Poemata of 1616 for which Heinsius' emblem series had been illustrated with new engravings. These new engravings and those for the
Thronus Cupidinis were made at about the same time by the Chris-
pijn de Passe workshop.

The last major Dutch work of love emblems entitled *Silenus Al-*
cibiadis, sive Proteus (1618) was by Jacob Cats, who introduced
realism and everyday life. The amatory emblems in Part 1 were
used again with moral applications in Part 2, then with religious
explanations in a third part. Cats freely used ideas and representations from his predecessors; but the homely, moralizing explanations in Latin, French, and Dutch, which represented man as a
member of a family and of society, set a popular trend for subsequent emblem books.

II Quaeris quid sit amor *(1601)*

Though it was never explicitly acknowledged by him, Heinsius' authorship of *Quaeris quid sit amor* can not be questioned:[7] The entire text of this collection together with "Het ambacht van Cupido" was embodied in his *Nederduytsche Poemata;* and, since its first publication, the introductory poem "To the Maidens of Holland" was signed by Theocritus à Ganda, Daniel Heinsius' playful pseudonym. The Greek name Theocritus is the translation of the Hebrew name Daniel, and Theocritus is also the name of the Greek poet most admired, studied, and emulated by the young Heinsius; the designation "à Ganda" ("from Ghent") clearly refers to Heinsius' birthplace, which the poet likewise fondly commemorated with the Latin epithet "Gandius." The date of publication of late 1601[8] makes this book one of his first literary publications—appearing even before his tragedy *Auriacus* of 1602.

Heinsius wrote the Dutch verses for twenty-four already existing copper engravings. His friend and editor Petrus Scriverius, who had been a student at Leiden since 1593 and like Heinsius was a member of the Dousa circle, informs us in the *Nederduytsche Poemata* that a "certain amateur" had selected the twenty-four emblems from the collections of the famous Dutch physician Hadrianus Junius and others and had engravings made from them for which the poet then supplied the needed verses.[9] The artist has been identified as the well-known engraver Jacques de Gheyn who had lived in Leiden since 1596 and came into close contact with the university and Dousa's circle.[10] De Gheyn was also a friend of Hugo Grotius and had provided illustrations for Grotius' first publications, Grotius in turn supplied captions for de Gheyn's works, and in the *Quaeris* collections three inscriptions bear his name.

The engraved title of this little book shows Cupid pointing his arrow toward a lady in contemporary dress. There are empty spaces designated for the coats of arms of each of a wellborn couple as well as for their names. It is an elegant and expensive book that was intended as a gift volume for well-to-do young men. The lengthy Latin title advertises its contents: "You inquire what Love is, what it means to love and to follow Cupid's army. Look into this book, you will learn: it shows you the garden of love and its delights—look: the engraver has a gifted hand."[11] This Latin invitation on the title page, as well as the playful Dutch address "To the Maidens of Holland," is inspired by Ovid's love poetry, while the twenty-four emblems and accompanying poems for the most part draw on commonplaces from classical and Petrarchist love poetry. Cupid is present in all but a few emblems illustrating different aspects of love in a variety of situations.

There were three different sets of engravings; the original twenty-four emblems designed by de Gheyn were used for the seven editions from about 1601–1612, all of which were made from the same copper plates and show a circular picture with varying frames. For the Leiden edition of 1613, *Afbeeldingen van Minne. Emblemata amatoria. Emblemes d'amour*, new oval prints were engraved.[12] These were used in four subsequent Leiden editions through 1619. Then the same emblems were engraved a third time in rectangular format in 1615, and these plates were used for *all* editions of Heinsius' collected Dutch poems, the *Nederduytsche Poemata* of 1616 and thereafter. The content is the same in all three sets with minor variations in some pictorial details and sequence; our description will follow the emblem series in the *Nederduytsche Poemata*.

The first emblem, Cupid riding on a lion with the Vergilian motto "Omnia vincit amor" (Love conquers all; *Ecl.* X, 69), which was already an emblem in Alciati, serves as a theme for the collection. The verses elaborate the paradox of a child conquering the strong. The following seven emblems (nos. 2–8) share the theme of love as fire (a flame or light): In emblem 2 Cupid blows with a bellows under a pot steaming on the fire; in the third emblem he rakes a fire under an oven serving as an alembic. Emblem 4 portrays a candle melting beside the fire. Cupid holds a burning torch upside down in emblem 5: "What nourishes me, consumes me." A salamander which from antiquity was regarded as capable of living in fire is sitting in flames in emblem 6. Emblem 7 with Cupid placing a lantern in a niche asks: "Who can hide love?" Emblem 8 shows a burning candle on a pedestal with moths immolating themselves in its flame. Just as the salamander was used as an allegorical representation for love, the moth or butterfly became one of the commonplaces for all-consuming love in lyrical poetry. This first group of emblems is clearly indebted to the Petrarchist tradition, not to Petrarch himself, but mostly to French intermediaries. Heinsius' lines faithfully explain the emblems, but they do not make direct use of quotes from Petrarch.

The next eight emblems (nos. 9–16) occur in pairs: Emblems 9 and 10 are taken from nature and compare the breath and beauty of a girl with the wind and the moon respectively; in emblems 11 and 12 love is likened to a bird in captivity. The allegory of bitter-sweet in emblem 13 is based on the wormwood growing out of a beehive; in emblem 14 another theme of nature is used, the twining ivy. Emblems 15 and 16 are both designed around the stag, the Petrarchist sign for the wounded lover.

Realistic situations from rural and domestic life are illustrated in another group of seven pictures (nos. 17–23): Emblem 17 depicts Cupid grafting a tree; emblem 18, the ditch being filled after the calf has drowned. In emblem 19 a vine bearing grapes and clinging to a dead tree signifies the union between lovers lasting beyond death; for Heinsius it means "Death conquers all, but Love overcomes even death." Love in bondage is the theme of emblems 20 to 23. In number 20 a realistic domestic scene pictures a mouse trapped in a cage and afraid to emerge, a huge cat lies in wait while Cupid is peeking around the corner. The Italian motto "evil weighs upon me, and the fear of worse haunts me" represents the initial line of a Petrarchan sonnet (Canz: 186); and Heinsius explains the emblem: "Als ick in liefde ben, dan ben ick als gebonden,/ Als ick daer buyten ben, dan ben ick gans geschonden" (When I am in love, I am bound. When I am out of it, I am grievously hurt, 90). Emblem 21 uses yoked oxen to demonstrate the bonds of love; emblem 22 shows birds willingly imprisoning themselves in a cage and in emblem 23 a blind-folded horse turns the wheel of a millstone. The last emblem (24) strikes a somber note. It shows an old man besieging a girl, while Cupid's arrow is on its way to a corpse in the foreground. An owl sits next to the couple, another one on the corpse. The belated amorous attempts of the old man, a "living corpse," are described in the poem. The Latin motto is a line from Alciati (emblem 84 in the 1550 edition): "Like the night owl among the graves, sitting on corpses." For the young lovers to whom Heinsius' emblem book was addressed this is an exhortation to enjoy love before it is too late. It is another version of the *carpe diem* theme, a fitting conclusion to the series.

Although an unidentified "amateur" had selected the emblems and Jacques de Gheyn designed the prints, in all probability Heinsius was responsible for the arrangement of the emblems; he certainly interpreted each one. Since the Cupid figure seems in some emblems (9, 10, 13, 14, 18, 20, 21) to be an isolated part of the picture and could easily have been added to the plates, perhaps

Heinsius suggested the explicit interpretation as love emblems? Several pictures and mottoes would have lent themselves to nonerotic interpretation and were in fact used in other emblem books. Heinsius organized these emblems from a conceptual point of view. He coordinated the sections according to theme and then framed the series with two basic statements: the omnipotence of love *Omnia vincit amor* in emblem 1 and the exhortation to timely enjoyment in emblem 24.

Nearly all emblems and mottoes can be traced to earlier sources, to the Hellenistic tradition (the *Greek Anthology*), to the Roman poets (especially Ovid), to Petrarch ãnd Maurice Scève, to Alciati, and Hadrianus Junius. De Gheyn's pictures show a great improvement over the schematic emblems of Alciati and Scève, which resembled hieroglyphic pictures. The scenes, landscapes, and interiors of Junius have been developed further toward a realistic presentation of a variety of everyday life scenes. The pictures show perspective and detail enhancing the motto; and the allegorical, abstract idea is visually elucidated in a manner similar to that of a proverb which explains and generalizes but does not provide a riddle or obscure the meaning.

Heinsius' lines further enhance this tendency toward realism, immediacy, and explanation. They abound in colloquial and proverbial phrases and provide a close reading of the picture from a personal perspective: It is mostly the "I" that speaks and relates an experience, then draws the conclusions in the final epigrammatic lines. Mythology (except for the Cupid allegory) is absent, the effects of love are explained in relationship to the pictures. The "Art of Love," appearing in useful and entertaining handbooks throughout the ages, has assumed yet another form in the De Gheyn-Heinsius emblem book in which the playful, optimistic atmosphere of the well-to-do Dutch upper middle class has left its traces. Petrarchist motives and paradoxes, though not chosen by Heinsius, abound (emblem 2–16); but a psychological, realistic approach begins to manifest itself in his verses containing truisms about love: The lover emerges as an individual with emotions, and at the same time he begins to be depicted in the context of the real world.

III   *"Het Ambacht van Cupido"* (1613)

For the series of love emblems "The Trades of Cupid" the pictures illustrating Heinsius' verses were presumably made after the poem had been written or on the poet's suggestions. The artist who

designed the oval prints has not been identified; and since they are
considered inferior in artistic execution to de Gheyn's, the artist was
probably a relatively unknown man. In addition to Heinsius' verses,
Scriverius supplied a Latin couplet and a French quatrain. Trilingual editions of emblems had been popularized by Otto Vaenius'
emblem books, among them the *Amorum emblemata* (1608) which
appeared with Latin, Dutch, and French; Latin, French, and Italian; or Latin, English, and Italian verses. Multilingual editions not
only appealed to a wider reading public, they were also an indication of the cultured readership in the Low Countries where people
read, and usually also spoke, several languages.

Even more so than in the *Quaeris* collection, each of the twenty-
four emblems in "Het ambacht van Cupido" centers around Cupid,
the personification of Love, presented in everyday occupations. The
Latin mottoes are based for the most part on concepts from Ovid
and the *Greek Anthology*. Emblem 1 shows two Cupids tossing a
ball, representing the earth, between them. The braced wrists are a
realistic detail pointing to a then-popular game, a sort of tennis. The
Latin motto, "Pila mundus Amorum est," is rephrased in the poem:
"The world is the ball, with which we play." The ball of fortune, a
traditional metaphor especially popular in Baroque poetry, was
adapted by Heinsius to refer to love and served as the theme for his
emblem series. The second emblem illustrates the motto "Love
preserves the harmony of things" showing Cupid as a cooper. The
fashioning of the vat by joining the wood with hoops is the concrete
concept in this mythological metaphor of the poem and the
emblematic picture. Among the other commonplace activities presented in this series are: Cupid at the spinning wheel (emblem 3), a
homely scene which is a presentation of a mythological tale; Cupid
playing dice (emblem 4); Cupid as an artist working on a girl's
portrait (emblem 5), a theme similar to Heinsius' Dutch verses for a
Latin motto; Cupid sowing seed and children's heads springing from
the ground as "The wondrous seed of love" (emblem 8); Cupid
playing with a top (emblem 9—"I am sustained by whipping").[13]
"Cupid drives the hoop: that is the game of love," as the Dutch
poem begins, is the theme of emblem 14; Cupid plays blindman's
bluff in emblem 15. In yet another game Cupid blows soap bubbles
in emblem 21 with the motto "Love's favor is a bubble" *(bulla
favor)*, an adaptation of Terence's *homo bulla* popularized in Erasmus' *Adagia:* "Man is a bubble" is often pictured as a child blowing
soap bubbles in paintings allegorizing the fragility of life.[14] In the

final emblem (24) Cupid is a tailor; "Omnia coniungo" becomes "I unite everything."[15]

With the first emblem, the world as a game of love, the theme for the series is set. The last emblem, love as a common bond, concludes the series with a summarizing statement. Cupid, the allegorized figure of love, is present in each emblem; and each shows a characteristic feature of love. The Latin mottoes are proverbial in character, often approaching a moral; they are clear rather than cryptic. The pictures represent realistic, everyday situations in contemporary Dutch life, showing Cupid at work and at play. Classical mythology and the poetic literary tradition have almost completely disappeared behind the contemporary occupations. Heinsius' arrangement of love emblems into a structured composition can be regarded as an innovation which has been compared to the development of the sonnet sequence.[16]

The Dutch verses give explicit descriptions of these realistic scenes, explaining the allegory in visual detail. Even if some emblems are based on Vaenius' *Amorum emblemata* (1608), the majority were conceived by Heinsius and inspired by his surroundings and the contemporary scene. They illustrate common situations of love, but the visualization of these maxims is realistic, concrete, and obvious. It is not the riddled conceit which can only be understood by a knowledge of certain signs, with mythological learning, or by an intellectual effort assisted by explanatory lines. In technique, but not in content, these emblems approach at times the iconic poems Heinsius wrote for the slender volume *Spiegel vande doorluchtige Vrouwen* (Mirror of Illustrious Women, 1606).[17] This was a moralistic and antiquarian picture series which had been designed by Jacques de Gheyn in the 1590s simultaneously with the love emblems for *Quaeris quid sit amor*. There are few earlier pictorial parallels for Heinsius' ideas in "Het ambacht van Cupido"; some did become long-standing favorites thereafter. The prominence of the winged Cupid with his bow and arrows, playful but realistic, involved in contemporary games and occupations, is a heritage of the Hellenistic-Latin tradition, in which love was depicted as a frolicsome boy similar to the representations in the Pompeian frescos. Thus, while in his first emblem series Heinsius was still bound to the literary, especially the Petrarchist tradition and to earlier emblematic representations, in "Het ambacht van Cupido" he created a genuine, partly original series of love emblems. Scenes and interpretations have replaced the earlier allegorical signs. Realism and detail, to be observed also in Dutch genre painting in the seventeenth century,[18] have supplanted classical and mythological subjects. Heinsius' poems were conceived as a verbal paraphrase for the picture; they no longer present a riddle but describe the pictorial device in great detail as if to exemplify *ut pictura poesis*.

CHAPTER 4

The Elegies

I Neo-Latin Poetry and the Edition of Heinsius' Poemata

F OR Neo-Latin poetry[1] the classical heritage of Greece and Rome
served as a model, as well as the Italian Renaissance authors
since Petrarch. Since the turn of the fifteenth century the scientific
and artistic aspirations of the humanists had invaded the North, the
Low Countries, and Germany. A thorough study of ancient authors
coupled with an intensive training in the classical languages, which
was pursued especially in the religious schools, provided the audience for Neo-Latin literature, a literature in which all countries of
Europe (except the territories under Turkish occupation) shared.[2]
Language, literary models, artistic and aesthetic goals formed a
common bond among the humanist poets such as the Frenchman
Michael Marullus (died 1500), the Italian Marcantonio Flaminio
(1498–1550), the Dutch Janus Secundus (1511–1536), the German
Petrus Lotichius Secundus (1528–1560), or the Pole Matthias
Casimir Sarbievus (1595–1640). National boundaries were of little
importance for the community of scholars and poets who had redis-
covered classical literature and culture and who under its guidance
strove for the education of the individual and a worldly existence.

Many Dutch authors of the early seventeenth century wrote in
Latin and the importance of this literature is especially evident for
Daniel Heinsius and Hugo Grotius, whose Dutch works remained
on a much more modest scale in scope and aesthetic perfection in
comparison with their achievements in Neo-Latin literature. As one
of the most distinguished classical scholars of his century, Heinsius
found it natural to write verses in Latin for an educated reading
public. When Hugo Grotius once asked him for a poem for a mutual
friend's wedding, he requested that it be in Dutch, so that the bride
would also be able to read it.[3] On that occasion Heinsius responded
with a suitable poem in Latin and also composed an epigram in

64

Dutch. Versification came easily to him, and he was constantly besieged with requests for dedicatory or occasional poems. The vast
amount of Neo-Latin poetry that he left behind attests to his popularity.

All his life, writing poetry was a favorite pastime for Heinsius who,
at the age of nine, according to his own testimony started "to scrib-
ble verses and to pour them out for any occasion."[4] The study of
Greek and Latin literature at school required practice in writing
compositions in the style of classical authors. While a student at
Franeker Academy, Heinsius wrote a poem about Hero and Lean-
der in the style of the Greek poet Musaeus, composed love poetry
and published a commemorative poem. With an epithalamium for
the wedding of Petrus Scriverius in 1599 Heinsius seems to have
entered Scaliger's circle in Leiden. A first collection of occasional
and "moral" verses[5] was appended to his drama *Auriacus* in 1602.
Later that year he dedicated one of his first accomplished love
lyrics, a bucolic eclogue in the manner of Vergil, to Janus Dousa,
the distinguished poet, co-founder, and curator of Leiden University. The years from 1602 until 1621 were to be Heinsius' most
productive period for writing poetry.

His first important collection *Elegiarum libri III, Monobiblos,
Silvae* appeared in 1603. Dedicated to Cornelis van der Myle, a
curator of the university and later son-in-law of Oldenbarnevelt, the
volume shows Heinsius as an already accomplished poet. It consists
of three Books of elegies, mostly love poems in thematic arrangement; the "Monobiblos" (single book, like Propertius) which continues the themes of the elegies; miscellaneous poems, in hexameter under the heading "Silvae" (forests, i.e. occasional poems); and
as a fitting conclusion to a volume which owed so much to Theocritus and Anacreontic poetry, an oration on the nature of poetry,
held in May 1603 when Heinsius embarked on his first lectures on
Greek poetry.

A second edition of Heinsius' Latin poems appeared in 1606. A
fourth book had been added to the elegies, while the "Monobiblos"
had undergone considerable changes, with the long mythological
poem "Hylas" appearing for the first time. In 1610 a third and
greatly revised edition came out in both Leiden and Cambridge; the
volume now contained five books of elegies, and several poems from
the first edition were replaced by new ones. The fourth edition of
1613 again incorporated change, and Heinsius informed the reader

in the preface: "Our playful kind of poetry *(lusus)* has been improved with great care and not a little has been added. What we published in the first edition has in part been censored, some appears further below, some at the end of the volume."[6] Thus in 1613 Heinsius' evaluation of his poetry had changed: Many of his early elegies (mostly from Books II and III) were relegated to the end of the volume under the heading "Youthful Elegies, which he wrote as a young man or as almost still a boy." The body of elegies had again been reduced to three books and underwent only minor stylistic changes in subsequent years.

The inclusion of a sizable number of Heinsius' poems in Gruter's collection *Delitiae poetarum Belgicorum* (The Delights of Dutch Poets, 1614) is an indication of their popularity. Then in 1617, four years after the last edition, a newly revised edition[7] appeared in Leiden which was followed in 1621 when Heinsius was 41 by yet another edition in which the most remarkable feature was the inclusion of the long didactic poem *De contemptu mortis* (On Contempt of Death). With this edition his creative period of almost twenty years paused. It was not until eleven years later that a new group of mostly occasional poems was appended to the poetic drama *Herodes infanticida* (Herod, Child Murderer, 1632). The edition of 1640 and the final edition of 1649, prepared by Nicolaas Heinsius, relegated all elegies written before 1610 and even the funeral poems for Dousa to the section of "Youthful Poems," while reflective and didactic poems gained preponderance and were put in a prominent place.

A body of Greek verses appeared separately in 1613 under the title *Peplus Graecorum epigrammatum* (Collection—literally: Athena's robe of state—of Greek epigrams) and at the same time was included in his poetry edition of that year and subsequent ones. This collection contained, besides occasional verses, Greek versions of Latin poems as well as fifty-seven epigrams in the manner of the *Greek Anthology*. They were translated into Latin by a German admirer of Heinsius in 1618, but their importance lies in the display of his extraordinary gift for language, as only very few humanists succeeded in writing flawless verses in classical Greek. The epigrams served as models for the writing of this genre which was extremely popular in the seventeenth century.

The editions of Heinsius' poetry from 1603 to 1649 reflect the poet's activities and his appraisal of his own work: He produced the most—and also the best—verses during the first two decades of the seventeenth century. In the early years, love poetry in conventional form reflecting his own aspirations and, in later years, verses characteristic of his intellectual occupation and social standing provide the major themes. He continued to produce occasional poetry throughout his life, and descriptive, contemplative, and mythological themes became increasingly dominant; he wrote no religious poetry in Latin, except for the verse poem in four books *De contemptu mortis*. His facility at versification and mastery of form are evident throughout his poetic production. Rather than following Heinsius' individual development as a writer[8]—which is, of course, discernible to a certain extent, but of lesser importance for the Neo-Latin poet who orients himself on classical models and their styles—we shall in this chapter discuss the major types, themes, and stylistic features of the elegies, then devote another chapter to some of his outstanding occasional poems, and one to the didactic poem *De contemptu mortis*.

II *The Elegy as a Poem*

The word "elegy" usually evokes the notion of a melancholy and meditative kind of poem. Neo-Latin poetry, however, followed classical literature in which an elegy was solely defined by its meter: a distich consisting of a dactylic hexameter and a pentameter. This metrical pattern with its gentle yet insistent musical quality was compared by Ovid to the rise and fall of a jet of water: "In six feet let my work rise and fall again in five."[9] A variety of themes and moods was conveyed in the elegy which more than any other poetic form revealed the poet's personality, his tastes, his experiences, his philosophy of life. The elegy did not compete with the epic. In the postclassical period, however, long mythological narratives appeared, such as Callimachus' elegies; and during the Augustan Age the elegy served as the preferred medium of Roman love poetry for Catullus, Tibullus, Propertius, and Ovid.

The Neo-Latin poets acknowledged this tradition and continued it. Janus Secundus (1511–1536) from the Hague speaks about his poetry through Elegy who appears in his famous poem "Somnium" (dream):

> Imparibus tibi nota modis Elegia pridem,
>   Ebria cum caneres lumina mollis herae,

Quaeque tuas curas, et quae tua gaudia novi, . . .
Adsumus Italia, tales nos terra remittet
  Aurea, quae nobis patria sola manet.
Quae cineres mutos vatum venerata priorum,
  Quos fovit gremio daedala Roma suo,
Parturit usque novos, et iura tuetur avita.[10]

(I am the Elegy with uneven rhythm, long known to you, when you sang about the seductive eyes of your tender girl. I have known all your sorrows and all your joys. . . . We come from Italy, which is our only true homeland; as you see us, the golden earth has sent us. Revering the silent ashes of the ancient poets, which the city of art brought forth from her womb, Rome gives birth to ever new ones and maintains the ancient customs.)

Janus Secundus then cites Italian Renaissance poets whose Latin poetry inspired him: Pontanus (1426–1503), Marullus (+1500), Bembo (1470–1547), the Strozzi from Ferrara, and Sannazaro (1458–1530). Dousa's translations of Secundus' poems circulated in his circle which used his *Basia* ("Kisses" published 1539), elegies, odes, and the epithalamium as literary models; and Petrus Scriverius published a complete edition of Secundus in 1619.

Heinsius, who in 1618 edited Secundus' prose account of his travels to France and Spain from the manuscript,[11] was intimately acquainted with this tradition. Like a prologue, the opening poem of his elegies, "He commends his Muses to Joseph Scaliger," characterizes their nature:

[10]   Pro iaculis frigus, pro face mittit aquas. (1610, V, 5, p. 125)

[11]   Perque vagos saltus, habitataque vatisbus olim

Antra, levesque umbras, priscaque rura feror . . .

[22]   Et mea lascivus carmina discit Amor. (1603, I, 1, p. 4,5)[12]

(Through vast forest, caves once inhabited by poets, light shadows, and ancient lands I roam . . . . And playful Amor is learning my songs.)

In the final elegy ("Operis conclusio") Heinsius states that he could have written about wars, battles, and kings, for his poetic talent (*furor*) was not lacking. In fact, he had treated those topics in the theater only the previous year with his *Auriacus* (1602). But love is the major theme in his poems since he met his girl Rossa:

> Candida simplicitas placuit, leviterque cothurni
> [20]   Pondere deposito, blandus amator eram.
> Risit, et ostendens gremium Cythereia mater,
> En ait orchestram, magne poeta, tuam.
> (1603, III, 14, p. 118)

(The splendid simplicity pleased me, and gently I put aside the weighty cothurn, became an enticing lover. Venus smiles; and showing me her bosom, she says, there is your stage, great poet.)

Heinsius not only defends his change from writing drama to poetry, but at the same time he distinguishes his poetry from the more exacting and more prestigious form of the epic, a topical distinction since antiquity. Homer, he explains in the introductory poem to Book II, was blind and unable to see the beautiful girls; thus he wrote about fierce warriors. Heinsius chooses differently:

> At mihi sunt dulces oculi spectari puellas:
>   Et minor hoc nobis magnus Homerus erat.
> [35]   Posteritas mea crede mihi, sua iactat Homerus,
>   Et rigidas acies et fera signa ducum.
> Dignior ille cani, levibus qui victus ocellis,
>   Tutius ut possit vincere, victus abit. (1603, II, 1, p. 43)

(But I have eyes to watch sweet girls, and great Homer was in this respect less than I. Believe me, my posterity, Homer tossed about his men, the rough battle lines and wild standards of the leaders. Worthier than an old man is he, who, conquered by fair eyes, sets out defeated to conquer all the more certainly.)

Not to be taken literally in any way as a rejection of Homer, such lines rather characterize the nature of his poems in the tradition of the Roman elegy. They are above all playful poems, games *(lusus);* Ovid was known as the "playful author of tender love-poems" *(tenerorum lusor amorum),* Catullus called his poems "trifles" *(nugae).* But like the works of the classical elegiac poets, Heinsius' verses are the product of a "conscious literary technique" *(doctus labor)* exhibiting clear thought in polished phrases and precise metaphors.

III   *Love and Poetry*

The major theme is love with all its inherited *topoi* from Greek and Latin poets, as well as Petrarchist commonplaces, most of which have appeared in the *Nederduytsche Poemata* and in the *Emblemata amatoria*. But while in the *Emblemata amatoria* such *topoi* are visualized in the emblematic picture and condensed to epigrammatic brevity in the verses, in the elegies they are often described in full in a scene which may hint at some personal experience or contemporary life. The girl Rossa ("the sandy-haired one")[13] is his inspiration for the elegies and "Monobiblos."[14] A situation is related when he describes how he took a walk in the city and saw the construction of large elaborate houses, luxurious showcases of their owners' wealth (1603, II, 7, "To his girl"). The poet does not strive for such riches but wants to build his own house "on the rosy cheeks of his girl"; and he imagines this house as an abode protected from the vicissitudes of weather and fortune, safe from rivals. In another poem (1603, II, 11) he sets out to dissuade his girl from a trip by boat; instead he offers to be the captain and in the imaginary voyage, he perishes together with her and enters the Elysian Fields to be crowned by Anacreon, the Greek poet of love and wine. He imagines himself leaving for France[15] and promises fidelity (1603, III, 2); he attempts in vain to leave Rossa (1603, "Monobiblos," 10), and the girl takes him away from his legal studies back to love (1603, "Monobiblos," 11). Common situations from the Roman love elegy and the Petrarchist tradition, such as the voyage, the dream, the crowning of the poet, building a house, the features of the girl, are narrated and combined with a reference to Heinsius' own life, such as the trip to France and the early aversion to legal studies.

Rossa is *both* the idolized beloved and a girl of flesh and blood, though she is not an easily identifiable individual. Often Rossa represents a projection of the poet's amorous feelings, a personification of love and poetry. Rossa is never pictured beyond the Petrarchist tradition of the red cheeks or lips, white neck and tender arms; Heinsius described his real and imaginary encounter with love in traditional literary forms. To look for the real Rossa is as futile as it is unjustified to reproach Heinsius as lacking feeling or experience. His poetic imagination was kindled by varying situations of love, real and traditional. "Why do you ask so often about my love and do not let me hide my flame?" (1613, I, 3, p. 6), the poet asks an inquisitive friend; only his poetry is important:

> [71]   Haec quoque Dii praestant, qui me facere poetam.
>   Dos hederae nobis, dos mihi carmen erit.

Caetera congnosces: sine nomine nomen habebis,
   Nec poteris flammae nescius esse meae. (1613, I, 3, p. 8)

(The gods, who made me a poet, have given me this: Ivy will be my dowry,
also my song. You will understand the rest: Nameless you will have a name
and be unable to ignore my flame.)

Two later elegies may actually refer specifically to an unhappy
love. As best man at Grotius' wedding in July 1608, Heinsius and
another friend both fell in love with the same girl, a relative of the
bride, Margaretha Luycz, who later married someone else.[16] "To
the Girl Who Married the False Rival" (1610, V, 7, pp. 98–99) is a
lament about the loss of his girl, Lucia. The concise poem of fifteen
couplets successfully blends the experience of a personal loss with
the traditional elements of elegiac poetry, rhetorical images, and
mythology. The opening couplet presents the situation; then in a
conciliatory mood—bitterness or invective is altogether absent from
Heinsius' elegies—the poet resigns himself with a generalizing
statement in the next two couplets:

[1] Quae placuit nobis, quanvis vix visa fuisset,
      Alterius nunc est facta puella viri.
   Nil iuvat ignavis animum consumere curis,
      Nil iuvat hic fati de gravitate queri.
[5] Vinceris aut vincis, lex haec certantibus instat.[17]
      In medio posita est aequaque palma iacet. (1610, V, 7, p. 98)

(She, who pleased us, although we hardly saw her, has now become the girl
of another. It is useless to destroy your mind with idle anxiety; it is useless
to complain about the severity of fate. You are conquered or you conquer;
this is the only rule of struggle. The palm of victory lies equitably in the
middle.)

The following five couplets contain an amplification, citing
mythological examples for lost loves and varying fortune in the
realm of Venus with the conclusion: "Errat et in regno Veneris
fortuna vagatur,/ Praecipue est illic quod Dea semper agat." (In
Venus' realm fortune roams and wanders; there it is important that
the Goddess always rule.) Then the poet addresses himself to his
own situation and the girl:

> Forsitan et demens nocuit secordia nobis:
>   Nec satis intentus, nec bene cautus eram,
> Alteriusque iacet, ne sit nullius in ulnis.
>   Et sapit, et venia digna puella mea est.
> [20] Quidquid id est, vires animumque a vulnere certum est
>   Sumere: sumenti sit Venus aequa mihi.

(Perhaps a foolish negligence has harmed me and I was not attentive, not eager enough that she be in nobody's arms; now she lies in those of another one. My girl regrets it and deserves forgiveness. No matter what, from this wound I shall certainly recover strength and courage: and when I recover may Venus favor me.)

This conclusion is amplified with metaphors from the hunt. Heinsius merely touches on images from the Petrarchist tradition familiar to the educated reader of his day and to the Dutch audience from the works of Janus Secundus, Dousa, or from Heinsius' own *Emblemata amatoria:* the hunter whose boar escapes, the fisherman who is unsure of his catch, and the birdcatcher who is successful with another bird. The poet restates his experience in these images integrating them into the theme of the poem and concludes with a final epigrammatic couplet:

> Non iacet incassum media venator in herba,
>   Si fugit, et primus vincula rumpit aper.
> Nec gemit infelix vacuos qui respicit hamos,
> [25]   Cum tremulum fallax linea sensit onus.
> Dum sedet, elapsamque sibi non cogitat anceps,
>   Saepe aliam rursus cassidae cepit avem.
> Tu quoque, si qua mea est, ignosce Walachria culpae,
> [30]   Inque alia nobis non inimica veni.

(The huntsman does not lie in vain in the grass, when the first boar breaks his fetters and flees. He does not sigh unhappily, seeing the empty hook, when the treacherous line has felt the trembling weight. While waiting and not thinking of the bird that escaped, he often gets another one in his chase. And you, girl from Walcheren, if I sinned forgive me and come friendly in the other one's place.)

Just like the hunter who does not give up, the poet has found another girl. He is comforted for the misfortune with a new gain. Even if we can assume that an actual experience formed the basis of the poem, there is nothing of the despair and bitterness of a Catullus over Lesbia or Janus Secundus over the loss of his Julia. Rather than reproaching the girl or himself, the poet submits to the rule of fortune with stoic equanimity. "In Venus' realm fortune reigns"; love is a struggle *(certamen)* with an ambiguous outcome and not to be taken too seriously.

The well-structured thoughts are presented in three major sections as in classical poetry. In verses 1–6 the poet presents the situation (a lost love) from which he generalizes about love; verses 11–16 amplify the idea of fortune and love with mythological examples; in the third section, verses 17–30, the poet turns to himself with *a)* the reproach, 17–20, *b)* experience gained amplified by Petrarchist imagery, 21–28, and *c)* the consolation, 29–30. The polished language is reminiscent of the Roman elegiac poets and is based on the main structural features of antithesis and balance, without becoming ludicrous or artificial. In his mythological digression Heinsius merely hints at several tales from the Trojan cycle, a technique similar to that of Ovid in his *Amores*. This is balanced by a second digression, the hunting imagery from the Petrarchist tradition, which likewise serves the purpose of illustrating the thought before it is pointedly phrased in the concluding couplet, a reversal of the initial situation and the opening lines. Formal mastery in the use of the classical and Petrarchist tradition when describing a personal and at the same time ever-recurring situation has led Heinsius to find his own style.

Love as a *certamen* (struggle) is a motif that occurs in endless variation in Heinsius' love poetry. Love as a form of military service was a common metaphor for Ovid as in the opening lines of *Amores*, I, 9: "Militat omnis amans, et habet sua castra Cupido;/ Attice, crede mihi, militat omnis amans." (Every lover is a soldier, and Cupid has his own camp; believe me, Atticus, every lover is a soldier.) After Ovid, metaphors from the realm of war and love became traditional; Petrarch's often paraphrased sonnet "I find no peace and bear no arms for war"[18] to which this theme is usually traced is merely another famous link in the propagation of the motif. Heinsius merges it with the pen-and-sword *topos*, defending his own position:

> Nos, Veneris pia turba, leves sectemur amores:
> [80]   Et, gremium dominae, sint mihi castra, meae.
> Hic ego versatos contemnam fortiter enses,
> Cunctaque quae fuerint spicula missa feram. (1603, I, 8, p. 23)

(Let us pious followers of Venus pursue tender loves; and the bosom of the beloved be my camp. Here I gravely spurn the busy swords, and I shall bear all the arrows thrown.)

He addressed these lines in 1603 to his brother Nicolaas who had returned from France in order to join Prince Maurice against the Spanish. Heinsius, with all his enthusiasm for the Dutch cause, kept aloof from fighting. Only one poem in the 1603 edition, "To the Dutch on Their Expedition to Flanders" (II, 5, p. 50–53), is an exhortation to battle to his compatriots though he is unsure if he himself is fit for battle: "Nescio ut immensos mea mens se tollat in ausus,/ Et gravius toto pectore surgat opus" (p. 53) (I don't know, if my mind equals the immense undertakings, and a work weightier than my heart arises). Heroism and patriotism are conspicuously subdued in the elegies. Love and poetry, a playful pastime growing out of the author's intellectual pursuits and personal lifestyle, are the themes of the elegies.

IV *Two Fountain Poems*

In Book III of the elegies two poems are written with a fountain as their subject matter. In theme and literary technique, the two elegies resemble each other closely so that they can be regarded as a pair, complementing each other. They embody all the characteristic features of Heinsius' elegies and belong to his most accomplished verses. The first is dedicated "To the Cupid in Brussels artistically fashioned next to the Labyrinth and spouting water from a fountain" (1610, V, 5, pp. 125–26). When visiting Brussels in 1609 during his trip to the South to take care of some family business in his hometown, Ghent, Heinsius must have seen this fountain in the gardens of the ducal palace.[19] Such a Cupid fountain had become a favorite decoration for a grotto in Renaissance gardens in Italy. A Cupid spouting water, not a natural but artificial creation, is the key idea on which the poem is based, the oxymoron of a cold Cupid or a burning god serving as a cool fountan (lines 1–6). Heinsius even changes Cupid's mythological origin: From the son of Venus and Mercury he beomes the child of a water deity, a nymph who inhabited the sea, rivers, and fountains:

> Non illum genuit claudo Cytherea marito,
>   E Nymphis genetrix illa vel illa fuit.

Non face, non iaculis, non saevis ignibus urit:

(Venus did not bear him with her limping husband, someone of the Nymphs was his mother. He does not burn with a torch, arrows, or savage fire: Instead of arrows he carries coldness, instead of a burning torch, water.)

The allusion in line 7 to Cupid's mythological origin is then expanded in six couplets (11–22) to other mythological figures who will enjoy this fountain, as the soothing and refreshing qualities of the water affect each god. After Heinsius has established the nature of the Cupid fountain as a place of rest and rejuvenation, lines 23–24 established another, related quality: its purity which is defined as an absence of erotic stimulation:

[23] Spicula quae cernis, sine vi sine vulnere manant,
       Et prohibet solam missa sagitta sitim.

(The spears you see flow without violence or wounding, and the arrow quenches the thirst alone.)

After allusions to three myths of illicit love (25–34), loves that could have been prevented by such a cold Cupid, the purity of the fountain is emphasized. The explicit statement "there is nothing more chaste than it [the fountain]" (29) is rephrased in the mythological concept that Venus herself, if she came, would realize this fountain was forbidden to her. Next, the surroundings of the fountain are described (35–46): The open path leading up to it is contrasted with the labyrinth of mythology and with Theseus' labors, while the shady setting of the fountain reiterates the theme of the poem. The dense foliage protects the refreshing coolness of the fountain keeping Phoebus' (the sun's) rays and impetuousness away. The cool setting is further enhanced by the water's origin from a deep spring:

Stat super armatus solis (quis crederet) undis
Et solas undas eiaculatour Amor.
Sentiat hunc, nullos si quis desiderat ignes,
[50] Frigoraque ardoris poscat amica Deum.
Sentiat hunc, ipsum si quis vitabit, Amorem:
Causaque nullius fiet Amoris Amor.

(Amor stands above armed only—who could believe it—with water and shoots forth only water. Whoever has no desire for flames should feel him, should ask the god of heat for welcome coolness. He should feel this Amor, whoever will avoid him. This god of love will not be the cause of any love.)

These final three couplets return to the statue of Cupid and to the theme of the elegy, the paradox of a "cold Amor," climaxing in the last line with epigrammatic succinctness.

The theme of this poem—the contrast between fire and water, love and chastity—is of course present in ancient literature and also a favorite with Petrarch. What distinguishes this particular elegy is the skillful variation of the theme based on the visual image of the fountain. Heinsius proceeds from a description of the "work of nature, or rather of art" (4) to involve the reader's attention with the direct command: "look," *(aspice)*. The juxtaposition of "art" and "nature," indicative of the fountain, is maintained throughout the poem, where the cold water, the shady setting, the winding path give rise to elaborate allusions to learned mythology. The fountain considered as a work of art denotes its artificiality in contrast to nature as well as the artful, artistic creation of men. For Heinsius, the latter does not consist of the sculptural qualities of the statue; we hear nothing about the kind of stone, for instance, nor about any details such as hair, features, and so forth. The mythological tradition, since it is not only a heritage from antiquity, but the creative expression of humanity, provides the artistic quality of an object like the fountain. Myths are alive and an integral part of poetic fantasy and vision. A mere allusion to a mythological figure will enhance an observation, add intellectual and conceptual quality to it.

Built on antithesis, the principle of contrast and adversity dominates the verses, the imagery, and the style. The path here is unlike the labyrinth of Minos: The water is pure, unlike Phaedra's passion and Hippolytus' death; the foliage provides cool shade, unlike Phoebus' heat. The play with antithetical words and phrases like *pro face mittit aquas* (10) (instead of a burning torch he shoots forth water) or *ianua clausa patet* (32) (a closed door opens to Venus) can be observed throughout the poem; it is a correllation to the antithetical theme. This, together with the numerous stylistic devices used (oxymoron, metonomy, alliteration, anaphora, adnominatio, parallelism, amplification), gives the poem a rhetorical quality. The poem is dominated by conceptualization, by traditional ideas in novel and

unexpected form. Heinsius' intellect was playing with a tradition
when he re-created the fountain in this elegy.

The other fountain poem is entitled "On a Very Pure Spring in
the Forest Near Geeraardsbergen" (1610, V, 7, p. 132–33). The
poet's grandfather Nicolaas Heinsius had been burgomaster of
Geeraardsbergen (Grammont) which Heinsius visited in 1609, and
he possibly also went to the spring nearby known for its clear water.
The poem begins with a long address: The poet as a wanderer
approaches the fountain in its tranquil natural setting which is contrasted to the vicissitudes of travel. He begs to be received, promis-
ing not to disturb the peacefulness. A series of six comparisons leads
to a description of the one quality of the spring, the attraction of its
pure water, and the poet repeats his earlier request (9, *accipe me*
receive me) with the same words in slight variation: [22]" Accipe
defessum nimiis solisque viaeque/ Aestibus, et siccam frigore pelle
sitim./" (Receive me tired from too much heat of sun and journey:
drive away my drying thirst with your coolness.) He prefers the
clear water to wine, a simple life to a luxurious one. From the
fountain the poet turns to himself, the wanderer, with observations
on natural simplicity, concluding with a traditional comparison to
earlier days for which he is longing.

> O ego sic possim tranquille ducere vitam,
>   Ignotus populo, cognitus ipse mihi!
> [40]   Sic mihi paulatim veniat non pigra senectus,
>   Tardaque mors, felix terminus ipsa sui.

(O if I could only lead my life so peacefully, unknown to the masses, aware
of myself. In such a way welcome old age would come to me after a while,
death slow in coming, and an end happy in itself.)

In the last five couplets (43–52)[20] the idea of a simple life is extended
to the praise of friendship and poetry. His poet-friend from Ghent,
Vrient, and his beloved are sufficient for him. Heinsius ends the
poem by hailing the spring as his source of poetic inspiration.

While an artistic creation was the point of departure in the poem
"To the Cupid in Brussels," nature, a spring in the forest, is the focal
point in this elegy "On a Very Pure Spring." Observations of an
object forms the basis for Heinsius' verses in both poems. Visual
perception of the spring—the dense foliage, green grass, clear

waters—is enhanced and interpreted in its essence with mythological references. From the beginning the poet has entered this elegy
by approaching the fountain as a weary wanderer to quench his
thirst. From a spring in the forest the fountain becomes a symbol for
the poet's creative imagination. Nature, the crystal spring, and his
love, Hyella the "clear crystal one," merge and become one as his
poetic creations, his love elegies.

The two fountain poems are similar in literary technique and
style. Both grew out of the tradition of classical and Neo-Latin
poetry. The "Cupid in Brussels" with its love/heat/fire and chastity/
coolness/water antitheses belongs to the Ovidian-Petrarchist poetic
convention. The elegy "On a Very Pure Spring" is in style and
concepts more akin to Horace's famous ode: "O fons Bandusiae,
splendidior vitrio,/ Dulci digne mero non sine floribus" (III, 13) (O
Bandusian spring more glittering than glass, worthy of sweet wine
and flowers). Horace pays tribute not only to an obscure fountain
but to poetry as well.[21] Just as Heinsius' poem is an invocation to a
spring, it can be considered an invocation to his own art.

Heinsius' elegy amplifies the fountain-as-inspiration motif; his
landscape is as ideal[22] as Horace's, with identical characteristics: the
oak tree, the hollow rocks, the crystal clear water, the murmuring
brook whose coolness is refreshing to cattle, the blazing sun.
Though these motifs are only hinted at by Horace with a single word
or phrase, they are extended and repeatedly pictured in Heinsius'
elegy. The other theme in Horace's ode, that of a sacrificial kid
whose blood will stain the waters, Heinsius has replaced with the
wanderer motif, the weary traveler seeking refreshment from the
fountain.[23] Heinsius thus introduces the human element, not so
much reflecting an individual experience as one with universal
significance. The fountain—poetic inspiration and creativity—is
shared by his fellow poets; but his personal return to the city of his
ancestors is a source of creativity and life for him. By means of a
direct address to the fountain combined with the symbolic merging
of the actual fountain and his poetry, Heinsius re-created the age-
old fountain motif.

V   *Themes and Arrangement of the Elegies*

Inasmuch as the elegies are individual poems in their own right,
their thematic arrangement is not altogether immaterial. The body
of elegies has been carefully grouped; the division in three (1603,

1613, 1617, 1621), four (1606), and five (1610) books followed the
model of the Roman and Neo-Latin elegists. Ovid's *Amores* contains
three books; Propertius' poems have come down to us in four; Janus
Secundus assembled his elegies in three books. The "Monobiblos,"
though its content varies in each edition until 1621, remains a single
book and is not integrated into the main body of the elegies, as had
been Janus Secundus' "Julia. Monobiblos" which served as Book I of
his elegies.

For Heinsius' elegies we can distinguish two major phases which
are represented by the editions of 1603 and 1613. In the edition of
1603 each book opens with a kind of prologue: an elegy dealing with
Heinsius' role as a poet and his poetic creations. "The Poet Commends His Muses to Joseph Scaliger" (I, 1) is not merely a flattering
address to the great scholar, but a statement of Heinsius' own aspirations and of his indebtedness as a poet to the stimulating model
and fatherly patron. He implores: "Rege vela pater: miserere
poetae/ Iuliade: vates regia turba sumus" (1603, p. 6). (Rule the
sails, father: Have compassion with the poet, offspring of Julius
Scaliger: we poets are a royal group.) Praise of Scaliger and his
literary achievements occurs in I, 7; I, 11; II, 2; II, 8 (especially
noteworthy, presenting Scaliger with a copy of his Silius Italicus
edition in 1602); and II, 13, while Heinsius' indebtedness as a poet
is treated variously in a pair of elegies addressed to Janus Dousa (I,
6; II, 14): In I, 6, Heinsius speaks of the multitude of poets and
poetasters and is unsure yet if he will succeed; elegy I, 14 gives the
triumphant answer: "Dousiaco nostri genio placuere libelli/ Ulterius
votis non licet ire meis" (p. 75) (My writings have pleased Dousa's
genius; my prayers need not go any farther). The programmatic
introduction to Book III shows the independent poet, a king in the
realm of the Muses. The lighthearted tone of this elegy also prevails
in II, 1 in which love poetry is defended against the serious epic.
Heinsius, the poet, and his work—there are allusions to it in almost
every elegy—is the main theme of I, 9, in which he dreams of
returning to Ghent with his Rossa, and in II, 10, in which his
scholarly endeavors come to life as poetic figures. His poetry also is
the common bond in the poems of friendship to the French ambassador Paul Choartus (III, 2), Hugo Grotius (III, 11), his brother
Nicolaas (I, 8), his friend Petrus Scriverius (I, 10), his fellow student
Elias Putschius (II, 4), and to Dousa's son Diederich (III, 4).

In the remaining poems—by far the largest group—the love

theme dominates; it is at times combined with a mythological fable
(I, 12; III, 6; III, 7) or with another imaginary incident (III, 7, walk
in the city; II, 6, the wind disperses the poet's elegies; II, 12, poetry
rescues him from the study of law). The love theme also dominates a
pair of nature poems, "To the Evening" (I, 5) and "To the Moon"
(III, 3). But the arrangement in the elegies is not a completely
inflexible one. However, certain poems are cornerstones: the introductory elegies and the "Conclusion of the Work." All themes occur
in these poems to be varied, alone or in differing combinations,
throughout the three books. Even complementary poems, such as
the Dousa elegies and the "nature" poems, are separated. Variation
within a cycle of major themes is the principle of the arrangement.
These in the order of importance, not of frequency, are:
poetry, the poet, friendship, love, and mythology.

A brief look at the cycle of 1613 shows that the cornerstones (I, 1,
and III, 14), remained unchanged except for stylistic alterations to
improve expression and meters. II, 1, is a different poem, but like
its predecessor a light-hearted jest about the poet as a servant of
Venus. III, 1, "About his Muses," has been replaced by a friendship
poem which also reflects Heinsius' nostalgia for Ghent—he had
visited there after the truce of 1609—and his poetic creativity. Book
I still contains two poems for Dousa in similar places in the middle
(I, 5) and at the end (I, 9) but they are different poems. Dousa had
died in 1604, and the themes of indebtedness and friendship are
modified accordingly.

In other changes in Book I, similar poems have been substituted:
The friendship poem to the French ambassador (I, 2)—now no
longer of importance[24]—has been replaced by the poem to Heinsius' brother Nicolaas (in 1603, I, 8); playful love poems in the
Petrarchist manner I, 3, and I, 4, are replaced by two poems from
Book III (12 and 13). Major new themes do not appear, but several
pairs of accomplished poems have been added: the poems on Ghent
(III, 1 and 9), on the loss of his girl (II, 7 and 8), and the fountain
poems (III, 5 and 8). The main principle of arrangement is again a
variation of major themes, a principle which applied to Ovid's
Amores and to many other Hellenistic and Roman books of poetry.

The "Monobiblos" remains a body, containing from thirteen to
fourteen poems, distinct from the elegies. Its prominent theme is
love: "Materies satis apta mihi est: feror huc, feror illuc:/ Praesidet
et puppi dux Cytheraea mea" (1603, 1, p. 127) (This subject is
well-suited for me: I am carried here and there: Venus presides as

the captain of my boat). The book is dedicated to one girl, Rossa, like Propertius' first book to Cynthia and Janus Secundus' Book I of his elegies to Julia. Themes come from Secundus' elegy 2 "Which young man invented the kiss" (a variation of Catullus) and from the Petrarchist tradition: elegy 3, the poet waiting in front of the girl's house. Various situations are explored to the end when a mythological poem to the stars (12) and a praise of Bacchus and of wine and women conclude the book.

The 1613 edition of the "Monobiblos" retained the structure of the original but its contents have been altered considerably. The love elegies in the Petrarchist manner have been reduced to four poems, elegy 2, 3, and 4 (in 1603 they were numbers 3, 2, 5 respectively), and the "Farewell to Rossa" which has been placed at the end as Heinsius moved farther away from the playful love elegy. Narrative mythological poems and descriptions now compose the main body, elegies 5–12, in which love is shown at different stages of life: the wedding (7), death of the spouse (8), and birth (10). The structure of the "Monobiblos" has been preserved in the main theme, only the variations have changed.

The elegies and the "Monobiblos" must thus be seen as a coherent, though flexible, body. Thematic variations and associative motifs are the characteristics of these cycles, which dominated lyric poetry, especially the sonnet of the Renaissance since Petrarch. Heinsius knew Ronsard's *Amours* and the poetry of the *Pléiade*. Although Heinsius relegated his elegies and "Monobiblos" to an ever less important place in his poetry, they still represent his best lyric productions and were recognized as such by his contemporaries and emulated in Latin as well as in the vernacular.

CHAPTER 5

The "Silvae" and Other Occasional Poetry

I Occasional Poetry

WRITING Latin verses for important occasions in a person's life was a popular custom which produced voluminous collections of often monotonous poetry. If we were to accept the verdict of scholars from the late eighteenth century up to the recent past who condemned these verses altogether as unoriginal products and insincere flattery, we would overlook an important body of poetry without consideration of its particular function and merits. For the humanist scholar-poets, the occasional verses provided exercise in versification—and many drafted lines attest to that—but they also represented a vehicle for genuine communication and expression for the poet, his friends, and contemporaries. Important events, such as births, weddings and deaths, a trip, a new appointment or the publication of a book, were usually the occasions for which such verses were written. They might also be the expression of friendship, of gratitude for hospitality, or of some thoughts or observations on their work, life, or current events. Most Neo-Latin poets collected such poetry under the title *Silvae* (lit: forests). Papinius Statius, a Roman poet of the first century, A.D., called a collection of his poetry *Silvae* which derived its origin from various occasions and contained as a characteristic feature descriptive poems. These were laudatory poems for gods, men, animals, rivers, and cities, and verses for various events in public and private life. These descriptive poems based on a wealth of rhetorical *topoi* greatly influenced form and structure of Neo-Latin occasional poetry.

The first edition of Heinsius' poetry in 1603 has one section entitled "Silvae, in which are contained miscellaneous verses." The title was retained until 1649, throughout the eight editions published during his lifetime, though the contents were continually increased, the arrangement was changed, and new poems were added under separate headings. The "Silvae" grew from thirty pages in 1603 to eighty-nine pages in 1621, when the most representative edition of Heinsius' entire Latin poetry (but not of the elegies) appeared,[1] although the total volume of his occasional poems remained fairly constant with 144 pages in 1603 and 155 in 1621. The editions of 1640 and especially of 1649 included still more recent poems. The elegiac couplet dominates his "Silvae" which show "except for the panegyric, a rather uniform character."[2] With other poems Heinsius tried his hand at various meters, imitating Latin and Greek forms.

II *Friendship Poems*

Friendship *(amicitia)* with other poets, scholars, and educated men who were socially or politically important played a major role in the writing of these poems. For Heinsius and the Leiden circle friendship was intimately linked with education and scholarship. Such poems could develop only among the educated, and only in the circle of like-minded men, like that of Scaliger in Leiden from 1593–1609, or Heinsius and his students and colleagues at home and abroad. For Heinsius and his age, education did not so much foster the development of individual talents or the realization of one's self as a unique, feeling human being; rather, education meant a growing into an international community of scholars pursuing humanistic studies.[3] *Amicitia* was the bond between these men. (Women, did not, of course, receive any education and were thus excluded from such friendships.) They aided one another or competed in their studies, their writings, and their pursuit of self-perfection. They corresponded and exchanged books for enjoyment and research and manuscripts for suggestions; and they wrote prefaces and dedicatory verses for their works. Few friendships were based on personal ties or shared experiences, though these were certainly not excluded; but individual ties rarely entered into or shaped the conventional forms of friendship poetry.

As a twenty-two-year-old, when Heinsius was about to establish his reputation as a scholar and poet, he addressed his revered model, the famous poet Janus Dousa, with a bucolic poem in the manner of Vergil's tenth eclogue entitled "Noordwijk, or Unhappy Love." As Heinsius stated in his autobiography: "Often he [Dousa] led him [Heinsius] away to Noordwijk, where they spent the days pleasantly mostly with literary pursuits,"[4] and Dousa of his own accord frequently visited young Heinsius and Scaliger when he came to Leiden from The Hague. The poem is a present, so Heinsius states in the preface, for an invitation; and the theme of the poem is related to Dousa's life; he, in spite of his active political life, had continued to write poetry. Heinsius' verses are to be a diversion from the pressing concerns of war and public strife. They also introduce Heinsius to the great master as an accomplished writer of bucolic poetry.

Grotius, a student of Scaliger's at the age of eleven (from 1594–97), and Heinsius were good friends until the religious and political differences at the Synod of Dort separated the two. "I revere you, you move my heart" and "Heinsius is my guiding star" ("Heinsius numen mihi")[5] Grotius wrote about the poetic efforts of his friend. And Heinsius presented Grotius with a poem when he published his tragedy *Adamus exul* (Adam in Exile, 1601) and said about the young genius with admiration:

> Senex ephoebus ille, quem Batavia
> Miratur omnis, optat Hetruscus sibi,
> Omnisque Gallus, ille dum puer fuit
> Vir esse cepit: Namque reliqui viri
> Tandem fuere: Grotius vir natus est.   (1603, p. 235)[6]

(A youth, yet already a mature man, to whom all Netherlands looks with pride, whom Germany wishes for herself and all of France; while still a boy he began to be a man. All others finally become men: Grotius was born a man.)

The phrase "Grotius was born a man" succinctly characterized the child genius and became an often-quoted description of Grotius.

As best man at Grotius' wedding in 1608, Heinsius composed the lengthy and lofty wedding poem, which still introduced his epithalamia (Book II of the "Silvae") in 1621, an indication of his continued esteem for Grotius. The poem, "About Hugo Grotius Freed by His Wife from the Prison to which He was Sentenced for Life," shows admiration for Maria Reigersberg's courageous deed. Grotius' death sentence had been commuted in 1619 to life imprisonment at Loevestein. His wife entered the prison hidden in a chest of books, donned his clothes, and let her husband escape in the chest. Even Grotius' enemies, who prevented him from ever living again in the Dutch Republic, admitted to her courage and she was released.

> Coniugis auspicio superas effertur in auras
>   Grotius, et geminum munus amantis habet;
> Pro tenebris lucem, cum lucis munere vitam;
>   Quae cum luce simul pene negata fuit.
> [5] At vos, o proceres, iam poenam mittite et iras,
>   Sub vobis pereat ne pietatis amor.
> Aeneae licuit medios gestare per ignes
>   Intactum Graiis dulce parentis onus.
> Eripuit tenebris proscriptum casta maritum
> [10] Thuria: nec fraudi res fuit illa viro.
> Iam mortem, morti modo non vicinus, et ipso
>   In tenebris letho non leviora tulit.
> Post vitam suus est. E morte renascitur ipsa.
>   Nascenti legem dicere nemo solet.   (1649, p. 410)

(Grotius is carried to freedom with his wife's help and has a twofold present of love: Instead of dark captivity luminous freedom, with the gift of light his life, which, together with light, had almost been denied him. But you, noblemen, now put aside your punishment and anger that the love of piety may not perish under you. Aeneas was allowed to walk through fire, unharmed by the Greeks, with the pious burden of his father. The chaste woman rescued her husband condemned to darkness: Nor was it a deceit for the husband. Not yet near to death, he suffered death and things worse than death while in captivity. Back to life again he is hers. She herself is reborn from death. No one is wont to impose the law on the reborn.)

Heinsius uses the contrast of darkness and light as metaphors for captivity and freedom; he appeals to the authorities for pardon and compares the wife with Aeneas who carried his old father Anchises from burning Troy, a favorite example of piety. Then he very pointedly equates the regained freedom with a rebirth, in contrast to imprisonment which is worse than death. The final point, that no man can impose the law on the reborn, reiterates the plea to the authorities. In an admirably concise form, Heinsius has described the wife's loyal deed as a rebirth: Now that Grotius has regained his freedom and Maria has regained her husband, their life can begin anew unimpeded by former events. These verses reveal the intensity with which implications of a specific event are interpreted and

reflected upon in an occasional poem. The event is analyzed intellectually as to its meaning and then generalized in two metaphors of
contrasts—light and darkness, death and rebirth signaling captivity
and liberation. Akin to the sonnet which culminates in an epigrammatic couplet, this is one of Heinsius' best occasional poems.

The lofty occasional poems in a panegyric tone have lost much of
the appeal they must have had for the contemporary audience. Such
a poem is the one which begins the "Silvae" of 1621 (published
separately in 1617) and is addressed to Heinsius' close friend and
brother-in-law Janus Rutgers who was leaving for a diplomatic post
in Sweden. The wish for a safe voyage is used as a topical metaphor
for life and for a prosperous career with Gustavus Adolphus. Rutgers
is praised for service in the defense of his own country, but now the
most powerful and greatest king of Europe is calling.

This poem to Rutgers is followed by the "Apotheosis of August
Thuanus," a long descriptive poem opening with a stately paraphrase of Thuanus' death:[7]

> Felix quem longae meditantem incommoda vitae
> Regnorumque vices, nec stantem legibus aulam,
> Tollit summa dies: fatoque occurrit, et ultro
> Eluctantem animam, poscenti indulget Olympo.   (1621, p. 3)

(Happy is he, who pondering about the troubles of a long life, about the
vicissitudes of kingdoms and the court disdainful of laws, meets his last day:
He approaches his fate and readily yields his struggling soul to beckoning
Olympus.)

The traditional beginning, an extension of the *beatus ille* combined
with the weariness of this world, serves as consolation for death and
leads up to the glorious reception in heaven. When Thuanus arrives
there, his eyes wander along an array of mythological, allegorical,
and historical figures, among them Religion:

> Religio, quae bellorum nunc maxima causa
> Pacis et obsequii quondam mitissima nutrix,
> Priscas ipsa suo iungebat foedere gentes:
> Necdum in mille vias nequicquam scissa modosque,
> Necdum picta comas, multosque imbuta colores.   (1621, p. 4)

(Religion, now the greatest cause of wars, once as the kind mother of peace
and allegiance joined ancient nations in a bond, not yet torn apart in a
thousand ways and manners, not yet adorned with hair of all colors.)

Religion is then compared to the many colors of the rainbow fading away into a ruddy glow after a thunderstorm, a reference to the bloody religious wars. Rarely does Heinsius deplore the religious feuds as openly; these lines are all the more significant as they were written in 1617 at the height of the Remonstrant controversy. Religion's kiss for Thuanus is a fitting tribute to his efforts for peace: After he has met War, Peace, and Liberty, the Muses crown him with a laurel wreath. Even Henry IV appears and congratulates Thuanus on his literary and political achievements.

With its lofty allegorical figures, lengthy descriptions, and elaborate mythological images, the poem is a tribute to a great scholar and influential statesman. The accomplished panegyric successfully blends classical and Christian elements. The setting is reminiscent of Aeneas' visit to the underworld where he meets with the heroes who fell at Troy and is then given a glimpse of Rome's future greatness. Heinsius uses this setting to survey Thuanus' accomplishments and to honor him in allegorical encounters that resemble a theatrical procession. In its elevated style the poem is dignified, but not stilted; it is one of the most outstanding in the "Silvae," which from 1621 on were reserved for the best commemorative poems (Books I, III) and epithalamia (Book II).

III *Commemorative Poems for Scaliger, Lipsius, and Dousa*

For the three great scholar-poets whom the young Heinsius had admired the most, Joseph Scaliger, Justus Lipsius and Janus Dousa, he composed three cycles of commemorative poems[8] in different meters and forms which transcend the traditional epicedium[9] in style and content. The unifying element in each cycle is the dedication to, and praise of, the deceased, though the poems are by no means all solemn in tone.

In dignified hexameters an "Apotheosis" opens the "Manes Scaligeri" which were written in 1609. The illustrious souls when freed from the dark prison of their bodies become constellations in the sky. Scaliger sits in their midst on Nature's lap and admires this new sight. Virtue takes him to the beautiful house of the heroes where he is rejuvenated. His father Julius Caesar comes to greet him, and he joins his ancestors as a new star in the sky. Here is another version of deification in which Heinsius describes the life after death not in Christian terms, but in a classical allegory.

The following three epitaphs[10] in the elegiac couplet, Heinsius' favorite verse, culminate in praise of Scaliger's scholarly achievements. In two plaintive poems, "Querela" (Lament) and "Threnus" (Dirge), Heinsius mourns the loss of his friend. He recalls happier days together in the ideal landscape of the Elysian Fields and wishes to rejoin him there; and he compares himself with a child who has lost his parents. The final poem is in the manner of Vergil's fifth Eclogue, the shepherd's lament over Daphnis' death, which among other poems of antiquity served subsequently as a model for funeral poems. Heinsius has taken the setting, the tone, and the language and expanded the bucolic poem. The shepherd Aegon mourns the death of Thyrsis:

> Carmina iam sordent (nam cui mea carmina cantem?)
> Et mihi discedens tamen haec armenta reliquit.
> Et dixit moriens: post me pulcherrimus Aegon,
> Aegon hos calamos mortis solatia nostrae
> Inflabit, tanto reliquis dilectior Aegon
> Quanto pulchra suo capra est villosior agno.   (1613, p. 142)

The following is a free rendering from the eighteenth century:

> Now flags my Muse; Whose Praises shall I write?
> When hence my Thyrsis took his hasty Flight.
> His latest Breath bequeath'd those Herds to me
> And said, My Heir shall beauteous Aegon be:
> He, with these Reeds, Coelestial Strains shall play
> And charm the Groves with his enchanting Lay.[11]

Heinsius is Scaliger's heir, as the executor of his literary works and manuscripts, as a scholar and poet.

In this cycle, Heinsius shows his virtuosity in recreating each of the major classical forms of commemorative poetry: the apotheosis, epitaph, death elegy, and eclogue. The three major themes, praise of the deceased *(laudatio)*, mournig *(lamentatio)*, and consolation *(consolatio)*, are carried through in this order with the eclogue ending on a consolatory note: Heinsius sees himself as the heir to the great man and is to continue the literary and scholarly tradition. The cycle is a monument to his patron and friend in style and in content. Some of the seemingly exaggerated idolization of Scaliger as the new constellation in the sky is not simply flattery, but a traditional motif from the deification of ancient heroes, such as Caesar and Augustus by Vergil, and a contrast to the mournful lamentation of the following poems, as well as an antithesis to the simple world of Vergilian shepherds which concludes the cycle.

The second cycle of commemorative poems which Heinsius wrote is the "Manes Lipsiani" concerning another great scholar, Justus Lipsius, who died in 1606. In the "Epicedium" all the people of the Low Countries are called upon to pay homage to Lipsius in spite of the war which separates the North from the South. After five rather undistinguished epigrams a "Playful Poem to the Little Bees" strikes an entirely different chord. The bees are called upon to settle on Lipsius' grave, to guard it and to sting any malevolent, envious people who attempt to steal honey from the grave. It is an allegorical homage to Lipsius whose style was considered "honey-sweet" *(mel- lifluus)*. From antiquity the bees were considered messengers of the Muses; and the poet gathering material was compared with the bee, his creation with honey.[12] The poets will guard Lipsius' heritage, detractors or thieves will be punished; this is possibly a reference to Lipsius' difficulties in compromising his Stoic and humanist ideas so as not to offend Catholic views. The last poem in the cycle for Lipsius skillfully combines a laudation with a description of his last unfinished work, "Thrasea." Lipsius had been working on a treastise on the Stoic philosopher R. Thrasea Paetus (put to death by Nero), and he forbade that the manuscript be published in its incomplete state after his death. In Heinsius' "Epigram on Thrasea" Lipsius arrives at the gates of the Elysian Fields and a huge crowd comes to greet him; among them are the Stoic philosophers Zeno, Cleanthus, Cato, and Thrasea. The last is horrified to see Lipsius and can only utter the sad words: "Quem Nero damnatum voluit, ne viveret unquam,/ Tu nasci prohibes, et iubet ille mori" (1613, p. 158). (Whom Nero wanted doomed so that he would never live, you refuse to give birth to, and he [Nero] seals his death.) In this final couplet Heinsius, as a master of the poignant phrase, makes Lipsius' refusal to allow his own work to be published responsible for the victory of Nero's tyranny. Heinsius' lines echo his contemporaries' disappointment at not being given yet another work on Stoicism from Lipsius' pen, although he had reconverted to Catholicism and shown his devoutness in several works. It was above all Lipsius the classical scholar and Stoic whom Heinsius revered and was indebted to. His tribute in a mastery of classical meter, form, and imagery was a very appropriate one. A personal, individual expression of grief was not to be expected. Neither was it customary in Neo-Latin poetry, nor was Heinsius' relationship with Lipsius a personal one.

Heinsius' third commemorative cycle, "Manes Dousici" honors

the poet Dousa, who died in 1604. While the first cycle introduced
classical forms of funeral poetry and the second cycle added philosophical ideas, the third emphasized poetic forms. It is not only the
longest, but also the most varied and interesting one. This cycle has
three sections: Two introductory poems consolatory in tone are followed by eight plaintive and twelve laudatory compositions. The
opening poem is addressed to Dousa's sons: "Vos etiam Dousam,
sed ne lugete parentem./ Plus proprio cuius Dousa parente fuit"
(1613, p. 160). (But you mourn Dousa, not the parent. For Dousa
was more than anyone's parent.) The theme, the importance and
meaning of Dousa, is stated and then varied throughout the cycle.
In the second introductory poem Heinsius sets his task:

> Hic quoque, quicquid ero, Batavorum extrema secutus
> Fataque fortunasque, et non ignobilis exul,
> Vocibus insuescam solemnibus, et tua clamans
> Nomina, supremos indicam liber honores. (1613, p. 161)

(Here now, whatever I shall be, having followed to the ultimate fate and
fortune of the Dutch as a worthy emigrant, I shall become accustomed to
the solemn songs, and proclaiming your name, I shall freely pay you my last
honors.)

Grief and mourning are expressed in the familiar imagery of a dark-
ening sky, silence, paling of the Netherlands, fear and stupefaction
in the poem "To the Members of Leiden University"; in "To the
Muses of Leiden," who grieve over the loss of their king; and in a
"Threnus" (dirge) in which the earth and the ploughman mourn a
cricket killed by the feet of a thoughtless wanderer.

A pair of epigrams, each consisting of ten lines, is especially
noteworthy. The first is written "To the Sun":

IV Ad Solem

[1]   Auriga lucis, ignei poli cursor
        Metator aethrae, temperator horarum,
        Aevi minister, circulator aeterne,
        Lustrator orbis, dissipator umbrarum,
[5]   Currus perennis igneaeque quadrigae
        Fraenator ingens, qui diem vehis purum,
        Rursusque vultum surripis tuum mundo,
        Et candicantis occulis comae flammam;
        Cras e lacertis Tethyos tuae rursus
[10]   Redibis; at nox occupat meum solem. (1613, p. 166)

(Charioteer of light, courser of the fiery heaven, limiting darkness, governor of hours, attendant of time, forever a wanderer, lightbringer of the world, destroyer of shadows, of the eternal car and fiery four-horse chariot the mighty tamer, who leads along the pure day, and again takes away from the world his face and from the eyes the flame of the gleaming hair: From the arms of your Thetis you will return again tomorrow. But night embraces my sun.)

The thought expressed in the poem is plain: The sun will return tomorrow from darkness, but not Dousa. One of the most famous renditions of the ever-returning sun versus death, the eternal night, are Catullus' lines: "Soles occidere et redire possunt:/ Nobis cum semel occidit brevis lux/ Nos est perpetua una dormienda" (Carmen V). (Suns can set and return again: But once our brief light is gone, night is perpetual and one eternal sleep.) In Catullus the motif is used, to be sure, in an entirely different context; the famous "Vivamus, mea Lesbia atque amemus" (Let us live and love, my Lesbia) is an exhortation to enjoy life while it lasts. Heinsius has used the idea for his poem's epigrammatic climax to which the preceding lines build. In ever new metaphors the qualities of the sun as eternal light (life) are described, a contrast to night (death) which holds the poet's guiding sun, Dousa. The sun is addressed in a series of eight nominal periphrases followed by another extended one, and then followed by two relative clauses containing three further periphrases—the clause in lines 7–8 contains two: the face and the flaming hair. Altogether, twelve periphrases, a favorite rhetorical device in Neo-Latin poetry, evoke the majestic and eternal nature of the sun—in stylistic contrast to the final two lines. The series of addresses is discontinued and the idea underlying the poem is expressed, but still in a periphrastic way. With "my sun" the poet himself enters his verses at the end and states his grief in a personal way, a stark contrast to the rhetorical metaphors of the preceding lines.

The poem "To the Stars" has the same structure:

V Ad Sidera

> Dulces alumni noctis, ignei fratres,
> Parvae cohortes, aurei poli cives,
> Qui per serenos aetheris vagi campos
> Molles choreas ducitis levi planta,
> [5]   Cum membra nostra molliter reclinata
> Victosque sensus occupat sopor lenis;

> Quid nunc, ut ante, per domum poli pictam
> Et e latebris fornicisque inaurati
> Puris fenestri tollitis sacrum vultum?
> [10]   Abite rursus non videbitis Dousam. (1613, p. 166)

(Sweet children of night, fiery brothers, small cohorts, inhabitants of the golden sky, across the serene fields of the immense heaven gently move on a light course, when our limbs are gently at rest and our minds overcome by soft sleep. Why then, as before over the sky's ornate house and from hidden places of the golden vault and the pure windows do you lift your sacred face? Go away, you will not see Dousa again.)

The poem proceeds from rest and peace to mourning in the last line, which finally gives away the reason for the mourning, that is, Dousa's absence. The address to the stars is much less weighty than the many nominal periphrases for the sun; here four metaphors are followed by a clause extending over four lines expressing "you appear at night." With the address to the stars and reference to "our limbs" the poet enters his verses as a person. Mythological references are absent, and the imagery—such as the expression "small cohorts"—is taken from classical Latin poetry. Rather than using one metaphor for the stars, the address is amplified by using a series, but one which is not as inflated as the periphrases for the sun. It should also be noted that in both poems Christian metaphors, which are so frequently associated with celestial bodies in seventeenth century poetry, are absent. This poem is really a transformation of Joseph Scaliger's "Ad sidera," in which he laments the absence of his beloved (*Poemata omnia*, 1600, p. 597), which in turn is based on Bion's Idyll XVI.

In ever-new comparisons, Heinsius continues the lamentation with another "Threnus" and with two more poems concerning the inspiration he received from Dousa. The theme of the third cycle is the praise (*laudatio*) of Dousa. Each of the twelve poems in this section honors one of Dousa's achievements: as a writer of Dutch history, as a defender of freedom, as a pious man, as a poet. A vision of Dousa's deification, "On the Harmony Which Dousa Seemed to Hear Shortly before his Death," concludes the cycle. Out on the tumultuous sea, Dousa sees a huge spirit which beckons him to approach and shows him a palace. The gods and constellations come, applaud his poetry, and make him a citizen of the celestial city. Since this apotheosis is presented as a vision and is narrated in some detail, it does not appear as exaggerated as the apotheosis of Scaliger, although the famous person's reception in heaven is a traditional setting for commemorative verses. What distinguishes this poem is the lively narrative of the voyage and of Dousa's vision.

The cycle for Dousa, written in 1604, is the most poetic and varied one of the three. The theme, set in the first poem: "What Dousa as a man means for the country," is demonstrated in a group of plaintive and a group of laudatory poems which culminate in an apotheosis. The reassurance of life and honors after death add the consolatory note. Laudation, lamentation, and consolation are the traditional three themes around which this commemorative poetry is built.

In Heinsius' three cycles, the first theme is the most important one to which the other two are subordinated. Although the motifs employed are topical in the sense that they all, in one form or another, belong to classical poetry and the Neo-Latin epicedia, Heinsius has re-created them anew in a eulogy of the three great contemporaries whom he emulated. It is the poetic re-creation of traditional themes and *topoi* in three varied cycles stressing scholarship, philosophy, and poetry that transformed these occasional poems into outstanding creations of that genre and age.

IV   *Rhetoric and Heinsius' Latin Poetry*

Heinsius' poetic production cannot be fully understood without considering its close affinity to the rhetorical tradition which provided its basic thematic, structural, and stylistic framework. Individual and subjective modes of expression were for the most part subordinated to traditional patterns. For the Neo-Latin author the science of writing poetry (poetics) was considered closely related to the science of oratory (rhetoric), and the essence of poetry consisted of the perfection of eloquent ideas in a metrical form. Rhetoric concerned the right choice of ideas and ways of expressing them. While the orator's goal was "to persuade and to move" *(persuadere et movere)* the audience, the poet's aim was "to please by imitation" *(imitando delectare),* a distinction formulated by Julius Caesar Scaliger,[13] the father of Joseph Scaliger and authoritative theoretician in the sixteenth century, who was likewise revered by Heinsius. In *invento* (the finding of thoughts), *dispositio* (structuring of the ideas), and *elocutio* (stylistic garb), corresponding to the modern

concepts of content, structure, and style, the poet was dependent
upon the rhetorical tradition. Poetry was an art which could only be
prefected by the study of the rules and practices in versification and,
above all, by the close reading and study of the classical models.
Having pointed to Heinsius' creative use of themes, ideas, and *topoi*
from the classical tradition in individual poems, I shall turn now to a
few major features of his poetic language (in an epigram) and structure (in a descriptive, mythological poem).

An early epigram, not in Martial's satirical vein but in the lyrical-
descriptive manner of the *Greek Anthology*,[14] embodies most of
Heinsius' characteristic and favorite stylistic elements. It is entitled
"To the Unborn Child Whose Mother Has Died":

> In Infantem nondum natum matre moriente.
> [1]   Hic tumulus matrem: natum tegit illa: sepulchrum
>   Terra tuae matri est, nate, sed illa tibi.
>   Mortuus in tumulo es quo vixti molliter ante:
>   Estque tibi tumulus, qui fuit ante domus.
> [5]   Sic tumulusque, domusque fuit tibi mater: et ante
>   Quam poteras natus esse, sepultus eras.   (1603, p. 192)

(This grave mound covers the mother, she the child. Earth is your mother's
grave, child, and she yours. You are dead in the mound where you lived
softly before. And she, who was your house before, is now your grave: Your
mother then has become your grave and your house. Before you could be
born, you were buried.)

The title of the poem itself contains alliteration—the *m* and *t* alliteration are carried throughout the poem—and assonance of *o* and *a*.
Alliteration and assonance are the most prominent acoustic features
in Heinsius' verses: Rhyme, used by some Neo-Latin authors but
not in classical literature, is never used. In addition *adnominatio*
(repeating a word, bringing together various inflected forms of a
word, or using words that are homophonous) adds to the homogeneous acoustic impression. In this epigram repetitions occur with
tumulus (4 times), *mater* (3 times in different inflectional forms), and
with *illa, tibi, ante, domus,* and *fuit; moriente* and *mortuus* are used
as are *sepulchrum* and *sepultus*. Such playing with words shows
mastery of the language, enhances the musicality of the verse, and
has an intensifying effect. It is employed in description as well as in
the pointed phrasing of a thought.

In the epigram, Heinsius uses the metaphors grave/mound womb/house with all the paradoxical implications possible. The idea of the unborn child buried with its mother is phrased in lines 1 and 2, then pointedly rephrased in lines 3 through 6. An antithesis underlies every line: 1. This is her grave—she buries the child; 2. Earth covers the mother—but the mother covers the child; 3. You are now dead—where you were living before; 4. What is now a grave—was formerly a house; 5. Your mother is to you both—a house and a grave; 6. You died—before you were born. Such an exploitation of one paradoxical metaphor creates a cerebral, artfully contrived epigram, always a major characteristic in Heinsius' verses, resulting from the constant use of antithesis and the ultimate exploitation of ideas in a metaphorical context. In this epigram these features are of course exaggerated by the very nature of its poignant form.

The elegy "Hylas,"[15] a re-creation of Callimachus' mythological Idyll XIII, may serve as an illustration for some of Heinsius' poetic devices such as circumlocution, metaphors, and similes which are also prominent in the longer descriptive poems, with mythology furnishing a rich source for these features. "In florem viridis protinus ibat humus" (1613, Monobiblos, 5, p. 99) (The green ground was soon going to come into bloom) is a circumlocution for spring; the moon is called "argentea Phoebe" (the silver sun); morning comes in the following description of Aurora driving her chariot: "cum se Memnonis Aethiopis/ Pegaseis super arva parens sustolleret alis,/ Et roseis lora flecterat articulis" (p. 99) (when the mother of Memnon, the Aethiopian [Dawn], with the winged horses rose over the fields and with rosy fingers held the reins). Seasons, times of the day, or fixed points of orientation are usually presented in a circumlocution or metaphor. For the contemporary reader, who was well read in mythology and trained in such rhetorical devices as the periphrase, this did not obscure the meaning but was appreciated for the new, the unusual way of expressing the obvious and ordinary. It stimulated vision and thought, for it had to be absorbed by the intellect and visualized before the inner eye in order to be fully understood.

The constant use of epithets and descriptive phrases further enhances the visual quality of Heinsius' poetry. Descriptions with elaborate modifiers are interspersed with the action. "Hylas" begins:

[1]   Cum Venus occultis Cinyridae saucia curis,
        Furtivo domini surgeret e thalamo,
      Languida nox prono factura silentia mundo
        Stillabat madidis roscida sideribus.   (p. 98)

(When Venus, hurt by secret love for Cinyras' son [Adonis], secretly rose
from her husband's bed, the quiet night, ushering silence for the world at
rest, dripped dew from the moist stars.)

The rendering of epithets massed together presents problems, since
we no longer use such an accumulation of descriptive modifiers. In a
typical description of nature such as this one, numerous pictorical
epithets are used mostly in a *hyperbaton* (a free word order separat-
ing what belongs together grammatically), a figure so prominent
with Heinsius that nouns and modifiers are rarely placed together
(as *languida nox*) but are mostly separated; for example, *nox* is
modified by *factura* and by *roscida* in the following line; *prono
mundo* is separated by *factura silentia, madidis sideribus* by *roscida.*
This feature of separation, peculiar to Latin and mostly inimitable in
even the Romance vernaculars, is carried to an extreme by Heinsius.
    The frequent use of similes also enhances the visual quality of
Heinsius' poetry. Increasingly important, more frequent, and
longer in his later poetry, the similes are always well integrated into
the context and the narrative flow. In "Hylas" the first simile compares the water to a bee:

[16]   Et strepitus densis murmuret e violis
          Occultus, qualis desertae rupis ab antro
          Vere novo florum conscia fundit apis.
        At circum faciles Nymphae choreas ducebant.   (p. 98)

(The gushing water murmured from under the dense violets, hidden, as
from a deserted, rocky cave the bee emerges in early spring, aware of the
flowers. And the lightfooted Nymphs danced around.)

In this simile the spring shares several qualities with the bee: It is in
a hidden place (the bee comes from a lonely cave) with *desertae,*
though in grammatical agreement with *rupis,* modifying *antro*
(lonely cave) in the stylistic device of *enallage* (change of words); it
gushes forth (the bee comes out, *fundit*); there are many violets,

flowers of love and flowers of spring (the bee senses the new flowers of spring, *vere novo florum*). The simile is also linked to what follows with the bee's flight anticipating the Nymphs' graceful dance. Heinsius develops a simile around the spring because it is of central importance to the story: Amor slips away and chances upon the hidden spring of the Nymphs, is enchanted by it, and loses his quiver and arrow, thus turning the waters into a love potion. The Nymphs drinking from the water are seized by desire and seduce the young boy Hylas. The use of the simile thus enhances one of the key motifs in the poem: the spring.

Three more similes in "Hylas" come at turning points of the story. Amor's loss of his arrow and quiver is likened to shooting stars disappearing in the ocean; the innocence of the sleeping Nymphs before they drink the magic water is compared to a drooping flower hiding in the leaves from the rain or heavy with dew; Hylas struggling with the waves and calling Hercules for help is illustrated with a description of a doe looking in vain for its mother when the wolf attacks it. The similes become increasingly longer and more elaborate: The first and the third similes illustrate an important motif (the spring, the sleeping Nymphs), the second and third similes illustrate turning points in the narrative (the loss of the quiver, Hylas is pulled into the water). They let the reader pause and reflect at prominent moments of the poem, a purpose for which Heinsius frequently uses similes. They are a major stylistic feature of his verses.

The list of rhetorical devices and metrical and poetic forms employed by Heinsius is almost as comprehensive as those used in classical poetry from early Greek to late, though not medieval, Latin literature. The most characteristic features of his verses are the musical quality achieved by the use of alliteration, assonance, and *adnominatio;* an intellectually structured content accomplished through the epigrammatic play with pointed phrases, antithesis, and parallelism in the presentation; and an imaginative visual expansion created by metaphors, circumlocutions, and similes which are integrated into the poem.

In a dedicatory poem to the 1613 edition of Heinsius' poetry Grotius complimented the author: "Vicerat antiquos: et cui contendere posset/Heinsius, haud quenquam saecula nostra dabant" (p. 17) (He has conquered the ancients; and our times have not brought forth anyone who could compete with Heinsius). Even though these

words are characteristic of the flattering admiration between
friends, they also reflect the poets' desire to rival and surpass their
classical models. Did the Neo-Latin poets then merely imitate the
ancient examples? Basing their concept on Quintilian, who introduced the idea into rhetoric, and for whom Cicero was the ultimate
model, Renaissance poetics treated *imitatio* (imitation) as the cor-
nerstone of poetry.[16] What was meant was not plagiarism, or slavish
adherence to established techniques but rather an innovative as-
similation and creative emulation of the classical tradition for original and occasional poetic compositions. The poet was compared to
the stream into which many brooks have merged, his work to the
honey collected by the bee from various blossoms. For Heinsius,
the classical philologist, this tradition came alive through intimate
acquaintance with classical works. They stimulated his creative
imagination and provided the literary forms for his poetry.[17] He
could, and did, draw on the techniques, imagery, and ideas of all the
major classical poets, above all Vergil, Catullus, Horace, Ovid,
Theocritus, and the Anacreontics.

CHAPTER 6

De Contemptu Mortis

I Origin and Arrangement

I N 1621 Heinsius published his last major work of poetry, *De contemptu mortis* (On Contempt of Death), a timely subject since the threat of death and destruction had acquired a renewed urgency for Heinsius and the Dutch Republic. After a period of relative stability and increasing prosperity during the first two decades of the seventeenth century, internal strife and new wars had shattered the tranquility of the young republic and of central Europe. In 1619 the clash over dogma within the Calvinist church had ended with the execution of the political leader of the losing Arminian faction, Oldenbarnevelt, and the prosecution of many adherents. The truce with Spain came to an end in 1621, when Flanders and Brabant were forced into a renewed war with their northern brothers as part of the last great attempt by the Hapsburgs to extend to its utmost limits the Catholic counteroffensive. A religious war which was to last thirty years flared up in Germany in 1618 with the defeat of the Protestant leader, Frederick of the Palatinate, the Winter King of Bohemia.

In this time of increased hostility and uncertainty, *De contemptu mortis*, a reflective poem of about thirty-nine hundred hexameters, was welcomed as a timely treatment of a pressing subject: death. Heinsius intended this work to be a philosophical handbook in poetic form, as is indicated by its arrangement: Each of the four books is preceded by subject headings *(argumentum)*, an elaborate prose summary *(argumentum doctrinae)* follows the poetry, and an index of some twenty pages of philosophical concepts and poetic examples concludes the work. Moreover, pertinent passages from Plato's *Phaido* with a Latin translation are attached. Such an arrangement easily enables the reader to seek out topics or examples of interest.

While the main body of verses forms the poetic center of the work, the prose sections contain informative philosophical material.

The philosophical and religious content of this work is of prime importance, while its poetic form is the artistic garb for the contemplative message. The themes must be considered within the proper tradition, as Heinsius attempts to reconcile Christian and classical thought: In Book I, the Platonic concept of the soul is explained; Book II deals with the nature of death, mostly in Stoic terms; Book III suggests that one must face death like a "Christian soldier," the biblical metaphor which has been a well-known *topos* throughout the centuries. Book IV sums up Heinsius' personal religious credo, the Christian dogma from a Protestant, mostly Calvinistic, point of view. Following is a brief summary of each book:

Book I: After an invocation to Jesus, Heinsius sets out to describe Plato's doctrine of the soul. The body comprises man's material, mortal part, but the soul is divine, immortal. At death the soul is separated from the body and achieves a true union with God. Thus people who gradually free their souls from the domination of their bodies, as did Archimedes and Socrates, do not feel nor fear death. When people rely on their senses, they perceive darkness in death; hence, many erroneous cults have arisen. Man's eyes should be fixed upon heaven, not upon the earth. When the soul is being separated, it strives for only one goal: union with God. Since the body and earthly things are obstacles in this attempt, all bodily vices must be weeded out. This is achieved by a simple life without luxuries, without drinking or eating excessively. God must be separated from human things, from the elements, and from corporeal things in order to be recognizable by the soul. We must look upon Jesus, the one who combined the spiritual and the material, whose death was transformed to eternal life. Mankind carries the seed of this union in itself and the contemplation of this objective is man's foremost duty in life. Men mistake fame or the propagation of children as their goal, while life slips away like a dream. But one can only remain untouched by death if one places oneself outside of its domain, that is to say, if one lives for one's soul and is dedicated to God and to virtue. For Plato, philosophy meant the separation of the soul from the body; he taught how to live and die.

Book II: Death is to be despised, because life on earth is a calamity during which man is exposed to all kinds of misfortune. The newborn's cries already deplore this fate of being born onto the earth, which fell into disgrace when Prometheus stole the fire, when Adam was expelled from paradise. Thus the Scyths rightfully bemoan their newborn babes and rejoice over their dead. The soul should be prepared with fortitude and constancy not to fear death, but to be contemptuous of it. The poets should be read with care lest they instill vain fear of death in men, as Homer does. The writings of the Stoics offer the best example, teaching that there is nothing bad except that which is not virtuous and that one's own nature is to be followed. Fear of death does not come from nature but arises in man's imagination. Death is feared by the crowd but not by great individuals like Socrates or Cato. One should look back to former times and how people suffered and died, as we still do today. A friend's or relative's death need not be mourned if we remember that we will rejoin him later; for the soul is immortal as was proven by ancient philosophers and the Scriptures and has been demonstrated by the poets. Death is inherent in birth for all beings in this universe; and though it is feared as painful, it is the end of all fears. While people die reluctantly and cling to their earthly possessions, death should be welcomed in an increasingly troublesome life. As a courageous horse is eager to fight on the battlefield, a man should be ready to fight his fear of death.

Book III: Like a soldier, man has to be educated to lose his fear of death. The soldier devotes his life to his country; he is taught to love his country, to steel his body from early childhood, to live his entire life like a military exercise. A soldier dies in the service of virtue; death in battle is the most honorable death. Many examples of virtue and constancy in history show how the spirit must fight and conquer. Death is a constant companion, and it does not matter where it strikes, for the soul will then finally be freed. Heinsius then addresses himself to the fate of the Netherlands, which have suffered so much in war; he prays for a happy peace at last. He himself was forced to leave his home in Ghent but found refuge in Leiden and the Dutch Republic, which he praises for its new federation with the Republic of Venice. He then hails Gustavus Adolphus, asking him to leave the Polish wars and come to the rescue of the Dutch against the Spaniards.

Book IV: The work climaxes in this book which is dedicated to Jesus. Jesus was prefigured in the Old Testament, from Noah to Isaiah; and even the sibyls knew of him. Just as the ancients awaited him until he was incarnated, we likewise should live in contemplation of his example. True faith, charity, and true repentance for our misdeeds will lead to him. Like a hunting dog in search of his prey we must search for Jesus' wisdom. The martyrs have shown us the way, with their fortitude in believing and their disregard for their physical bodies. God's love was revealed to them: They aspired to heaven and their souls fought with their flesh. They refused to marry, to propagate; they traveled to mountains, deserts, lived in caves and graveyards; they observed Christ's passion on the cross and wished for their own death like fearless leaders on the battlefield. Jesus' birth, life, and triumph in death is described, and the work ends with a prayer for redemption.

II   *Stoic and Platonic Concepts of the Soul*

The title *De contemptu mortis* reveals Heinsius' attitude toward death; it is not one of fear but rather of contempt. This is important because in the Christian tradition the close relationship of sin and death had been emphasized. St. Augustine had given a concrete interpretation to the biblical statements by considering death as a punishment for personal sin and for the original sin of Adam and Eve. Thomas Aquinas also adopted this view; and throughout the Middle Ages death was regarded as a punishment, a view to which Luther as well as the religious men of the Reformation and the Baroque still adhered. Death was a first warning of the Last Judgment, at which the resurrection or condemnation of the body was to be decreed. Heinsius' concept of death is different: To him death is a transformational stage in which the soul is separated from the body and its real life begins. As the natural end of all living things, death is inherent in life from its inception. This Stoic concept is explained in detail in Book II, in which Heinsius explicitly refers to the Stoic writers and describes the most prominent Stoic example of death: the suicide of Cato the younger in 46 B.C. at Utica after losing the battle against Caesar. A Senecan phrase serves as a motto for the work: "Totius vitae remedium est contemnere mortem. Nihil triste est, cum huius metum effugimus" (The remedy for all our life is to despise death. There is nothing sad left, if we flee this fear).

While Heinsius accepts the Stoic view of death as being essentially a natural phenomenon, at the same time he embraces the Platonic concept of the soul and points to Plato's "unique contribution . . . , which is the soul's dissolution from the body and its union with the highest good *(summo bono)*"[1] at the time of death. Heinsius appended to his work, along with a Latin translation, pertinent portions of *Phaido*, the dialogue of Plato which is often treated as though it demonstrates the immortality of the soul.[2] Plato's object is to justify faith in immortality as a rational faith by showing that it follows naturally from a fundamental metaphysical doctrine. The divinity of the soul is being maintained; its survival of death is a consequence of this inherent divinity. Like Plato, Heinsius maintains that the soul strives for a union with its divine origin; it can be obstructed by the senses which are dominated by material and corporeal things. Hence one should endeavor to separate the soul from bodily things, for it does not perish together with the body in death. Heinsius explicitly refutes the Epicureans, whose dogma is called "absurd and harmful to mankind" (p. 106), and offers proof in fourteen points that the soul is indeed immortal. Even if some of those arguments taken from classical philosophy and Christian dogma seem naive and had already at his time been refuted (e.g., the soul cannot be destroyed by any of the four elements since it moves in circles), the important tenet is the existence of the divine quality of the soul. This represents Heinsius' unshakable belief. Like Plato, he is passionately sincere in his faith in personal immortality. Heinsius neither shares the medieval fear of the sinner's damnation and modern scepticism about the existence of a divine spark in man, nor does he question the existence of a divine spark as such.

The Church fathers and Christian dogma have repeatedly been influenced by Platonic ideas, yet the Church fathers usually did not subscribe to the idea of the natural immortality of man, but rather awaited a judgment over mankind and the resurrection of the flesh. Heinsius advocates that one should follow one's nature "to be carried without fear or terror wherever one is ordered by nature like the stars and whatever else lives in this world theater" (p. 102). This assurance of man's divine origin and destination leads to an almost optimistic acceptance and world outlook and provides the strength for his contempt for death. The *memento mori* (remember that you must die) had been a major theme in religious poetry since the Middle Ages.[3] Such poems suggested a contempt for the world and for all human life, showing their vanity and worthlessness. For Heinsius, the contempt for the world has been averted and transformed into a contempt for death.

III *Lipsius' Stoicism and Heinsius*

Heinsius' view on death also includes a stern ethical command and a deeply religious feeling. Not only in his concept of death as a

natural phenomenon but also in his ethics Heinsius has embodied
Stoic ideals. The soul, he writes, "must be fortified against death by
firmness of mind *(fortitudo)* and steadfastness *(constantia)*" (p. 91).
To be sure, these are the frequently proposed virtues of seventeenth century man who is supposed to face his fate with courage
and endurance. There was a renewed interest in Stoicism during the
Renaissance, but it was above all Justus Lipsius who had revitalized
and popularized the Stoic concept of steadfastness in his widely read
didactic prose treatise *De constantia* (On Constancy)[4] in 1584,
which was followed by his authoritative Seneca edition in 1605 and
scholarly presentations of Stoic philosophy, such as the *Manuductio
ad Stoicam philosophiam* (1604).

In *De constantia*, Lipsius describes how on his flight from his
Belgian fatherland he receives consolation in the doctrine of constancy. He shows that the source of affliction does not lie in exter-
nals, but within man in his own fearfulness. Constancy is the companion of reason; it is opposed by inconstancy and delusion of the
mind. Man has to recognize the necessity for submission to fate,
which is inevitable, universal, and sanctioned by the divine. *Constantia*, the guiding principle of the Stoic concept of life, becomes
through Lipsius' influence an undisputed virtue for the seventeenth
century. There is a genuine personal involvement in his didactic
work; philosophical advice is phrased in plain, understandable language illustrated by historical and contemporary examples. The illusion of a conversation, in which the apprentice Lipsius learns from
his older friend, is successfully maintained throughout the work and
contributes to its immediacy. This work was probably just as
influential in popularizing Stoic philosophy as were Lipsius' more
scholarly works on the subject, with the exception of *De constantia*.

Heinsius was certainly well acquainted with the writings of Lipsius, who had left Leiden for Louvain in 1591. Next to Dousa and
Scaliger, Lipsius was the person he most admired during his early
years and for him he composed a series of commemorative poems
after his death in 1606.[5] By 1621 when Heinsius was writing *De
contemptu mortis*, it became evident to him that his views differed
in several vital points from the Stoicism advocated by Lipsius. A
central concept for Lipsius is fate *(fatum)*, the order of the universe
willed by God in which evil *(mala)* only exists in the false, pre-
judiced opinion of men *(falsa opinio)*. When man acquires correct
understanding *(recta ratio)* and judgment *(judicium)*, he realizes

that evil exists only in his imagination. Constancy, a noble and unshakable strength of the soul *(rectum et immotum robur)*, guides the wise man in resisting chance *(fortuna)* which is shown to be a mere illusion.

Heinsius, too, discusses constancy at great length as the companion of reason as opposed to inconstancy and delusion. But while for Lipsius reason is at the center of man's life, enabling him to free himself from the bonds of self-imagined, illusionary evils, the Calvinist Heinsius proposes a firm faith in the grace of God. Heinsius does accept from Stoic ethics the central virtue, constancy, as a guide for the Christian life; but his world outlook remains emphatically Christian. He goes beyond the rational ethics which Lipsius has provided and adds another dimension, which was for him and his religiously oriented contemporaries of the seventeenth century yet more important: the direction toward God. A personal God does not appear in Lipsius' treatises; rather, God is in the background as a ruler and sustainer and at the same time as the law of the world, while endless misfortunes of past and present generations are pointed out as a comfort to the individual in his own miserable state. For Heinsius, life's definitive goal is that step in the direction of God. He cites the martyrs' unshakable faith and their later rewards for their firm stand. In this way he interprets biblical history, the well-known events of the Old and New Testaments, as either prefigurations of Christ or late imitations of Christ whose exemplary life amidst God's grace is to be remembered by men in all their actions.

IV *Faith and Redemption*

Heinsius' propagation of the idea of faith and redemption was directed against Lipsius' insistence upon reason; but he also voiced the Calvinist dogma of predestination as it had been reasserted at the Synod of Dort in 1619 in opposition to the Arminian interpretation.[6] The Remonstrance of the Arminians stated that the election or condemnation on the day of judgment was conditioned by the rational faith or nonfaith of man; that grace was not irresistible; and that believers, though able to resist sin, were not beyond the possibility of falling from grace. For the Arminians, human dignity required an unimpaired freedom of the will, a freedom which was in no way mitigated by divine acts or decrees. The opposing Counter-Remonstrants, among them Heinsius, maintained the dogma of ir-

resistible grace and the impossibility of falling from grace; they
understood that for the Arminians it was reason, rather than alien-
able love, which was chiefly determinative of human choice.

Not with theological discussion, but rather with exemplary
presentation of faith and with related interpretations from the
Scriptures, Heinsius expounds his personal credo, which coincides
with Calvinism as it had been upheld by Gomarus and the Synod of
Dort. In poetic form Heinsius states:

> Unum hoc praecipue, si quae est fiducia vero
> Et coelo demissa iuvant praecepta, monebo
> Assidue: quantum precibus contendere fas est,
> Posce fidem, posce intrepidus, certusque potiri.
> Illam coelicolum genitor, cum numine terram
> Fundaret, solidumque undis includeret orbem
> Edidit, auxilium lapsis in Tartara rebus.   (p. 64)

(Above all one thing, if there is any reliance on truth, and if heaven's
precepts please you, I shall admonish constantly: As much as is possible in
prayer, ask for faith, ask intrepidly, and possess it firmly. Faith, the Creator
of all, when He created the earth by His will and surrounded the earth with
water, gave as a help for those fallen to Tartarus.)

It is this fervent inisitence on belief rather than reason that attracted the reader of the religious seventeenth century to this work,
an interest that was still shared in Protestant-Pietistic circles in
Germany during the first half of the eighteenth century, as a German translation of *De contemptu mortis* by Ludwig Friedrich
Hudemann as late as 1749 asserts.

V   A New Christian Soldier

The contents of Book III seem somewhat different from the
mostly philosophical and religious subject matter that has preceded
it. When Heinsius compares a Christian's life to that of a soldier, he
uses the Pauline concept of the *miles Christi* (2 Tim. 2:3 and Eph.
6:11–17).[7] In the Middle Ages the knight represented the union of
the worldly and the spiritual; *miles dei* (soldier of God) was the title
of the knight of the orders. The Emperor Maxmilian I of Austria
(1493–1519) who repelled the Turks was still hailed by this name. In
Albrecht Dürer's engraving *Knight, Death and Devil* of 1513 he
pictured a Christian knight who, because of his courage, does not

fear the devil or death. Like a specter with glowing eyes and a white garment, death approaches the knight and shows him the hourglass. But with a serene face the knight rides on.

Erasmus' widely read *Enchiridion militis christiani* (Handbook—literally, small sword—of the Christian Soldier, 1503), in which he outlines his concept of evangelical devotion, also uses the metaphor of the Christian soldier who must prove himself in the world as the soldier does on the battlefield. Eighteen years later, Martin Luther preached on the sixth chapter of the Letter to the Ephesians, the same lines upon which Erasmus had based his *Enchiridion*. The difference in their religious concept is evident in their description of this Christian soldier. Luther's warrior is the faithful vassal, who takes up arms for his Lord, is inseparably linked to Him, and derives his strength exclusively from Him. For Erasmus, the Christian soldier also needs wisdom and knowledge; and he recommends to him the study of the classical poets and philosophers, especially Plato.

Heinsius certainly knew Erasmus' works, and he greatly admired his compatriot whose writing was generally held in esteem in the Low Countries, while at the same time it was attacked by the Catholic as well as the Protestant camp. He mentioned him explicitly in his autobiography[8] and edited his *Colloquia* in 1636. Yet Heinsius' warrior has assumed an entirely different role and interpretation. The metaphor has been secularized and modernized, and the warrier closely resembles the patriotic soldier fighting for his homeland in the War of Independence with Spain. Heinsius' Book III is a tribute to his new brand of patriotic citizen and soldier. He pictures this soldier's training from earliest childhood: abstinence from the luxuries of life, courage and zeal, fearlessness of death, in traditional terms. Patriotism and the warrior's service to his country are glorified: "Praecipue, dulcem patriae primaevus amorem/ Imbibat . . ." (p. 43). (Above all in his first period of life let him imbibe the sweet love for his country.) The spirituality and inwardness of the Christian soldier, as Erasmus and Luther had viewed him, have given way to a robust, successful, worldly soldier reminiscent of the Dutch burgher defending his religion, country, and possessions against the hired, often unpaid, and mutinous mercenaries of the Spaniards. The secularized Christian soldier serves the goals of this world, that is to say, his country; his courage has become a virtue in itself and the contempt of death, now in the service of worldly reasons and aims, is his professed goal.

While using literary models from antiquity,[9] Heinsius pictures the warrior in contemporary society; he represents a reality in the patriotic Dutch Republic. For Erasmus, the spiritual life of the individual Christian is at the center of his treatise; for Heinsius the metaphor of the Christian soldier is but a metaphor with a long tradition, an outward garb as it were, for a new moral and worldly content.

As a fitting climax to Book III, Heinsius laments the war and his fate as an exile, praying for his country which has suffered so much:

> Sed potius Pax laeta veni: tibi moverit arma
> Hactenus, et multo lassarit funere Mavors
> Flandorum populos, contemptoremque Batavum
> Lucis, et in toto meditantem proelia ponto;
> Usque vel oceano qua Sol devexus, ad Indum
> Volvitur occiduum, nostroque obvertitur orbi.   (p. 55)

(Happy Peace, come soon: against you Mars has taken up arms until now and with much killing wearied the people of Flanders and the despiser of Dutch liberty, who plans to attack everywhere on sea: Everywhere, from the ocean where the sun pales, to where it returns in the Indian East, and turns to our land.)

Heinsius' subsequent appeal to Gustavus Adolphus to protect the Dutch is personally and politically motivated since his brother-in-law Janus Rutgers was in the service of the Swedish crown and he himself had been appointed as Royal Historian of the Swedish Court. More important, the Protestants in northern Europe looked to Gustavus Adolphus for help against the Catholic kings of France and Spain. Gustavus Adolphus is seen as a "Christian soldier."

VI   *Form and Style*

The artistic form of *On Contempt of Death* is patterned after the most poetic, didactic poem of antiquity, Vergil's *Georgics*. These four books on farming, describing the four major forms of agriculture in the Augustan period, are of great beauty as poetry in spite of the often dry and technical subject matter. Vergil's poetic treatment of a technical subject influenced subsequent didactic poetry. That Heinsius chose to model his work on the *Georgics* rather than on Lucretius' *De rerum natura* is understandable, since he disliked the Epicurean philosophy expounded by Lucretius. Moreover, Vergil's patriotic inclinations, evident in his praise of Italy and of Octavian and his victories in the East and his praise of farming and the countryside are akin to the ideals of Heinsius. Using the Vergilian hexameter and arranging his subject matter in four books of about the same length as Vergil's, Heinsius closely follows the structure of that work. This is particularly evident in the parallel arrangement of the material: The proems and closing passages of *De contemptu mortis* correspond to those of the *Georgics*. The philosophical discussions of Stoic and Platonic concepts in Books I and II parallel Vergil's technical advice on the crops, the vine, and the olive. Heinsius turns in Book III to "describe the laurel wreath gathered for the people of the Low Countries from the highest peak of Pindus" (i.e., the seat of the Muses; p. 41) and concludes with the praise of Gustavus Adolphus; Vergil hails Octavian's conquests in his third book. In Book IV Heinsius expounds the story of Christian salvation from the prefiguration of Christ in the Old Testament to the redemption of mankind, while Vergil's account on bee-keeping is followed by the Aristaeus myth.

This use of the Vergilian structure must be viewed, not as a slavish reproduction or a lack of originality, but rather as a creative reinterpretation of the classical form. The Vergilian poem is a vehicle that Heinsius fills with a new content, modifying it at the same time in many ways to serve its new purpose. While following the basic arrangement of the four books, Heinsius presents in each a kaleidoscopic panorama of the subject matter in which each idea is explained in a series of examples.

In the opening lines of Book I Heinsius uses verbal and stylistic correlations which reveal the affinity of his work to Vergil:

> Quid mentem eripiat tenebris, quid pectore lutum,
> Seu mors sponte sua vocat, seu tela adversa minantur,
> Eximat attonitis, animasque asscribat Olympo,
> Sanguine lustratas, terrae pelagique potentis,
> [5] Et fati, nostrique canam. Tu virgine natus,
> Et vitae Rex ipse, fave. Tu maxime, vati
> Auxilium, tu finis eris. Tibi nostra carina,
> Sistat in offensum supremo in littore cursum.
> Namque tibi Graiorum omnis sapientia servit,
> [10] Et Musae quaecunque tibi famulantur, et omnis,
> Ut semel exorta est tua lux animoque refulsit,
> Interit extemplo, longeque avertitur, error. (p. 1)

(What takes our mind away from darkness, or sorrow from our hearts, whether that death suddenly calls, or menacing weapons threaten, what removes our terror, and joins to heaven our souls, tried by bloodshed on earth and on the powerful sea, and about our own fate I shall sing. You, Son of the Virgin, and King of life itself, favor me. You will most of all assist the poet, You will be the aim. In You our keel should come to rest, shipwrecked at our last landing place. For all of Greece's wisdom serves You, and every Muse attends You; and all error, once Your light rises and illuminates the mind, dies away at once and is vanished.)

As Vergil had done in the opening lines of the *Georgics*, Heinsius presents the topics of his work in the first four and a half lines and then proceeds to invoke divine help, describing the nature of the deity. While Vergil carefully follows a certain order and form in the pagan gods he addresses, Heinsius' invocation climaxes in a description of Christ's supreme rule heightened by contrasting concepts such as "light" and "error," "arise" and "die," Christ being "the end" versus our "shipwrecked course." Poetry (the Muses) and knowledge (all of Greece's wisdom) exist for the service of Christ. In spite of their classical form, the opening lines reveal Heinsius' religious orientation. Vergil addresses his patron Maecenas in the second line, while the second half of his proem is devoted to Octavian. Heinsius likewise reserves the second part of his introduction (lines 13–38) for contemporary matters, and in them addresses Rutgers, his brother-in-law and the Swedish ambassador, to whom the poem is dedicated.

The stylistic devices in this poem are for the most part those of Heinsius' earlier Latin poetry. Numerous examples given to illustrate philosophical points are described at great length. Similes illuminate the text (e.g., men are caught by death as the unaware dove by a hawk, p. 17; the soul strives for its divine source as an arrow speeds toward its target, p. 31; the soul weighted down by the body is like a noble horse under the farmer's yoke, p. 38). Descriptive passages are mostly based on either classical literature or the Bible. They range from heroic narratives (e.g., the description of Aeneas' shield and other Homeric passages in Book III) to idyllic and religious ones. Books I and II especially contain numerous idyllic passages as contrasts to the author's descriptions of death.

Increasingly, the religious fervor becomes more noticeable in the language. The description of the Last Judgment concluding Book I is a model for the Baroque style used with this favorite topic in religious poetry of the seventeenth century:

Scilicet et rerum nunc foecundissima tellus
Una parens frugumque eadem, pecudumque virumque
Stabit, anhela, tremens, squallanti torrida vultu,
Flammarumque globos liquefacta ad sidera mittet,
Cum gemitu fluviorum, atque indignantibus undis.
At super horrendo mugitu, maximus aether
Concutiet trepidantem; abruptis undique nimbis
Fulmina praecipitans, tempestatesque coruscas,
Et late ambusti volvent incendia montes.   (p. 18)

(And then the earth, now abounding in all things, the sole parent of all fruits, cattle, and men, will stand breathless, trembling, torrid with its parched face. She will send balls of fire to the melting stars, with her rivers groaning and her floods indignant. And the great Heaven above with a horrible roar strikes the trembling earth; with violent torrents sending out lightning and flashing storms and far and wide burning mountains tumble in conflagration.)

The prophecy of future destruction is contrasted to the pleasant present; personification, parallelism of the members, hyperbolic expressions, the unusual word for the common let the lines swell up to a fervent entreaty.

The recurrent use of the imperative when admonishing the reader to consider this or that point (e.g., in Book II, pp. 26–27) underscores the didactic nature of the work. It is the moral and religious advice for a Christian life, phrased in poetic language and illustrated with examples from antiquity and the Bible, that attracted readers to this work. Martin Opitz, after visiting Heinsius in October 1620 (Heinsius may then have been engaged in writing *De contemptu mortis*), conceived his *Trostgedichte in Widerwärtigkeit des Krieges* (Consolation in Adversity of War, 1633), which resembles the Heinsius poem in its organization, passages on fate and war, and Stoic-Christian concepts.[10]

Heinsius' didactic poem is not a dry accumulation of knowledge, but his presentation of wisdom to be used for a religious life is phrased in the hymnic tone of the religious epic, akin to the *Lofsanck van Iesus Christus* of 1616. There were also French influences on this work; Marot's *Psaumes* and, above all, Du Bartas' hymnic didactic epic on the creation *La Sepmaine*.[11] Though the enormous popularity of *La Sepmaine* in France had vanished by this time, partial Dutch translations and imitations were appearing in 1609, 1616, 1621, and 1622; and Heinsius had written a dedicatory poem for the 1621 translation by Zacharias Heyns. Its prophetic and panegyric tone was used by Heinsius especially in Book IV, but Heinsius' work is not an epic with a narrative description. It is rather a philosophical presentation of a religious life. His Christ hymn and then *De contemptu mortis* mark the beginning of his intensive preoccupation with the Bible in scholarship and writing. It should also be noted that he did not take sides nor openly advocate reconciliation in the clash of Protestant denominations among themselves or with Catholicism, as did Hugo Grotius in his propagation of the irenic movement with *De veritate religionis Christianae* (In Defense of Christian Religion, 1627).[12] Heinsius' was a search for religious truth through a scholarly reading of the Bible, a philological approach to the New Testament.

CHAPTER 7

Neo-Latin Drama: Auriacus *(1602)* and Herodes Infanticida *(1632)*

I Auriacus *and Neo-Latin Drama*

A S a twenty-two-year-old student at Leiden about to begin his professorial career, Daniel Heinsius wrote in the preface to his first dramatic attempt *Auriacus, sive libertas saucia* (William, or Wounded Liberty): "A tragedy is the most dignified and noble work of literature. Roman writers and Greek authors before them, have proven that with many arguments."[1] Tragedy, Heinsius maintained, was a royal literary genre in which only kings and princes appeared: Its language was elevated above the speech of the common people. Even the statesman Sophocles had found it worthwhile to write dramas. But while, according to Heinsius, antiquity employed only plots from mythology and did not possess a true historical drama, he wanted to combine historical truth with what he considered to be the supreme literary genre of the ancients.

Such a defense of drama was indeed called for in view of the Calvinists' and Mennonites' opposition to theatrical performances.[2] Being a Latin school drama, the work also had to pass university censorship. According to a decree of December 30, 1595, the performance of comedy or tragedy had to be sanctioned by the rector and four officials, thus ending a period of what appears to have been lively presentations, including plays by Seneca and Plautus. The *Auriacus* received a dispensation and was performed toward the end of 1601 and in January of 1602. Scaliger, Grotius, and Petrus Bertius, a regent of the States' College, were in the audience as Heinsius tells us in the preface.[3]

Heinsius' first dramatic attempt belongs in the rich tradition of Neo-Latin drama in the Netherlands. Before leaving the Low Countries to escape the Inquisition, William Gnapheus (1493–1568) dramatized the parable of the Prodigal Son in *Acolastus* (1529), a blend of a biblical theme with a classical form that became exemplary for the dramas of the entire century. The fourteen plays of Georg Macropedius (ca. 1475–1558), a member of the Brethren of Common Life and a director of the Latin school at 'sHertogenbosch, Liège, and Utrecht, dealt mostly with biblical events, such as *Susanna* (1540), *Passio Christi* (ca. 1545), and *Josephus* (1544). His version of the everyman theme made him famous throughout Germany and, to a lesser extent, in the Netherlands. The biblical dramas of the "Christian Terence," Cornelius Schonaeus (1540–1611), later principal of the Latin school at Haarlem, were used as textbooks in Dutch schools because of the elegant Latin and the moral views presented in them. Classical trends in biblical drama became more pronounced toward the end of the sixteenth century. In their dedicatory poems for Heinsius' drama Dousa and Grotius refer to two model plays, George Buchanan's *Jephthes sive votum* (Jephthah, or The Vow, 1554) and Muretus' *Julius Caesar* (1550). Buchanan (1506–1582), a Scottish emigrant living in Paris, had used features from Euripides' tragedies in his dramatic version of the Old Testament story of Jephthah. Muretus' (1526–1585) historical play was modeled after Seneca, the author whom Hugo Grotius emulated in his first drama *Adamus exul* (Adam in Exile, written 1601).[4] Grotius was only eighteen when he wrote his play on the Fall of Man; and though he later dismissed it as an immature attempt of his youth, it was acclaimed by his contemporaries and provided a model for a renewal of the Latin school drama in the Christian and Protestant tradition. More than half a century later it still served as the structural model for Vondel's Dutch drama *Adam in ballingschap* (Adam in Exile, 1664), one of the best examples of the close relationship in theme and literary technique of Neo-Latin school drama and Dutch tragedy in the seventeenth century.[5]

II   *Historical Background and Plot of* Auriacus

For his drama *Auriacus* Heinsius chose an event from recent Dutch history: the assassination of William the Silent of Orange on July 10, 1584 by a fanatical young Catholic from Brabant, Balthasar Gerard. After the inglorious failure of the Duke d'Anjou as a military leader, William, who had been instrumental in the union of the seven northern Dutch provinces, was about to accept the offer of

Holland and Zeeland to be their leader in the struggle against the Spanish when he was killed in Delft. William's death, though not instigated by Philip II, was a severe setback to the cause of the young Dutch Republic. Louise de Coligny, William's fourth wife, was the daughter of the Huguenot leader Gaspard de Coligny, who, together with Louise's first husband, was murdered in Paris during the infamous Bartholomew's Day Massacre in 1572. In 1600 Maurice, William's son, had won the battle at Nieuwpoort. Heinsius' play, written in 1601, is a timely tribute to Maurice, who appears in the concluding scene of the tragedy as a young man vowing to avenge his father's death with the destruction of the Spanish. The drama appealed to contemporary audiences because of its content: a patriotic challenge to avenge the murder of William of Orange against the Spanish.

Before Heinsius' play, the assassination had already formed the subject matter of several poetic works.[6] In 1586 the young Calvinist Georgius Benedicti Wortelius (1563–1588) from Haarlem, a student at Cambridge, Leiden, and Heidelberg and Janus Dousa's friend, published *De rebus gestis Illustriss, Principis Guillielmi* (Life of William the Silent), a heroic verse epic in the Vergilian manner. Heinsius' plot seems to have been influenced by this presentation of William's death: In both works a personified Inquisition instigates the murder to help Philip II; Balthasar Gerard wavers before carrying out the assassination and tells the story of his father's death at the hands of Alba's soldiers; and Louise ominously remembers her first husband and her father. In 1598, some years after Wortelius' epic, a dramatization of the assassination by a young Calvinist minister from Delft, Casparius (Caspar Ens), had appeared entitled *Princeps Auriacus, sive libertas defensa* (Prince William, or the Defense of Liberty). Heinsius' title, *Auriacus, sive libertas saucia,* seems to have been inspired by Casparius, but otherwise the latter's moralizing and pious drama with its amorphous structure, cumbersome plot, and awkward versification cannot compare with Heinsius' accomplished play. In every aspect Heinsius' drama bears witness to his intensive reading of the classical authors. His five-act tragedy closely adheres to the unities of time, place, and action.

Act 1: Prince William, the leader of the Dutch freedom movement opens the play with a long monologue. After an invocation to the powers of nature, William ponders over human life, the separation of the immortal soul from the body by death, and man's desire for wealth and honors. He has been called to defend his country's liberty at sea and on land against Alba and Philip II who are to be defeated like a lion by a hunter. In a similar way the mighty giant Typhaeus struck by Jupiter's lightning was buried under Mount Aetna. William has not fought for himself but for his country; he was born to serve his people. A chorus of old Flemish refugees extols the Netherlands and laments the uncertainty of fortune and the lot of those who remained behind—while hinting at imminent future disasters. Their love for the homeland and desire for peace support William's claim that the country needs a strong leader for the defense of their liberty against the Spanish.

Act II: Accompanied by three Furies, a personified Inquisition holds a chalice with human blood. After an invocation to the goddess of the Lower World, Persephone, Inquisition presents herself as a fourth destructive power created by the Spanish to aid the Furies. Philip's vengeance demands a new victim, the Netherlands; Rage, Hate, and Insanity will lead the way. In an effective contrast, the following scene shows William's wife, Louise de Coligny, with her infant son and an Old Man. Addressing the new day, fearful of what it may bring, Louise ponders the future of her innocent child. The Old Man attempts to comfort her, to discount her premonitions as a woman's fearful, false dream. He argues that the future cannot be known and that her husband, whose courage he lauds, is safe in the city. The chorus appears again and praises the beauty and innocence of Holland versus the ravaging Spanish.

Act 3: Balthasar Gerard, the murderer, appears in a state of utmost agitation, confusion, and despair. He does not know if he should carry out his plan or what he should do, comparing himself to a raft abandoned to the waves and the wind. Fate will lead him. When a suspicious guard questions him about his intentions, he tells of the loss of his father, who fought for his belief, and of his mother's death from sorrow. The guard advises him to overcome his sorrow and, rather than mourn, to avenge his father's death by fighting against the Spaniards. Gerard enthusiastically takes up the suggestion of revenge. In the next scene, William asks his wife why she is so fearful and pale. He has escaped many dangers and describes himself as the protector of the Dutch; but Louise is still afraid, pleads with her husband to be cautious, and reminds him of her father's assassination. William looks to the future unafraid and addresses his infant son as the coming leader and avenger of his father should his fate call him prematurely. The chorus concludes the act with a praise of love and marriage.

Act 4: The murderer surrounded by the Furies and Inquisition deliberates about his intentions in a long monologue. Torture will await him, but he decides to fulfill his promise and to carry out his revenge. Inquisition then steps forward and appeals to the powers of darkness and destruction to assist with the "funeral of the Dutch." In the second scene, Louise is frightened by a dream; her attendant tries to comfort her, but she remains suspicious of a stranger from Brabant. The third scene shows Gerard intent on committing the murder. William appears with a long monologue on the passing of all things, on the uncertainty of what the future holds, on the destruction that men bring upon each other, especially now with firearms. At that moment, the murderer comes forward and shoots William who commends his people and family to God while his life expires. A prefect sends guards in all directions to look for the murderer in different parts of the city. The chorus praises the power of the Netherlands and is disturbed about a yet unknown disaster.

Act 5: Louise mourns her husband and is comforted by her attendant. The chorus joins in the mourning and is overwhelmed by grief. Then Wounded Liberty appears and bemoans the death of the hero. The universe and the constellations also mourn the dead warrior, who terrified the Spanish and was felled by deceit. Liberty leaves the earth where man is only a monstrous being. In an epilogue, Prince Maurice appears upon his return from Leiden and vows to avenge his father's death.

This last appearance has been added,[7] Heinsius informs us in the Preface to the Reader, because friends had asked him why he had introduced the infant son Frederic Henry and not Maurice. For his drama, Heinsius had wanted to adhere to the Aristotelian unity of time and place: Since it was a well-known fact that Maurice was away when the assassination occurred, Heinsius would have had either to violate the unity of time in his drama or alter historical truth. Moreover, in his frailty and defenselessness the infant Frederic Henry served as a contrast to the cruel event and offered his mother the opportunity to lament her (and the Netherlands') fate and lack of protection. Because he did not want to appear stubborn, Heinsius added the epilogue spoken by Maurice who somewhat resembled a *deus ex machina*, Heinsius contends. It made the play more theatrical and patriotic and emphasized its contemporary context.

III   *A Fate Tragedy*

Since the plot of *Auriacus* was familiar to the reader or audience, the dramatization held little suspense. Each of acts 1 through 3 consists of two long scenes and a chorus; the fourth act contains the assassination as the climax in its third scene. Act 5 contains the appearance of the allegorical figure, Liberty, and an epilogue. Monologues, long scenes with little dialogue, and a general lack of action except for the murder on stage contribute to the static nature of the play. It is a discussion of an event and the persons involved in it rather than a dramatic presentation. William bravely faces his fate, sealed from the beginning, though as yet unknown to him, while Louise, his fearful feminine counterpart, is filled with dreams and premonitions. In his first monologue (1.1), William deliberates about man's lot and about his own calling:

> . . . labitur velox dies
> Ipsisque ab annis mensibusque ducimur,
> Fatique summam pervenimus orbitam;
> Denascimur semper, et finem suum
> Breves citato provocant anni gradu. (p. 7)

(. . . the day quickly glides away and we are led by the very years and months, and we go along the last path of fate: We perish forever and short years hasten the end with quick succession.)

The inevitability of fate and death is introduced as the major theme of the drama, the entire course of action being conceived as an inescapable occurrence. William has been called into the struggle by his country. The chorus (1.2) takes up the theme in referring to the refugees' young and yet unborn children who are destined to a life in exile. The Furies and Inquisition (2.1) represent the evil forces which are set upon the destruction of the Dutch, while Louise cannot suppress her ominous fears and premonitions: "Omnia et scio, et dolet,/ Timere posse, dum dolet, timeo tamen,/ Metusque causae nescius, causa est metus" (p. 29) (I know all and it hurts to be able to fear; while it hurts, I still fear, and unaware of its cause, fear itself becomes the cause). The Old Man uses rational arguments against this fear of uncertainty (William is in his castle; it is a safe city; he is a cautious person) which rather enhances the threat of the fateful event, though there are no discernible indications for it.

A key scene is Gerard's encounter with the guard (3.1). Gerard appears beside himself at the outset of the scene:

> Quo? quo? quis urges? huccine anne illhuc feror?
> Utroque certe; saeva tempestas dei
> Intus redundans cordis exercet salum:
> Exaestuatque mens; et incertus ferit
> Ardens tremensque pectoris votum tumor. (p. 34)

(Whereto? Whereto? Who urges? Am I driven here or there? In both directions; the savage storm of the god surging inside disturbs the sea of my heart. My mind is inflamed: an uncertain burning, great passion shakes the vow in my breast.)

He appears afraid to carry out his plan. For a moment the guard seems to be able to prevent the murder with his suspicion and the suggestion of revenge against the Spanish. But the well-meant advice only helps Gerard to strengthen his original intention to kill Prince William.

The scene between Louise and William (3.2) represents another moment of retardation: Her fears, her dream, her suspicion of the stranger from Brabant (the murderer Gerard) cannot persuade her husband not to leave for the banquet. Immediately before the assassination the murderer once again is in doubt and fear (4.1):

> Dubitamus anime? caeca concilia advocas?
> Hac hac eundum est. cernis, has cernis fores?
> Haec te beatum referet, aut nullum via. (p. 59)

(Are you in doubt, my mind? Do you advise the dark plan? There, there I must go. Do you see this gate? This path will bring you back happy or not at all.)

The phrase "I must go" *(eundem est)* occurs throughout the play; it indicates the necessity involved in each person's actions. In the first scene William uses it to demonstrate his calling as a ruler (p. 9); Inquisition admonishes Gerard with these words (p. 22); in the murder scene Gerard begins his monologue with this phrase (p. 66). The fateful deed must occur; this is the major theme of the play and Heinsius' interpretation of the historical event. Like the classical hero, especially Seneca's characters, William meets his predestined lot. For the Calvinist Heinsius a fatalistic view of the historical event prevails.

IV   *Patriotism Subdued*

The play's secondary theme, political freedom, is much less developed than the subtitle "Wounded Liberty" would indicate. William the Silent himself in his manifesto of 1568 had expressed the idea of *libertas ergo* when he declared that the liberties of towns and provinces were not benevolent grants by the monarch but contracts binding prince and people. William is a martyr to Dutch liberty in the contemporary view of the United Provinces. In Heinsius' play William is the defender of freedom:

> Belgia his cervicibus
> Inclinat, incubatque et invitum trahit
> Seges laborum vasta, patriaeque onus
> Fluctusque nostrae: Sancta libertas vocet,
> Et servitutis foeda detrectat iuga
> Mens nata magnis; nec sibi; sed omnibus
> Quoscunque regis insolens premit tumor. (pp. 8–9)

(The Netherlands rest on these shoulders, the vast fruit of our endeavors weighs upon me and drives me against my will, the woes and disturbance of my country: Holy Liberty calls, the base yoke of servitude is spurned by my mind born for great things, not for itself, but for all those whom the insolent pride of the king [Philip II] oppresses.)

With these lines, the political significance of the struggle is demonstrated; it is the black-and-white projection of tyranny versus holy freedom, of the "savage Spaniard" *(saevus Iber)* aligned with the Furies and the forces of evil against the happy, innocent Dutch (the theme of the chorus in act 1, scene 2). Throughout the play these positions are fixed. The emphasis shifts to William, the fatherly, patriotic ruler; praise of him is contrasted with the machinations of Inquisition and the Furies. The appearance of Wounded Liberty in the end underscores the grief of the Dutch and the evils of this world, and the political theme comes again to the foreground:

> Valete cives, sancta libertas abit,
> Abivit ille, quem videtis hic tamen,
> Abivit ille, praevium a terris sequor.
> Valete cives, sancta libertas abit. (p. 84)

(Farewell citizens, Sacred Liberty is leaving. He has left, whom you still see here. He has left, and I follow him who leads the way from this earth. Farewell, citizens, Sacred Liberty is leaving.)

With Liberty's long monologue enhanced by Prince Maurice's epilogue, Heinsius closes on a strong patriotic note. In this aspect the play is dogmatic, uncomplicated, and predictable. Heinsius' patriotism is, however, much more subdued than in the play of another emigrant: Jacob van Duym's *Het moordadich stuck van Balthasar Gerards* (The Murderous Plot of Balthasar Gerard; Leiden, 1606).[8] In large part a reworking in Dutch of the Heinsius play, it pleads the cause of the Flemish emigrants and the fight for the freedom of all the Netherlands.

V *Three Main Characters*

Only three characters in *Auriacus* are drawn in some detail: William, the murderer, and Louise. They reveal themselves in monologues or long speeches but show little or no development or interaction. Rather, each of the three exemplifies a state of mind: William shows stoic calmness and constancy, Louise the sadness and intuitive fear of the future of a woman, Gerard anxiety and a compulsive passion for the evil deed. Heinsius presents these states of mind with psychological insight.

In his first monologue William recognizes the power of fortune which may change at any time. He is the courageous leader against the Spanish: ". . . ibimus tamen; neque/ Servire nostrum est. Regiam tendens viam/ In dura virtus sponte prorumpit" (pp. 9–10) (. . . Nevertheless we'll go; I cannot be a servant. On its royal path virtue breaks forth by itself in hard times). The monologue serves as exposition of the play, and the prince does not so much praise himself as demonstrate the steadfastness that he preserves in spite of his wife's premonitions. With Stoic arguments he assures Louise (3.2) that he does not fear death nor the enemy's treachery and points to his son as his avenger should he die, referring to the natural cycle: "Dies diei cedit, atque annum novus/ Reducit annus,

ultimusque saeculi/ Finis, futuri primus est aevi gradus" (p. 68)
(One day gives way to the next, and the new year leads away the old;
the end of a century is the first step of a new one). With Stoic
calmness William then meets his fate.

Louise and Gerard are conceived of as contrasts to this steadfastness. Both have supportive figures (the Old Man and the attendant
for Louise, the guard for Gerard) to draw out their thoughts and
emotions. As a woman, Louise can express sorrow and fear. Her
child is always on her lap, as Astyanax is on Andromache's in Seneca's *Trojan Women*. In the last act she can completely dedicate
herself to mourning; for like Hecuba she has nothing worse to fear.
In the dedicatory poem to the play, Grotius compares her to the
mourning women of antiquity, Electra and Antigone. In contrast
with the scene of the Furies, Louise appears with the infant child
whose innocent happy sleep she wishes for herself. A conversation
about the nature of dream and sleep ensues in which the Old Man
explains to her that it is fear of darkness that terrifies her, and he
tells her that a false dream "puts out the flame of reason like a cloud"
(p. 27). But she cannot be soothed by his rational arguments concerning her husband's safety and remains the typical prophetess of
antiquity who cannot suppress the premonitions and anxiety which
turn out to be justified. Louise pours out her feelings which portend
imminent, fateful events. And while there is no development or
action, it is the Old Man's function to elicit her state of mind.

Likewise the murderer opens his heart and lets the audience see
his agitated state of mind. It is far too simplistic to dismiss him as a
sly, fanatic villain. Heinsius takes great care in showing that he is
hesitant to the last, conscious of the dark forces he is to serve, afraid
of evil, yet unable to tear himself away. He is the condemned sinner
unable to follow the right path. The detailed story (told to the guard)
of his father's death for his religion and his freedom must have been
moving for a Dutch audience at that time.[9] Upset and shaken by this
event, Gerard goes "quo sors agit, Deusque" (p. 27) (where fate and
God drives him); it is a blend of the classical fate concept and Christian predestination. The Furies have taken possession of the murderer as the avenger of his father's death as they did with Orestes
and Medea; but Gerard is not a cold-blooded villain. A misguided
piety and desire for revenge overcome his moral scruples and fears
of death; Gerard thus represents a person who is irrationally driven
to evil.

Although these three characters lack development and argue rather than act, they are conceived with an interest in their moral and psychological motivation. Modeled on prototypes of classical heroes within a Stoic and Christian moral context, they are a new type of rounded character, not mere stereotypes. Louise especially is in many respects an innovative female character drawn with much more insight than the few stereotyped women in Neo-Latin and vernacular drama at the time. Heinsius' later discussion of character portrayal and analysis of classical drama in his theoretical work on tragedy of 1611 underscores his perceptive eye for psychological motivation.

VI *Allegorical Figures and the Chorus*

The figures Inquisition and Liberty support the contemporary political theme of the play, while the chorus scenes[10] are modeled on the chorus of classical drama. Neither was an innovation by Heinsius, but both elements are well integrated into the play. Inquisition, the leader of the Furies, represents the dark side of religion (*religio noctis*, p. 22). She is a creation of the Spanish; and the chalice of human blood she is holding visually underscores her bloodthirsty language. The appearance of Liberty who joins in the mourning contrasts starkly with Inquisition. Both are allegorical figures representing an idea, but Heinsius did not use Liberty or Inquisition as his mouthpiece. Inquisition is the fourth Fury whose appearance in classical drama—for instance, in Seneca's *Medea*—was nothing unusual. As a group collectively representing the forces of evil, the Furies have a function similar to that of the Guards in act 4 on the one hand and the chorus of the Dutch on the other, acting as a collective body rather than as individuals.

Liberty in her only appearance sums up the essence of the play; actually she neither argues nor discusses freedom but merely mourns the evil deed and the loss of the prince. Her long speech is rather an extension of the chorus, a prophetic end like the conclusion of a Senecan tragedy.

The allegorical figures cannot really be regarded as a remnant from medieval drama.[11] Allegorical personifications used in the seventeenth century were no longer major but supporting elements in the dramatic structure. In classical dramas (e.g., Aeschylus and

Seneca) spirits of the deceased or apparitions appeared with a similar function. Liberty, a new concept of the Renaissance, and such
allegorical figures as Irene (Peace) or Mars (War) were often employed in dramas with contemporary subject matter to represent
ideas, not stereotyped persons. The use of the chorus most clearly
reflects Heinsius' intention of reviving the form of the classical
drama. The chorus' lines continue themes, mood, and to some extent the action of the preceding scene. Thus the chorus is function-
ally integrated into the play and has become a vital element. In its
first appearance the chorus continues William's thoughts about the
role of fortune, admonishing its children: "casusque tuos/ Disce, et
saevi fulmina fati" (p. 14) (Learn about your calamities and the
savage strokes of fate). The idyllic description of the homeland is
contrasted to the Furies' appearance thereafter. In the second act
this contrast between the "raging Spanish" and the peaceful Dutch
is further explored; in the fourth act, following the scene between
William and Louise, trust and love in marriage are pictured before
the murderer and the Furies appear again on stage. The chorus thus
is an integral part of the drama, a retarding element given to reflection and emotion at important points in the play. In the last act, the
chorus mourning William unites several themes of the play: William's roles as husband, father, and prince of his people; the unpre-
dictability of fortune; the evils of this world. The lyrical element is
especially evident in the choral lines that describe the country:

> Cernis, cernis per inane leves
> Nare columbas, expersque metu
> Placida ut campos perrepat ovis.
> Tuque o tepidi conscia veris
> Quae nocturno carmina fundis
> Ebria rore:
> Quae sub tremulis Zephyri tenui
> Flamine ramis, tua tecta colis,
> Parvosque lares, nutantesque
> Strepitu tenui suspirantis
> Leniter aurae, florumque leves
> Incolis umbras, blanda cicada.
> Non te trepido quatit infelix
> Turbine Mavors. (pp. 30, 31–32)

(You can see over the wide plains, the doves sail free from fear as the
peaceful sheep wanders across the fields; and you, feeling the warm spring,

you pour out your songs at night drunken with dew. And you who make your home under leaves rustling in the gentle breeze of the wind and care for the small hearth, making gentle tones and inhabiting the light shadows of the flowers, charming cricket. Unhappy Mars does not strike you with his trembling assault.)

Bucolic tones are audible in these lines which are very similar to Heinsius' poetry from the early years. The chorus is the most independent and innovative feature in Heinsius' drama.

VII *A Senecan Tragedy*

In its dramatic technique, the play shows the influence of Seneca whose tragedies Heinsius was to edit in 1611 and to analyze in his theoretical work on tragedy of the same year. The action is as static and undramatic as in Seneca's *Medea*.[12] Both are subdivided into five acts each of which begins with a long monologue. Heinsius' chorus, however, does not interact with other characters as does the chorus in Greek tragedy but is much more integrated into his play than is Seneca's. *Auriacus* contains few scenes and only a few major actors. Almost all characters introduce themselves with long speeches and then only address another person present. Reflection and declamation fill the rather skeletal action; descriptions and discussions have replaced action. These are the most important features in the Neo-Latin drama in the Senecan tradition because they entail a concentration on the spoken word, on the psychology of the characters, themes, and ideas, and a departure from intricate action and elaborate staging. The result was a solemn, dignified, and stationary play with immobile figures but a highly sophisticated language,[13] which deeply influenced Dutch, German, and French classical drama of the seventeenth century.

Contrary to the Horatian principles, Seneca displayed acts of cruelty on stage: Medea kills her children as does Hercules; Phaedra and Jocasta kill themselves. Heinsius shows the murder on stage—the only event in his play—and William dies in the middle of his speech. Unlike Seneca's characters, the murderer does repent; a conversion, so characteristic of the Neo-Latin biblical drama, does not occur. Seneca presents the characters of Greek mythology as cruel and brutal half-heroes, half-criminals with gigantic passions, like his Hercules, Medea, and Theseus. The pathos of Greek heroes becomes a frenzy *(furor)* in Seneca; his characters act in passion and despair, driven by anger *(ira)* and violent impulse *(impetus)*. Hein-

sius' murderer does not quite reach such stature, but he appears in a
rage bordering on derangement. In his frantic wavering between
good and evil, his passion for revenge wins out; and, aware of the
consequences, he shoots William. The furor displayed by Hercules
or Medea served as a model for these scenes and the portrait of
Herod in Heinsius' later play.

The metric patterns of the choral lines (such as trochaic tetramet-
ers and melodic use of repeated exclamations) show more the
influence of Greek tragedy than of Seneca. In a revised edition
which Heinsius planned around 1608–1610 but did not carry out,[14]
he intended to elaborate on the Greek features. The dialogue, on
the other hand, shows stylistic patterns similar to Seneca's. Lengthy
dignified invocations open all the monologues and longer speeches.
Heinsius frequently employs similes,[15] some extending over eighteen verses (the subterranean fires in 3.1; the pale moon in 3.2; the
sword resembling the iron courage of the hero in 4.2). Comparing
the hero to the hunter chasing the lion (as in 1.1) is a Senecan simile
from the epic tradition of Homer, but most of Heinsius' other
similes are independent in that they explore a new aspect in the
comparison. In his later play and his poetry similes are even more
elaborate and more frequent. In addition, all the rhetorical features
characteristic not only of Seneca but of postclassical Latin literature
are also present. Hyperbole, circumlocution, and epigrammatic
poignancy especially characterize the dialogue and contribute to the
sparkling declamatory qualities of the play. The spoken word thus is
already the most important feature of the play in this early work. It
is the tradition of classical stylistic and conceptual features that is
continued in Van Hogendorp's *Treurspel vande moordt begaen aen
Willem* (Tragedy of the Murder Committed Against William) which
in 1617 was the first play performed at Coster's famous theater, the
Nederduytsche Academie in Amsterdam. It is clear that the literary
and intellectual significance of *Auriacus* was not limited to the circle
of Leiden professors.

VIII *Developments in Neo-Latin and
Dutch Drama 1602–1632*

In 1632, thirty years after his first youthful attempt, Heinsius
published his second drama *Herodes infanticida* (Herod, Child
Murderer), a model tragedy by a famous classical philologist.[16] Important developments had taken place during these three decades in
Neo-Latin drama, and a classical Dutch drama had emerged. In

1605 with the Seneca edition of Justus Lipsius, then professor at the University of Louvain, the revival of Stoicism was complete. Seneca's rhetorical style became a model, together with Tacitus, countering the Ciceronian movement of the Renaissance. Still, Lipsius freely criticized Seneca for his conceit *(affectatio)*, pompous style, and bombast *(tumor)*. He saw in Seneca's sententious lines "sparks rather than a real flame."[17] He praised above all Seneca's *Medea* and *Phoenissae* but regarded *The Trojan Women*, often considered Seneca's best tragedy, as the concoction of an inferior poetaster. Joseph Scaliger defended *The Trojan Women* especially. He considered this drama in dignity *(majestas)* equal to Attic tragedy and in elegance *(cultus)* and brilliance *(splendor)* superior to Euripides.[18] Heinsius with his discerning literary taste and critical intuition, when characterizing Greek and Roman tragedy in his *De tragoediae constitutione*, put *The Trojan Women, Hippolytus,* and *Medea* above the others. He criticized the many repetitious and loquacious dialogues; the lack of characterization and economy in the *Hercules Oetaeus;* the sententiousness and declamatory pathos in the *Thebais;* and the rhetorical pomp which detracts from characterization as in *Thyestes.* Such views became the guiding principle for the entire century in which *The Trojan Women* was considered Seneca's best tragedy. Almost everywhere in Europe the tragedy in the vernacular, from Jodelle and Garnier, Kyd and Marlowe, to Corneille, Shakespeare, Calderón, Hooft, Vondel, Opitz, Gryphius, and Lohenstein, began in the manner of Seneca.

By using recent history as the subject matter in his Neo-Latin tragedy *Auriacus* (1602), Heinsius encouraged other writers to do the same. The Dutch Theodore Rhodius (ca. 1570–1625), a Calvinist like Heinsius, dramatized the murder of Coligny, the beginning of the Bartholomew's Day massacre, in *Colignius* (1614), adhering strictly to neoclassical form and the unities. Seneca was his model for style and characterization and Greek tragedy for the formal composition of the choral passages. Louise de Coligny resembles very much the character of the same name in Heinsius' play; she is fearful with premonitions, while father and husband appear as energetic, strong, stoic personalities like William the Silent, fighting the forces of tyranny and evil. Other Neo-Latin historical tragedies followed; and though less dependent on Heinsius' *Auriacus*, they embodied the prominent features of Senecan drama. The Louvain professor Nicolaus Vernulaeus (1583–1649) wrote and performed in fourteen

historical dramas between 1609 and 1648. The Dutch Johannes
Narssius (1580–1637), later court poet in Sweden, presented events
from the life of Gustavus Adolphus in his *Gustavus saucius*
(Wounded Gustavus, 1627). Hugo Grotius' second tragedy *Christus
patiens* (Suffering Christ, 1608), though dealing with a biblical
theme, followed the rules of Roman drama which Grotius later
ranked lower than Greek tragedy when writing his *Sophompaneas*
in the manner of Euripides in 1634.[19] With these dramas, stylistic
and aesthetic criteria became of major importance, while the traditional goal of Neo-Latin school drama, serving as a means of educ-
tion in the classical languages as well as in character formation,
receded more and more into the background. Considerations of
structure, language, style, and characterization became of ever-
increasing concern to the writers and the theoreticians of neoclassical tragedy.

During these decades the great dramatists of the Golden Age of
Dutch literature began their dramatic attempts. Cornelis Hooft
(1581–1647), an admirer of the Leiden scholarly poets, wrote his
historical dramas *Geeraerdt van Velsen* (1613) and *Baeto* (written
1617) after the example of Seneca. His characters are more the
personification of ideas than they are living people though they
present the problems of authority and governance with a strong plea
for tolerance and unity. Joost van den Vondel (1587–1679), the great
dramatist of the seventeenth century, read Seneca in the original.
The Roman became an important influence on Vondel's dramatic
style after the early drama *Pascha* (Passover, 1610) and on his subsequent play *Hierusalem verwoest* (Jerusalem Destroyed, 1619).
Especially his *Gysbreght van Aemstel* (1637) employs a classical
form with five acts, choruses, and strict adherence to the unities.
Vondel's own dramatic theory, that the pictorial aspects are more
important than the plot, accounts for the lack of dramatic action.
With the preponderance of speeches, lyrical choruses, and static
characters this drama is a creative continuation in the vernacular of
major features of the pictorial, rhetorical Neo-Latin tragedy for
which Heinsius' *Herodes infanticida* served as another model play
in 1632.

IX   *Plot and Structure of* Herodes infanticida

In the dedication of *Herodes infanticida* to the poet Constantijn
Huygens, his former student, Heinsius explains the structure and

intent of his drama in the Aristotelian manner: "The divine genius of Aristotle has covered almost everything necessary for a correct and ornate construction of a tragedy . . . I admire those who write in the manner of the ancients but still do not condone everything. Critical minds reserve their own judgment" (pp. A2, A3).[20] Not slavish imitation, but creative continuation based on the artistic principles of ancient drama is the goal.

Act 1 consists of one long prologue spoken by an angel who praises Bethlehem, the birthplace of Jesus, and tells the story of the sins of men and their fall from paradise. After receiving God's commandments, the people of Israel become unfaithful and fall into idolatry. Jerusalem is turned into a shrine for gods from Phoenicia, Babylonia, and Egypt, while the Roman Empire adopts the polytheism of the Greeks. The true god will be incarnated and born in a stable, and the Child will be the savior of this world. Representing the divine perspective, the messenger of God warns the mothers of Bethlehem and predicts the events in their major aspects. A chorus of Prophets and Pious Men praises Egypt and the Nile as the benefactor of Egypt, suggesting that they prepare to receive the Child.

In act 2 Joseph, looking at his infant son in Mary's lap, marvels in a long monologue at the story of the "offspring of heaven" who is still unaware of the fate destined for him by God; and he praises Mary and the virgin birth. Mary is frightened and with tears in her eyes looks at the Child who smiles in recognition of His mother. Noise is heard and the three Magi appear and tell of Herod's desire to see and to kill the Child. Lamenting the treacheries of this life, especially at court, and the wickedness of proud Herod who defies God and fate, Joseph and Mary now intend to return home. In "the upper part of the theater" the heavenly host appears showing the Child in the cradle and hailing the birth of Christ. The chorus of Prophets and Pious Men praises Bethlehem's glory and the King of Kings, who will not rule the lands but the universe.

With act 3 the action begins. Herod feels threatened by Rome, by the star which has announced an eternal ruler; he fears for his throne and vows to defy fate and heaven. Whoever the Child may be, he will kill it. The messengers sent out by Herod to gather information have found nothing. Herod wants to know about the Child and his Kingdom and is told about the rumors among the people who believe in the end of the Roman Empire and the advent of the Redeemer of all nations. Herod vows by the Furies that he will find the new ruler and feed His limbs to the vultures. He will kill this Child even though he was born in a manger and adored by shepherds. The chorus of Old Jews praises the joys of a peaceful life in the country, not wanting to believe in Herod's fury nor Roman falsehood.

Act 4 opens with Herod's wife Marianne accompanied by the Fury Tisiphone returning from the underworld and appearing to Herod in a dream. She reminds him of his crimes. The Furies show him the ghosts of those he murdered. Herod has an infernal vision: Jerusalem collapses, the sun darkens, and he sees his wife and the Furies beckoning while the earth opens to devour him. He wants to fight but finds himself chained while the Child steps onto His throne. He calls the Jews and Romans and the Emperor Augustus for help; he even implores his wife for her forgiveness, but only his victims appear. A short dialogue between Anna and Joseph shows that the Child has been taken to Egypt. Then the action returns to Herod's palace, where the king has overcome his fear and commands his soldiers to kill all male infants up to the age of two. His attendants are shocked. An Old Man pleads for reason and tries to avert the blood bath, but Herod wants to preserve his throne at any cost. A chorus of Roman soldiers dreams of a return to their homeland and praises the innocent.

Act 5 opens with three mothers from Bethlehem in utmost despair pleading to God to save their children and offering their own lives in return. The soldiers kill the children before their mothers' eyes. In the next scene, Herod is anxiously awaiting a report of the massacre. After the messenger's minutely detailed description Herod rejoices in the security of his throne only to learn that the Child has escaped to Egypt. In a last fit of anger, he vows to conquer Egypt, to destroy the pyramids if necessary, and to sacrifice the last of the line of Judah. Mothers from Jerusalem burying their children deplore the fate of the innocent and their own fate. In an epilogue the angels proclaim the wisdom of God and state that from the blood of martyrs a new race will be born that will overcome mortal tyrants and ascend to heaven.

Framed by the prologue and epilogue of the angels, the drama employs three choruses and only one fully developed character, Herod. There are two scenes: One is Bethlehem, where the Magi and Joseph appear and Christian dogma is pronounced; the other is

Herod's palace. The two localities are at the same time the two
levels of the play: One is a place of salvation and eternity and the
other of condemnation and time. The choral songs are hymns not
bound to any locality. Only when Herod appears are some concrete
and dramatic elements evident.

The play can hardly be regarded as having a coherent dramatic
plot. It falls into two parts: scenes in which dogmatic statements or
observations on human life are uttered and scenes developed
around the tyrant Herod. Thus acts 1 and 2 are a play in themselves.
The story of the Child Savior holds the two parts together and
permeates the play as much as the wrath of Herod adds a dramatic
element to it. What Heinsius wanted to show was not an intricate,
dramatic event, but a comprehensive perspective on life from a
Christian point of view. In his preface he had described his plot as
"straightforward, not intricate" (rectum est, non involutum, p. A4)
meaning that "it is brought to its conclusion without manifest reversal of fortune or without recognition," as he had explained in *De
tragoediae constitutione*.[21] Sophocles' *Ajax* and Seneca's *Hercules
furens* had this type of simple plot augmented by fitting episodes. In
Herodes infanticida dramatic action has been amplified by pictorial
description: for example, Herod's dream and the report of the massacre range from the very naturalistic and crude to the religious or
idyllic songs of the chorus concerning, for example, the fall of men
and the rural life. These episodes and the portrayal of Herod are
among the most interesting aspects of the drama as is also the
greatly admired rhetorical style of its dialogue.

X *Herod, the Unbeliever and Sinner*

Herod was already a familiar figure in the medieval Christmas and
mystery plays. The cause of Jesus' flight into Egypt and of the death
of the innocent children, the king was represented as the typical evil
scoundrel characterized by hypocrisy, cruelty, rage, and verbosity.
During the sixteenth and seventeenth centuries Sixtus Betulius'
drama *Herodes sive innocentes* (Herod, or The Innocent, 1538) was
followed by numerous works on this theme of which the epos by
Marino *La Straghe degl' innocenti* (The Murder of the Innocent,
1620) was the most famous.[22] Heinsius' drama introduced the
Marianne story by letting her ghost appear and prophesy Herod's
damnation.

Herod is the only rounded character in Heinsius' play; the messenger, attendant, and Old Man merely serve to elicit Herod's response or to render a description. He is the tyrannical ruler, proud, unrestrained, unreasonable, the very opposite to the intelligent, heroic Prince William.[23] Herod's obsession with the fear of losing his power leads him to defy God: "Sint fata, sint consulta, sint coeli minae" (p. 30). (Let there be calamities, let there be decrees, let there be threats of Heaven). Herod will not submit, even if his father were to return from the grave and bid him to; he will eradicate this fearsome belief and destroy this Child as a vulture seizes his helpless prey (p. 31). Still, Heinsius shows Herod in a moment of insecurity when he utters a helpless prayer, more a demand, to a higher power:

> Quicumque rector, quicquid ubicumque est tenes,
> Seu te vestusta Solyma porticibus colunt,
> . . . .
> Seu numen hic mentimur, et coelum tenes,
> Tarpeie genitor, orte Saturno patre,
> Qui cuncta iam Romana, qua Sol it, vides. . . . (p. 34)

(Whatever ruler you may be, whatever you may rule, wheter they revere you in the temple in ancient Jerusalem . . . or we falsely believe god is here, and you inhabit the sky, Capitoline Jupiter, offspring of Saturn, who oversees the Roman Empire, as far as the sun travels. . . .)

Herod is the unbeliever, the man who lacks faith, the most important attribute for any Christian, and thus he is doomed. He is only certain of the powers of evil which he subsequently invokes:

> Furiaeque veteres, noctis antiquae genus,
> Et quas perempta coniuge addidimus novas,
> Natisque caesis; vos, Deae, testes voco
> Sceleris futuri. uenta consilia execro
> Abominorque. Quidquid immane, efferum,
> Inusitatum, mens adhuc intus parit,
> Fugio proboque: sponte, et invitus, sequor. (p. 36)

(Ancient Furies, offspring of the age-old night, and the new ones added by my wife's death and the murder of my children, you goddesses I call to witness my future crime. I abhor slow decisions and fear. Whatever fierce, savage, unusual thing my mind is brooding upon, I flee and I accept it; willingly, and yet against my will, I follow.)

His intention to kill the one "with a thousand deaths" (p. 36) is sealed. Although Marianne's appearance frightens him, he is intent on destruction:

> Dum vita superest, pateat ad crimen data:
> Nedum ociosa lubeat ad mortem rapi.
> Nec dum inferos subimus. Hanc posco moram:
> Immane liceat agmen animarum prius
> Praemittere umbris. (p. 41)

(While life still lasts, it may be given to crime: and not idly do I want to meet my death. We do not descend to the underworld. I demand this delay: may I be permitted first to send a huge band of souls ahead of me to the world of shadows.)

Even the hellish horrors of the underworld cannot move him to accept the Child. Since he is rejecting Jesus, the Savior, the moment of appeal to his wife (he gets down on his knees and begs for forgiveness) cannot save him, for he has rejected God. Herod then is not only the tyrannical ruler who with hubris elevates himself above fate as did the defiant hero of the ancients, but he is also the doomed sinner who refuses to accept the coming of Christ by intending to destroy the Child. The Old Man vainly attempts to counsel moderation; again Herod rejects God by putting his power and throne above the Child and God: "Regnum regenti numen, ac sceptrum reor./ Quod restat, umbra somnii, ac sermo merus" (p. 52). (A ruler's god is his empire and his scepter, I say. What is left, is the shadow of dream and empty words). Herod, the tyrant, has become the prototype of a man without belief who rejects the advent of Christ. Such a figure, usually a king, is the opponent of the martyr in the martyr tragedies that were popular in the seventeenth century.

XI *Neoclassicism and Baroque*

Especially in the choral songs Heinsius shows his mastery of classical form. He introduces three different choruses: Prophets and Pious Men appear at the end of acts 1 and 3, the Old Jews and the Roman Soldiers conclude acts 2 and 4 respectively. A group of mothers of Jersalem appears near the end of act 5 with a comforting reply to the mothers of Bethlehem. Here the same Horatian meter is used as in the other choral passages, but this part is not designated as a choral song. As a retarding and contrastive element the chorus describes idyllic scenes, such as the Nile and Egypt, the Savior's birthplace Bethlehem, the innocent life in the country as opposed to the court, and peaceful Italy. These passages are more independent of the play's action than were the chorus parts in *Auriacus*. They enhance the descriptive qualities of the drama; and by showing the peaceful earth and the wonders of the creation, whether in Egypt, Italy, or Palestine, they underscore the religious message of the play, the innocent beauties of God's earth as opposed to Herod's man-made massacre and the horrors of hell. In style and literary technique they follow different models. The choral passages written in Horatian and Greek meters use a simple poetic language expressing a serene state:

> Felix, quisquis tacitum vitae
> Securus iter tenet, ignotus
> Rerum dominis, nec sublimi
> Cognitus aulae, qui sepositus
> Rure paterno, non turbatae
> Populi strepitu fremitque tubae
> Pacis alumnus, messibus hornis
> Vacuos curae supputat annos. (p. 36–7)

(Happy is he, who safely holds the silent course of his life, unknown to wordly lords, not knowing the high court; who on his paternal land far away from the throngs of people and the sound of the trumpets follows peace and with annual harvests counts his years free from care.)

A model for the entire choral passage in act 3 is Horace's famous epode II, "Beatus ille, qui procul negotiis/ Ut prisca gens mortalium/ Paterna rura bobus exercet suis . . ." (Happy is he, who far away from cares, like earlier generations ploughs his paternal fields with his oxen) which had become the *topos* for a happy country life as opposed to the life at court. Heinsius' choral passage is a paraphrase of the main ideas and images of Horace's epode, adding only the rejection of courtly life. The idyllic, lyrical character is also present in the other choral passages which echo the bucolic tones of Vergil. The Roman soldiers conclude their praises of Italy with a restrained enjoyment and satisfaction:

> Cras serum est. Hodie datur,
> Quod totum annumeres tibi.
> Vita, aut carpitur, aut perit.
> Victarum Dea gentium,
> Quam pulcher Tiberis lavit,
> Quis me restituat mihi?
> Quis me restituat tibi (p. 58)

(Tomorrow is too late. Today is given; that only is allotted to you. Life is either enjoyed or it is lost. Goddess of the vanquished, whom the beautiful Tiber bathes, who will restore me to myself? Who will restore me to you?)

Heinsius not only expresses the soldiers' longing for their homeland but also a quest for spiritual renewal which the Savior will fulfill.

In utmost contrast to such lines are two scenes that employ all the characteristics of the elaborate style and visual detail of the Baroque. When Marianne's ghost appears, Herod is in utmost fear and agitation (4.1). His frenzy is similar to the exaggerated state of mind of the murderer in *Auriacus*. But now a vision of the underworld, the hell Herod is doomed for, is evoked. It is a favorite topic of the Baroque to describe the sufferings of damnation. Herod sees his own fate:

> Viscera intueor mea,
> Immanis atrox tortor, atque idem parens.
> Hinc longus ordo, teter, atratus, sedet;
> Damnatque, iam damnatus, autorum necis.
> Quid ille, vultu immitis, ac virga gradum
> Firmans labantem? Fallor! an tremulum caput
> Fessumque senio veteris Hyrcani procul,
> Adhuc cruentum, video? Iam satis est, Deae,
> Poenarum, et ultra. (p. 45)

(I see my flesh fierce, hideous, I am tortured, and obey. Here a long line, black, clothed in mourning is sitting. He condemns and is already condemned, the author of the bloodbath. Who is that with a fierce face, supporting his failing steps with a cane? Am I mistaken? Or do I see the trembling hand tired from feebleness of the old Hyrcanian nearby, still bloody? Goddesses, it is enough punishment and more than enough.)

To show Herod's fear when confronted with his crimes and future punishment is the goal of this scene. The psychological portrayal of the character, a sinner faced by his deeds and called to justice, serves a didactic purpose. This is more important than the description of the underworld which is merely hinted at. Heinsius uses the underworld of antiquity as equivalent to a Christian concept of hell, which he did not describe in the realistic terms often found in Baroque literature.

It was the appearance of Tisiphone and the Furies in a biblical drama, the mixture of Christian elements and pagan mythology, that became the source for a dispute over *Herodes infanticida* with Jean Louis Guez de Balzac, former student of law and history at Leiden and a well-known literary figure since the appearance of his letters in 1624.[24] Constantijn Huygens, to whom the drama was dedicated and who had maintained a correspondence with De Balzac since 1632, had sent him a copy in 1633. After some exchange of comments through Huygens, De Balzac's Paris publication of his *Discours sur une tragédie de Monsieur Heinsius intitulée Herodes infanticida* (Discourse on a Tragedy by Mr. Heinsius Entitled Herod, Child Murderer) in 1636 brought the dispute into the open. He objected to the mixture of Christian and pagan elements as a travesty and accused Heinsius of violating the religion of his ancestors and corrupting discipline in his country. He refused to view the Furies symbolically but did praise the drama's moral thesis, the angel's discourse, and the nativity scene. De Balzac's is a moral-religious point of view demanding coherence in plot and message and historical verisimilitude in the presentation of a drama.

But his haughtily polite and servile tone, intended as a challenge to Heinsius' authority in Aristotelian criticism, angered the Dutch professor, who was also displeased because the *Discours* had been addressed and sent to Huygens and not to him. Later in that same year Heinsius published his response in Leiden, *Epistola, qua dissertationi D. Balsaci ad Heroden infanticidam respondetur* (Epistle in Answer to De Balzac's Dissertation on Herod, Child Murderer, dated June 1635, publ. 1636), in which he poured fourth a series of arguments and quotations from religious poetry, the Church fathers, and the Bible, to prove the tradition of the symbolic use of classical mythology in Christian writings. He further explained the role of the Furies in his play as representing Herod's vices personified on stage, just as the Furies in Euripides must be seen as prefigurations of what the Christians later called conscience (pp. 144–45). The dramatist used the Furies to arouse the passions of the audience, especially fear, which Aristotle considered the essential goal of tragedy. For the ancients the Furies were the same as devils for the Christians and in such a spirit they were referred to by the Church fathers and other Christian poets. As to the mixture of angels and Furies in the same drama, Heinsius points out that it does not happen in the same scene. Herod is a representative of the Roman, that is, pagan, world (pp. 173–74). He has fallen into idolatry and thus, though actually king of the Jews, could be treated like a Roman, while Marianne certainly was not a saintly woman and could have returned with the Furies from the Lower World, albeit from its upper level where those souls to be redeemed by Christ were waiting.

It is clear that Heinsius meant to show two worlds in his play: Bethlehem, the redeemed world, and the pagan world of Herod the sinner. The actual historical appearance of religions was for him immaterial: They all embody the divine world order since God and His adversary are ever present regardless of their different manifestations in heathen religions. Irenic and ecumenical sentiments were strong among the humanists of the Dutch Republic who were fighting the parochialism of the renewed religious fervor of denominations in the seventeenth century.

This dispute also signaled an attack on the humanists and philologists who were accused of living in the past and upholding pagan values. In the long-standing quarrel of "the ancients and the moderns,"[25] De Balzac represented the emancipation of vernacular, religious, and national literature versus Heinsius as the supporter of the humanist supranational "ancients." Even though the dispute helped to undermine Heinsius' hitherto unquestioned authority in Neo-Latin poetics, his play was subsequently widely read and his revised edition of *De tragoediae constitutione* of 1643 was studied intensely. The French poets adhered to a strict separation of classical mythology and religious subjects; De Balzac's view, which reflected already existing literary tastes in the 1630s, prevailed. The Counter-Reformation's renewed emphasis on Christian dogma gradually eliminated antiquity's pagan gods from the language and imagery of vernacular writings.

No objections were made to the crass and grossly realistic scenes such as the messenger's report about the massacre of the children. In 108 lines minute details of the slayings are given:

> Hic cerebri jacet
> Putamen. illic vulnere afflictum caput.

> Hic pes cruentus; sanguine hic foedae manus:
> Hic membra lacera; truncus hic impos sui. (p. 62)

(Here lies the skull, there a wounded head, here a bloody foot, here hands
spattered with blood, here limbs chopped off, here a lifeless trunk.)

Bloody descriptions of the devastations of war only reflected the
reality of the religious wars in France, the Low Countries, and
Germany's Thirty Years' War. Besides the mark of savage times
literary models affected the crass realism of Heinsius' scene.
Marino's epic *La straghe degl' innocenti* (The Murder of the Innocent, Paris, 1620) contained a vivid description of the massacre with
details which appear in Heinsius' drama as well as in other contemporary versions of the theme, such as the Jesuit Bidermann's epic
Herodiados sive innocentes Christo martyres (The Herodiad, or The
Innocent Christ Martyrs, published 1622). The unusual realism and
individual details, though belonging in the literary tradition as well
as to contemporary painting, stand out in Heinsius' play as features
of the Baroque. They are quite distinct from the other scenes and
localities of the religious events, which show an eternal serenity
based on classical models.

XII *Senecan Mannerisms*

Stylistic features of the dialogue are indebted to Seneca even
more than in *Auriacus* where the use of long similes in the manner
of the Homeric epic has already been noted. Seneca's similes can
easily be grouped according to the area of comparison: The hero is
likened to other historical or mythological heroes; comparisons are
taken from *a*) the nautical realm, *b*) the plant and animal kingdoms,
c) the elements (fire, snow, wind, rain, clouds, etc.). Heinsius stays
within this range, often employing a novel point of comparison but
completely abandoning mythological comparisons, a favorite technique in his poetry.

Heinsius' calculated use of similes can be seen in the middle of act
3, the center and first climax of the play. When the legate attempts
to dissuade Herod from his rash decision to kill the children, he
cautions the ruler with a series of five similes: The lion who does not
attack the weak calves in the herd but rather challenges the bull; a
captain who steers his raft across the stormy sea not with force but
with skill; a fierce, impatient horse throwing off the intemperate
rider and perhaps even dragging him to death if the rider gets

caught in the stirrups; the huge elephant who can be guided by a little boy. With a fifth comparison he advises Herod:

> Ne sperne modica, quisquis imperii regis
> Momenta: Nec cum saeva tempestas ratem
> Fert, contumacem stringe luctando pedem,
> Ventisque et undae naufragum indulge latus.
> Quin potius animi vela turgentis lege.
> Consilia plus efficere, quam vires, solent. (p. 35–6)

(Whoever rules should not disregard even modest commotions: and when a vicious storm carries the raft, don't haul the wind with force, nor give the winds and waves the side for shipwreck, rather fold the sails swollen with wind. Skill achieves more than strength.)

The sententious last line sums up the legate's advice which had been exemplified by similes. In this extended sequence of two nautical and three animal similes Heinsius describes the ruler as he should be and characterizes Herod indirectly: He is the lion attacking the young (the Child) and then the rider dragged to death by the unbridled horse. The similes add to the static, descriptive nature of the play; the swelling up of a single idea into a series of comparisons is a feature common in Baroque drama.

Like Seneca, Heinsius favors nautical and animal comparisons. The people at court are likened to vultures (p. 23); Herod is a vulture (p. 52) and a hungry lion (p. 61); the mothers try to protect their young like hens (p. 63), they rage like tigresses deprived of their cubs (p. 62). Such similes had become standard points of comparison, just as the universally employed nautical metaphors were especially popular in the seafaring Netherlands and used by both Erasmus and Heinsius. Nautical metaphors compare the life at court to water of unknown depth (p. 23); Herod resembles a sailor close to Charybdis (p. 48); he is calm but uneasy after his dream as is the sea after a storm (p. 47). Heinsius has a tendency to elaborate such standard comparisons into little scenes; for example, when comparing the messengers looking for the Child to the hunter on a fresh track (p. 31), or the fall from God to a girl giving in to love without waiting for marriage (p. 12). The source and range of comparison are traditional and limited; comparisons are integrated into the drama and enhance its epic character in the Senecan manner.

In two scenes Heinsius' dialogue is closely patterned on Senecan

stychometry.[26] In the conversation between Anna and Joseph each
iambic line is begun with Anna's question and completed by
Joseph's response; usually the break lies with the caesura after the
second or third foot. Thus a laconic exchange of condensed phrases
ensues:

> An. Quo rapitur aetas prima? Ios. quo suadet salus.
> An. Vix natus, et nunc exul? Ios. ut fugiat necem.
> An. Quis innocenti vim parat? Ios. saevus, nocens.
> An. Quis machinator caedis? Ios. Herodae furor.
> An. Quid casta mater? Ios. comes abeuntem premit.
> An. Deserta cunctis. Ios. Regnat, ubicumque est pater.
> An. O spes suprema! O vota. Ios. spem firmet fides. (p. 46)

A. Where is this early age thrown? J. Where safety advises. A. Hardly born,
and already an exile? J. To escape death. A. Who intends violence for the
innocent? J. A savage, a wicked one. A. Who plots the murder? J. Herod in
his fury. A. Where is the chaste mother? J. She holds him on the flight. A.
Deserted by all. J. Wherever the Father is, he reigns. A. O highest hope! O
promise! J. May faith give us hope.)

In Herod's conversation with the Old Man, the epigrammatic
density is heightened by the antagonism of the two agents:

> Sen. Cur Res timetur? Her. Rex timet. Sen. Regno, an sibi.
> Her. Utrique. Sen. puer est. Her. et fuit, quisquis regit.
> Sen. Ignotus orbi. Her. nempe, quem natus movet.
> Sen. Parce immerenti. Her. nempe, quo fiat nocens.
> Sen. Plebs vana trepidat. Her. amplius sperat tamen.
> Sen. Regemque fingit. Her. Rege sublato, cadet.
> Sen. Ne crede famae. Her. saepe neglectam nocet.
> Sen. Et cede populo. Her. saepe permissus sibi
> Regum tiaras transtulit populi furor. (p. 51)

(Old Man: Why is the king feared? Herod: The king fears. Old Man: For his
empire, or for himself? Herod: For both. Old Man: A mere child. Herod:
Every ruler was once a child. Old Man: He is unknown to the world.
Herod: Did not his birth move someone? Old Man: Spare the innocent.
Herod: Then he will harm us. Old Man: The masses fear in vain. Herod:
They hope even more. Old Man: They invent a king. Herod: Without a king
they fall. Old Man: Don't believe the rumor. Herod: Always the disre-
garded hurts. Old Man: Give in to the people. Herod: The people's fury, if
unchecked, has transferred royal crowns.)

Reminiscent of the famous dialogue between Medea and her nurse (*Medea*, I. 166ff.), these lines operate similarly with the technique of condensation and epigrammatic brevity. A two-line sentence breaks the staccato at intervals and the scene then goes over into longer exchanges. Often a phrase carries a sententious meaning, a hidden reference to Jesus' life such as the people crowning a king and then deserting him. It is this intentional ambiguity, the inference of a second meaning behind the literal one, which is characteristic of Seneca's rhetorical style as emulated by Heinsius.

Some further rhetorical elements based directly on Senecan dramatic style should be pointed out. Characteristic of Seneca's prose was the dissolution of long sentences into short phrases (*minutissimae sententiae*) which created his aphoristic style and was also employed in his dramas. Heinsius' tendency toward a skeletal, condensed phrase can be observed throughout the play, especially in long declamatory passages:

> Tranquila pavidos sceptra, magnanimos decent
> Afflicta. vires mens ab adversis capit,
> Languet secundis. Saeva, praedura, aspera
> Armant feroces fata, cedentes premunt. (p. 30)

(Tranquil reigns are fitting for cowards, troubled ones for great men. The mind draws strength from misfortune, it languishes in happiness. Savage, harsh, rough calamities arm the strong, they oppress the weak.)

Herod is explaining his position and the benefits of a reign of terror. The thought is broken down into short cola, parallel sentences which vary the content by revealing other aspects without adding a significantly new statement but rather elaborating the basic idea and generalizing it. A sententious phrase, or series of phrases, results.

At moments of tension in the play short phrases interrupt the flow of the speech. The mothers of Bethlehem eject short cries:

> Quod fugio? Utroque fugio, nec fugio metum.
> Defecit animus. lux abit. corpus solo
> Exanime, lapsis viribus, fessum cadit. (p. 59)

(Shall I go here or there? What I am fleeing from threatens everywhere. I flee everywhere but don't flee fear. My mind leaves me. The light goes away. Lifeless and tired falls the body to the ground without strength.)

Such staccato passages in the dialogue contrast with the rhythmically flowing choral songs.

Heinsius thus re-created the pointed, argumentative, rhetorical style of Seneca. The language in its often cryptic phrasing compensates for the lack of action and the loose plot. The rhetorical style received the attention of dramatists to such an extent that the play has become a rhetorical exercise. Johann Klaj (1616–1656) used acts 3 through 5 for a German verse adaptation centered around the character of Herod: *Herodes der Kindermörder/ Nach Art eines Trauerspiels ausgebildet* (1645, Herod Child Murderer, conceived in the manner of a tragedy).[27] Omitting the scenes in which Herod does not participate as well as some of the dogmatic framework, the dramatic work becomes a still life of Herod, a picture. Here the development from a dramatic play to a "picture in words," from action to declamation, has been completed.

CHAPTER 8

De Tragoediae Constitutione:
Heinsius and the Seventeenth Century

I   De Tragoediae Constitutione: *Genesis and Content*

THE importance of Heinsius' Latin tragedies is paralleled by
his theoretical work, a coherent prose commentary on Aristotle's concept of tragedy, which grew out of his philological study of
the works of Horace and Aristotle in connection with classical poetics. In 1610 he had published the collected works of Horace, to
which he had attached Aristotle's *Poetics* in a new arrangement
which he himself proposed.[1] In the same year he issued his text of
Aristotle's *Poetics* again, together with a Latin translation of this
work and annotations.[2] Only a year later this edition was reprinted,
this time with the addition of his treatise on tragedy.[3] Then an
intensive stylistic revision and amplification, which however did not
affect the ideas of the original treatise, appeared in 1643 under the
now commonly used title *De tragoediae constitutione* (One Plot ⌊lit.
On arrangement] in Tragedy).[4] It preceded the Aristotle edition, a clear indication that it contained the author's theoretical
statement on tragedy. It was a reassertion of Heinsius' literary
achievements and a reply to his critics in the ongoing controversy
caused by his drama *Herodes infanticida*.

   De tragoediae constitutione established Heinsius' reputation as an
Aristotelian literary critic of renown. While classical philology has
not accepted his rearrangement of the Aristotelian text of the *Poetics*, Heinsius' treatise formulated clearly the basic tenets of Aristotle's views of tragedy. As an editor of the *Poetics*, he made sweeping
transpositions of major sections on the basis of a more logical and
coherent argumentation, which he missed in the Italian editions of

the sixteenth century.[5] For instance, Heinsius thought that chapter 6 containing the definition and parts of tragedy should be followed by the discussion of the quantitative parts of tragedy (isolated in chapter 12 in the received text) as chapter 7. The next four chapters, 8–11 (i.e., 7–10 in the received text) then deal logically with the construction of the plot. Chapter 12 (11 in the received text) treats parts of the complex plot, peripety and recognition, but Heinsius left off its final section to be placed after chapter 13 (chapter 16 of the received text) where the topic of recognition is properly concluded. These and other far-reaching transpositions were made by Heinsius on the basis of a thorough study of the content and logical structure of Aristotle's presentation. Heinsius had progressed from the philological method of textual criticism, emendation, and stylistic observation, in which only individual words or lines were considered, to a comprehensive consideration of the text. In his notes to Horace's *Ars poetica* in 1610, in which he had also advocated the transposition of passages on the basis of a more coherent argument, he had answered those philologists who were clinging to the letter: "It is not the task of the true critic to throw out a letter in one place, or strike an insignificant syllable in another, nor to eliminate a word or emend it, but rather: to arrive at sound judgment about the author and his work. This is the sign of solid and strict erudition."[6] Heinsius had left the restrictive confines of classical philology and turned to literary criticism in the modern sense: the comprehensive analysis of the text.

The treatise on tragedy was conceived as an epistle upon the request of Rochus Honerdus (1572–1632), the Dutch statesman and author of the Neo-Latin tragedy *Thamara* (1611), as Heinsius stated in his preface addressed to Honerdus.[7] The work intentionally lacks a scholarly apparatus, rather it is an "epistle," a prose treatise, though a lengthy one, in which extensive examples and references have been eliminated in favor of a more concise treatment of the nature of tragedy and its parts. Written from a practical point of view, it comes close to being a handbook for an author aspiring to write a Latin tragedy. Heinsius puts down what he has noted about tragedy "according to the intention and ideas of Aristotle" *(ex mente atque opinione Aristotelis)*.[8] In his concern to attain clarity, brevity, and order he divides the work into seventeen chapters (a misnumbering in 1643 skips 15 and thus arrives at 18 chapters), each one preceded by a short outline and a reference to the prior and following argument.

The introductory chapter, "The Utility of this Doctrine," stresses that writing a tragedy requires, besides talent and rhetorical training, civil wisdom. Chapter 2 contains a definition of poetry according to Plato as imitation and a definition of tragedy according to Aristotle as a purgation of emotions: "Since this Muse [tragedy] is primarily engaged in arousing passions, Aristotle therefore thinks its end is to temper these very passions, and to put them back into order. The passions proper to it are two: pity and horror. As it arouses these in the soul, so, as they gradually rise, it reduces them to the right measure and forces them into order. Accordingly, Aristotle called this the 'expiation' of the passions, or emotions, unless one prefers 'purgation' " (11). A definition of tragedy follows: "Tragedy is an imitation of a serious and complete action, which is of just magnitude, pleasantly ornamented with speech, harmony, and rhythm; in such a way that each of them functions in its particular part; and which, not by narrating, but through pity and horror induces the expiation of the very same passions" (14). The various aspects of this definition are then fully discussed in chapters 3 and 4. The principal part of tragedy is its plot; action *(fabula)* is its soul. It has to be whole and complete; it must have unity: "An action becomes one only from actions so interrelated that if one of them is posited, another follows out of either necessity or verisimilitude" (26), as for instance in Sophocles' *Ajax* where all events truly belong together.

The tragic poet uses material which differs from the historian's, for he is more philosophical and exacting; he can employ real or invented subject matter as plot, as long as it is verisimilar (chapter 5). Then the complex action is further explained with its essential parts, peripety ("a change of fortune," 36) and recognition as exemplified in both Sophocles' and Seneca's *Oedipus* (chapter 6). Various modes of recognition are discussed, of which the principal one "gradually arises from the very subject matter and the argument itself without any sign" (42, chapter 7). The third part of the complex fable, emotions, has to arise from the plot itself, not from the actors (chapter 8–10). These emotions, namely, terror and fear, are aroused by the man "who errs unawares . . . in such a fashion as to comprehend what he did either afterwards or beforehand" (50, 53). A discussion of the turn of fortune in an action, usually from prosperity to calamity, concludes the principal part of the treatise, the nature of the plot. With chapter 11 Heinsius proceeds to the more technical discussions of how such a plot is to be constructed.

Characters and episodes are to be added; then complication and denouement are to be construed. Other important aspects are the exposition (chapter 13), characterization (chapter 14), the ideas (*sententiae;* chapter 15). Remarks on style, music, stage props and apparatus, and some related matters conclude the treatise.

De tragoediae constitutione serves as a handbook explaining what a tragedy in the tradition of antiquity is; numerous examples from primarily classical authors illustrate the major points. Heinsius aimed at an explication of matters basic to tragedy in a straightforward manner, as he explained to Honerdus: "We, however, have acted just as people, who, in entertaining a close friend (especially if they receive an unexpected visit in the country), immediately set before him home-grown dishes: a few eggs from the nest and with them the hen herself, then greens, turnips, sprouts, and other common things of that kind, and last—the main course—gay looks that bear witness to an honest and liberal heart" (153). Together with his own plays the treatise served as a guide for the basic concept of tragedy. That the treatise was far more lucid than his own dramatic attempts were successful is another matter. Heinsius saw clearly the difficulties for a biblical drama: "Especially if the argument is taken from truth or from Scripture . . . changing nearly everything is a violation of conscience. Obviously, there is more liberty in the fables: and hence, everything here is said with this in view" (54). It is curious that the weakest part in his tragedies, the construction of the plot, takes the largest part in his theoretical discussion.

II *Aristotelian Concepts*

Foremost for Heinsius, however, was an adequate interpretation of the Aristotelian doctrines. Consequently, his treatise has been considered mainly for its role in Aristotelian interpretation and scholarship. Heinsius interprets Aristotle's concept of catharsis in relating it to the two tragic emotions, pity and fear. Here catharsis is not considered an aesthetic but a moral aim of tragedy. The emotions, pity and fear, are reduced to an adequate middle plain (*mediocritas*). Heinsius states that they are not expurgated in order to prepare for a contemplative life, as the Pythagoreans and Platonists had advocated, in a sort of medical process. Rather, the expiation through tragedy leads to a middle plain of life in which reason controls the emotions: "In order to begin that life which most closely approximates immortal God (this consists in contemplation alone, because it is the work of the mind), Pythagoras used to induce beforehand a kind of purgation like physicians employed. By this, the passions (which are emotions and stirrings of the soul) would be gradually alleviated" (11). For Aristotle the passions were neither virtues nor vices. Just as the physician on the battlefield because of long practice is no more upset than necessary and has learned to apply treatment, or as a veteran soldier has learned to face the enemy calmly, the theater is "a kind of training hall for our passions which (since they are not only useful in life but even necessary) must there be readied and perfected" (12). It is the repeated experience of catharsis through viewing a dramatic performance that makes the spectator feel less horror. This is the dominating emotion, rather than empathy or pity; and Heinsius' own tragedies with the murder on the stage in *Auriacus* and the realistic description of the murder of the children in *Herodes* give vivid examples for the evocation of horror in the audience. Tragedy does not induce apathy,[9] but rather "it allays terror and pity in the mind, and teaches these two passions to obey reason as is necessary" (15).[10]

The didactic-moralistic nature in Heinsius' view of catharsis has overwhelmingly been accepted.[11] Heinsius' notion of catharsis rests on the principle of like purging like: Tragedy must first arouse pity and fear in the mind of the spectator and then through continued experience purge these emotions. Catharsis has become the final end of tragedy. Heinsius has dropped the Horatian duality of *docere* and *delectare;*[12] teaching is no longer an end of tragedy and nowhere does he discuss or imply the possibility of the transmission of a doctrine in a play, a practice which was important in the Latin school drama of the Jesuits.

In his approach to tragedy with catharsis as its focal point, Heinsius had freed himself from most of the technical and rhetorical discussion of the Italian commentators of the sixteenth century which dominated Aristotelian exegesis and poetological discussions. Besides codifying the rules of unity, of time, place, and action, they had interpreted Aristotelian catharsis to mean that either all harmful emotions were to be cleansed from the spectator's soul or that these were to be considerably modified. A third reading, proposed by Francesco Robortello,[13] defined catharsis as referring to the emotions of pity and fear characteristic of tragedy, which are not cleansed but moderated and brought into proportion. Heinsius followed this interpretation of the crucial passage in Aristotle's *Poetics:* "Tragedy not by narrating but through pity and horror induces the expiation of these very passions" (17).[14] This rendering has been incorporated almost verbatim into his definition in *De tragoediae constitutione*.

Neither the originality nor the correctness—or lack thereof—in Heinsius' reading of Aristotelian catharsis should be used to judge his *De tragoediae constitutione*. Interesting as these questions may be for the history of literary criticism and classical scholarship, it suffices to point to Heinsius' comprehensive grasp of Aristotle and poignant rendition for the dramatic poet and reader of his day. The treatise mirrors his wide reading and solid training in ancient and Renaissance literature and philosophy, as well as his practical experience with writing drama. It contains his fine critical observations concerning certain metaphors and the mixture of comic and serious language in Buchanan's *Jephthes* (chapter 17): It describes the rhetorical qualities of Euripides (pp. 195–96) and compares him with Sophocles, and it discusses his favorite drama, Sophocles' *Electra*. But more important, the treatise leaves behind a rhetorical interpretation of Aristotle's *Poetics* and of drama as a whole and turns to a comprehensive view of the poetic argument making *pathos*—clearly conceived of as "emotions"—the focal point of the Aristotelian treatment of tragedy. *Pathos* becomes the organizing principle on which the unity of tragedy is based. It was precisely this view which became dominant in the seventeenth century. It was absorbed in England by Milton, helped to shape neoclassical theory in France where Heinsius' work was of great influence after 1630,[15] adopted in his native country by Vondel, and also advanced in Germany. Martin Opitz in his *Buch von der deutschen Poetery* (1624) based his cursory remarks on tragedy on Julius C. Scaliger's *Poetics*, yet referred the reader to Heinsius' work. The great German dramatist of the seventeenth century, Andreas Gryphius, who attended some of Heinsius' lectures at Leiden some time after 1638, was influenced by *De tragoediae constitutione* and Heinsius' dramas.[16] Lessing's agreement with Heinsius on the definition of tragedy in its essence and goal in key passages in the *Hamburgische Dramaturgie* underscores the continued relevance, if not influence, of Heinsius' critical approach into the eighteenth century.[17]

III   *The World Is a Stage*

In the time immediately following Scaliger's death Heinsius once more laid down his thoughts on tragedy in the oration *De utilitate quae e lectione tragoediarum percipitur* (On the usefulness derived from the reading of tragedy) given as an introduction to his lectures on Sophocles' *Electra*.[18] It was in a way a defense of the theater in the young Calvinist state in whose orthodox circles there was much opposition to performances. At the same time Heinsius surveyed the essence of tragedy, comparing it to the phases of human life: The prologue corresponds to man's birth which is already painful and accompanied with cries; the protasis, or beginning of the plot, resembles early youth; the epitasis, in which the crucial confusion is born, represents adulthood; and the catastrophe is old age. For Heinsius life is "a full tragedy in all its parts, of which God is the director, the plot is grief and calamity, the actors are miserable mortals. Men and women are the chorus; the props are gold and silver, the costumes varied and assembled for a high price; everything belongs to someone else and is borrowed, often to be returned all of a sudden. This earth is a theater in which nature has placed men."[19] This tragic view of life finds a fitting expression in the "world is a stage" metaphor omnipresent in the sixteenth century and even more persuasively illustrated in the age of Baroque, extending from Shakespeare to Calderón.[20] Vondel phrased it succinctly in the epigram that was placed above the main entry of the first national theater in the Netherlands, the Schouwburg of 1638: De weereld is en speeltooneel, / Elck speelt zijn rool en krijght zijn deel. (The world is a stage, everyone plays his role and gets his part.)

For Heinsius the recognition of the vanity of this world in which only God is eternal, is expressed in this metaphor; it is not pessimism in the modern sense. He opens his oration with the paradoxical definition of tragedy attributed to Georgias of Leontium by Plutarch: "Tragedy is a deception in which he who deceives is more honest than he who does not deceive; and he who is deceived is wiser than he who is not deceived." Illusion *(fallacia)* then becomes for Heinsius the essence of this life as expressed in the metaphor of the tragedy on a stage. For the age of Baroque he could not have described human vanity more aptly than he did in his oration in 1610: "What is man? If you ask that, Pindar will answer: the sleep of a shadow. What is man? Socrates will say, this or that image. What is man? Calamity itself, Herodotus remarks. What is man? The occasion for misery, as Philemon says. What is man? A falling leaf, as Homer says. What is man: the paradigm of feebleness, a prey of time, a pawn of fortune, the image of change, a balance of envy and calamity; and beyond that nothing, except some slime and gall, as will be said and has already once been said by Aristotle."[21]

IV *Heinsius the Man*

"Quantum est quod nescimus" (How little we know) was Heinsius' lifelong motto in the tradition of the Greek sceptics. His last years were shadowed by declining fame and the gradual waning of his creativity and health, so that his student and friend Constantijn Huygens could write an epigram using this motto, with the lines: "Ultima lento subreprens inscitia morbo/ reddidit infantem, nec sine laude senem"[22] (His ignorance of late creeping up in a slow illness has again rendered him a child, an old man not unpraiseworthy). This cruelly reveals what his contemporaries witnessed, the progressing senility of his last decade, a slow death. At a time when any form of mental illness, and often physical shortcomings as well, were still greeted with derision or worse, Heinsius' sharp physical and mental decline from about 1640 influenced much later judgment.

When he sided with the Counter-Remonstrants, when he married Ermgard Rutgers from a powerful Orangist family, and when he served as secretary to the Lay Commissioners at the Synod of Dort, from then on Heinsius had been the object of personal attacks on his character, his manners, and his work. In a satirical work which he wrote in 1621 in the manner of Varro's Menippean satires, Heinsius imagines himself in a dream transposed to the moon and from there surveying the earth and answering his critics.[23] But the negative view has persisted. Heinsius has been accused of preventing the eminent scholar Casaubon from being offered Scaliger's chair after his death in 1609,[24] of opposing Salmasius' appointment in 1631 and intriguing against him,[25] of exhibiting an "egotistical penchant for compromising his ideals" in his friendship with Hugo Grotius,[26] all because of his exaggerated pride and insatiable greed for money.[27] This image of Heinsius the man is being carefully revised in recent research. Envy of his early success and widespread fame seems to have been the reason behind some of the criticism. "Livor abi" (Envy be gone) is the traditional theme in his first elegy (in 1603, I,1). Envy and detraction by one's critics is a major topic in Renaissance writings which reflect the direct opposite of the friendship cult: the development of bitter animosities.

What emerges from Heinsius' writings is that he was from the beginning an extremely gifted student of languages and of classical literature and an equally hard worker who had to make his way for himself, first against his father's wish that he study law rather than classics, but also as a Flemish refugee from a somewhat politically disgraced family.[28] Heinsius had to prove himself in order to enter Dousa's circle and to gain the total admiration and patronage of Scaliger which he achieved because of his extraordinary talents as a scholar and writer. Climbing the academic ladder in Leiden University was made possible only through his continuous scholarly activity and productivity as well as his reputation as an inspiring teacher and orator. Scaliger's patronage helped, but without Heinsius' own outstanding talents his success would not have been possible. He never seemed much interested in contemporary political issues; at the center of his attention were his writings, reading, and research. His publications and letters give evidence of high self-esteem, much of it professed in standard phrases of the age, but not of haughtiness, aggression, or maliciousness toward others. He never traveled abroad (except for a visit to his hometown of Ghent and to Brussels during the Truce), though he had invitations to France, to England from Casaubon, to Sweden, and was courted by Venice. The security of the Dutch Republic, its prosperity and freedom, by far outweighed the uncertainty of new countries, friends, and surroundings for Heinsius. And since he never left Leiden, his productivity and excellence were expected and taken for granted, while he faced an ever-increasing work load.

His religious convictions, though never involving him in a militant advocacy of a specific dogmatic point of view, were conservative, as was true of the great majority of the Flemish Calvinists who had fled to the North. His turn to religious matters around 1617 was a major change in his development but not as abrupt as it may appear. The increasing religiosity of the age, for which the Synod of Dort was merely a visible sign rather than a point of origin, the rigors and honors of the prestigious Leiden chair, and marriage into a powerful Orangist family at the age of thirty-seven must bee seen as factors contributing to Heinsius' almost exclusive occupation with scholarship, especially biblical scholarship. As a truly devout Calvinist and as an eminent scholar, his concept of service to mankind was to achieve the best understanding possible of the biblical text rather than to serve a particular dogmatic faction. Reflective, reli-

gious, and philosophical leanings are apparent in his Dutch and
Latin writings from the very beginning. The tradition of Renaissance love poetry and games—Heinsius never acknowledged his
authorship of the love emblems—went out of fashion after Dousa's
death, when the aristocratic gallantry of the sixteenth century came
to an end and was replaced by the strict religious and bourgeois life
style of the seventeenth century. Heinsius' later years are not a
reversal, an abrupt change from an earlier life of passion and feeling
to one of intellect and discipline, but the gradual maturing of a
gifted and industrious man, influenced by his social status and his
era, long before his physical and mental decline began.[29]

V *The Scholar-Poet and the Seventeenth Century*

Evaluations of character and personality are largely subjective, as
Heinsius' reputation illustrates. It is above all the literary work of
the author that made an impact on his age and that still speaks to us
today. Heinsius' fame during the seventeenth century rested especially on his superb knowledge of classical texts, his command of
Latin and Greek, and his scholarly works. As the spiritual heir to
Scaliger and to some extent to Lipsius, he helped establish Leiden's
fame in classical philology, continued by such eminent scholars as
G. Vossius, Gronovius, Burman, Hemsterhuis, and Runkehn.
Heinsius' philological work is considered "uneven."[30] His Greek
editions (Hesiod, Theocritus, Maximus Tyrius, Aristotle, Nonnus)
were valued during their day because they made unknown manuscripts of little-known works available, often with Latin translations
and annotations which greatly aided the understanding of the text,
because Heinsius had an intuitive gift for language and for literary
and poetic values. He had learned from Scaliger and further developed the treatment of classical texts as literary works, not merely
editing them in antiquarian fashion with grammatical or lexical observations.

While the far-reaching transpositions of passages in his editions of
Horace's *Ars poetica* have since been rejected, his essay *De satyra
Horatiana* succinctly defined the nature of satire as distinct from
comedy, on the model of Horace whom he preferred to Juvenal.
Satire is a kind of poetry in which, according to Dryden's translation
of Heinsius, "human vices, ignorance and errors, and all the things
besides, which are produced from them in every man, are severely
reprehended; partly dramatically, partly simply, and sometimes in

both kinds of speaking; but, for the most part, figuratively, and occultly; consisting in a low familiar way, chiefly in a sharp and pungent manner of speech; but partly, also, in a facetious and civil way of jesting."[31] Heinsius had proposed a model definition which was generally accepted and repeated until the end of the eighteenth century. Thus his Horace and Aristotle scholarship, along with *De tragoediae constitutione*, had left their marks on literary criticism of his and the subsequent century. The recent English translation of the last-mentioned work and the thorough studies by Sellin and Meter attest to its importance for the understanding and development of seventeenth century drama, especially in France, England, Germany, and the Netherlands.[32]

Though his poetic achievements are best judged by the criteria of his own age, a nineteenth century observer—in the age most critical of Neo-Latin poetry—had to admit: "His excellence consists of a small, but visible portion of talent, which pervades his verses and gives to their best parts a pleasing and equable . . . beauty."[33] Largely through Martin Opitz, Heinsius' Dutch *and* Latin poetry exerted a far-reaching influence on the early German Baroque. Although Heinsius is clearly indebted to humanism and the Renaissance, to Dousa, Janus Secundus and the Neo-Latin poets, to Scaliger, Lipsius, and the classical scholars of the sixteenth century, to Ronsard and the *Pléiade,* and above all to classical literature itself, his own works began to show Baroque features almost from the beginning.[34] The often swollen style, lengthy descriptive episodes, tendency toward exaggeration, the lament over the vanity of this world coupled with an exhortation to enjoyment, all these features are prominent in the writings of the seventeenth century. As one of the great scholars embracing philosophy, literature, and religion— but not the sciences—Heinsius continued in many respects the work of Erasmus, representing the ideal of an international union of humanist scholarship and learning while the age itself was proceeding toward religious and national consolidation and fervor.

Notes and References

Short titles are used for Heinsius' works; fuller titles can be found in the Selected Bibliography under Primary Sources. A reference to the "Short-title Checklist of the Works of Daniel Heinsius" in Paul R. Sellin, *Daniel Heinsius and Stuart England* (Leiden, 1968), pp. 203–252, has been added if necessary for identification, the number referring to the number in the checklist. All other books and articles listed in our Selected Bibliography are cited in the Notes by the author's name only, or—if necessary to avoid ambiguity—by the author's name and a short title. Only the works specifically referred to are listed due to the exigencies of space. The spelling of Latin u/v and i/y and other peculiarities have been standardized in accordance with modern practice; the seventeenth century Dutch spellings have been preserved. Abbreviations have been eliminated; obvious misprints and wrong pagination have silently been corrected. All translations, unless otherwise noted, are mine.

Chapter One

1. Autobiographical vita in Meursius, pp. 200–8; best biographical account by Sellin, *Heinsius*, pp. 3–68; Ter Horst's dissertation is biased against Heinsius the man and his work; J. H. Meter adds new insight into Heinsius' personality and early intellectual development, pp. 9–76; still informative is L. Roersch, "Heins (Daniel)," *Biographie Nationale . . . de Belgique* (Brussels, 1880–83), vol. 7–8, col. 854–74. The unpublished thesis by Frans Steyaert, "Daniel Heinsius. Polyhistor, Dichter en Poeta uit de eerste helft der zeventiende eeuw" (Leuven, 1970) contains familiar biographical material with, at times, questionable interpretation (pp. 1–192).

2. On the Dutch exiled communities in England 1567–1603, see L. Forster, *Janus Gruter's English Years* (Leiden, 1967), esp. pp. 25–68.

3. The chorus in his drama *Auriacus* (1602) mourns his fate and lost native land, then returns to praise the new home in Holland. See chapter 7, below.

4. Letters from Scaliger to Daniel Heinsius of August 1599 and May 1600 seek to animate an apparently ill young Heinsius by stimulating his

brilliant mind with philological questions; the letters are testimony to Scaliger's immediate recognition of Heinsius' talents. Meter, pp. 30–31.

5. See now J. J. Woltjer's Introduction to *Leiden University*, pp. 1–19, for a comprehensive survey of the early years.

6. Only after the Synod of Dort did orthodox Calvinism gain the upper hand; the board of curators was changed and liberal professors of divinity and philosophy were replaced.

7. *Leiden University*, p. 18.

8. For an impressive account of his untiring scholarly activity see Sellin's Checklist which records about 160 editions and reprints of 26 classical and patristic authors and over 40 works or editions in the areas of modern philology, theology, history, and other writings.

9. Lecturing in Leiden since 1581 until his death in 1614, Vulcanius was active in preparing readable texts without many emendations and Latin translations of Greek authors—for a wider humanistic reading public. His interest in Callimachus and bucolic poetry was continued by Heinsius, who enjoyed a good working relationship with Vulcanius, in his edition of Theocritus' *Idyllia* and *Epigrammata* in 1603.

10. Meursius, p. 206.

11. The son-in-law of the famous Antwerp printer Plantin had purchased the Leiden shop in 1585 after the fall of Antwerp. The relationship between the Leiden Plantins and the university is traced by E. van Gulik, "Drukkers en Geleerden.—De Leidse Officina Plantiniana (1583–1619)," in *Leiden University*, pp. 367–93. On Heinsius' places of residence see H. J. de Jonge, "Peregrinatio Heinsiana . . . ," *Jaarboekje voor de geschiedenis . . . Leiden*, 65 (1973), 51–67 and 68 (1976), 47–52.

12. See S. Hartz, *The Elseviers and Their Contemporaries* (Amsterdam, 1955).

13. See E. Hulshoff Pol, "The Library," in *Leiden University*, esp. pp. 423–32, on Heinsius' librarianship; being able to draw only on his three printed catalogues and the accounts of the treasurer to the university, the author concludes "his term as Librarian was not a very fortunate one and he fell short on many points. It should also be remembered that it was only a part-time occupation for a man who was deeply involved in many other fields" (p. 432).

14. In a letter to Casaubon of March 28, 1609, Heinsius described Scaliger's last days *(Is. Casauboni Epistolae*, Rotterdam, 1607, no. 454). An edition such as Aristotle's *De historia animalium*, presented a difficult task, since only scattered notes existed and Heinsius had no interest in physiology; the work finally appeared in 1619 with another editor. Meter, pp. 203–5, evaluates Heinsius' editorial commitments: Heinsius did acknowledge in his subsequent editions when notes or texts were based on Scaliger; he edited Scaliger's letters, "all that could be found," in 1627.

15. Sellin, pp. 21–32, correctly pictures him as "a cultured and en-

lightened but consistently orthodox member of the Reformed Church"
(p. 21) against the prevailing view that he was a turncoat.

16. Heinsius wished to refrain from all the recent theological disputes;
he did not consider himself a theologian. On the value of his commentary
and the attacks on it as plagiarism of Scaliger's unpublished notes and other
works, see H. J. de Jonge, "The Study of the New Testament," in *Leiden
University*, esp. pp. 93–100. However, Heinsius was not the editor of the
famous Elzevier New Testament, as H. J. de Jonge had assumed in *Daniel
Heinsius and the Textus Receptus of the New Testament* (Leiden, 1971); see
his correction of this thesis in "Jeremias Hoelzlin: Editor of the 'Textus
receptus' printed by the Elzeviers Leiden 1633," in: *Miscellanea Neotes-
tamentica*, ed. T. Baarda et al. (Leiden, 1977).

17. F. F. Blok, *Nicolaas Heinsius in Dienst van Christina van Zweden*
(Delft, 1949).

18. The presentation of the polemics by Sellin, pp. 39–51, is now supported by Salmasius' biased letters about Heinsius' work on the New Testament, and Salmasius' relationship with I. Vossius *(Leiden University*,
pp. 96–97, and pp. 356–59).

19. Sellin, p. 68. For Heinsius' portraits see R. E. O. Ekkart, "Icongrafie
van Daniel Heinsius," *Faarboek Centraal Bureau voor genealogie* (1974),
46–62.

Chapter Two

1. "Vber des Hochgelehrten vnd weitberümbten Danielis Heinsij
Niderländische Poemata," *Teutsche Poemata*, p. 25.

2. L. Forster, "Iets over Nederlandse Renaissancelyriek vóór Heinsius
en Hooft," *Tijdschrift voor Nederlandse taal- en letterkunde*, 83 (1967),
274–302.

3. J. A. van Dorsten, *Poets, Patrons, and Professors* (Leiden, 1962),
esp. pp. 1–18, 77–130; Chris L. Heesakkers, *Praecidanea Dousana. Mate-
rials for a Biography of Janus Dousa Pater (1545–1604). His Youth* (Amsterdam, 1976).

4. *Nederduytsche Poemata*, 1st ed. (Amsterdam, 1616), p. 62; all future
quotes are from this edition and will be cited in the text by page. This
edition is reprinted in my *Daniel Heinsius. Nederduytsche Poemata*,
Nachdrucke Deutscher Literatur des 17. Jahrhunderts, 32 (Berne, 1978);
see the Introduction for further bibliographical and philological detail.

5. See Chapter 3 below.

6. Sellin, "Daniel Heinsius' *Nederduytsche Poëmata* . . . ," in pointing
to the date of the printing privilege (28 Oct. 1615) and of the dedication (29
November 1615), concludes that the book already appeared in late 1615.
However, the 1616 imprint on the title page may also suggest that, although
the printing was concluded by late 1615, the production of the title page
and the binding of the volume had delayed the actual publication to early
1616. Bibliographical description of the first and second edition in this

article can be found on pp. 243 and 245; for a listing of all editions see Sellin's Checklist 40–45, 55, 58. In the 1622 and 1650 editions the *Lof-sanck van Iesus Christus* precedes the poems. As Scriverius explains to the reader (only in the 1st ed., p. 23), haste and misunderstanding (the volume was printed in Amsterdam) let some errors creep in which were then corrected in the 2nd ed. of 1616. On Scriverius see now P. Tuynman, "Petrus Scriverius. 12 January, 1576 — 30 April, 1660," *Quaerendo*, 7 (1977), 5–45.

7. D. Hoek, *Haags leven bij de inzet van de Gouden eeuw. Rondom Mr. Jacob van Dijck 1564–1631* (Assen, 1966), pp. 111–267.

8. Referring to Horace' *Sat.*, I, 10. On the structure of this preface and its influence on the early German Baroque preface, see Bornemann, pp. 210–21.

9. Rank et al., *Bacchus en Christus*, p. 14.

10. Anna Roemer Visscher (1584–1651), daughter of the Amsterdam burgher and poet Roemer Visscher, was praised as the Dutch Sappho for her poetry (mostly sonnets and songs). Cats, Vondel, Hooft, and Huygens also addressed poems to her.

10a. Though the importance of the collection has commonly been recognized, no adequate discussion of the poems exists. G. A. van Es evaluated their contents for the poet's character, *Barokke Lyriek van protestantsche dichters in de zeventiende eeuw* (Groningen, 1946), pp. 6–13, incorporated in his *Letterkunde*, I, pp. 19–32. Ter Horst, p. 43, considered the poems shallow and superficial; Smit, p. 78, preferred by far the religious hymn. Weevers, pp. 78–88, discusses certain stylistic features and their influence on Martin Opitz; Bornemann, pp. 59–93, 156–81, and 202–21, presents German renditions of several poems. Steyaert (see Chapter 1, note 1, above) explains the content of five poems in detail (pp. 272–358).

11. For the meaning of the term "elegy," here derived from Neo-Latin poetry, see Chapter 4, note 10.

12. The "Elegie, ofte Nacht-clachte" (published 1607) is a partial reworking of his own Latin poem, "Monobiblos" 2, *Elegiarum libri III* (1603); more in my edition of the *Ned. Poem.*

13. C. Ypes, *Petrarca in de Nederlandse letterkunde* (Amsterdam, 1934), p. 157, traces several mottoes of the emblem series to Petrarch, but does not mention these poems. Heinsius freely uses metaphors employed in Renaissance love poetry since Petrarch, drawing on Italian, French, and Neo-Latin as well as Anacreontic and Ovidian images and phrases; however, a *single* model or source need not be present. The research on Petrarchism has been summed up by G. Hoffmeister, *Petrarkistische Lyrik* (Stuttgart, 1973).

14. Sellin, Checklist 344. This 1603 Heidelberg Theocritus edition is a reissue of the text and notes by Scaliger and Casaubon published in 1596 to which the separately paginated and signed notes by Heinsius had been appended; in 1604 a new edition in quarto (Sellin, Checklist 344) also contained a text revised by Heinsius.

15. *Poematum nova editio*, 1606, p. 114 i.e. [214].

16. *Theocritus*, ed. A. S. F. Gow (Cambridge, England, 1952), II, 221.

17. E.g., "plum" for "sloe," 38, 1. 6 (my numbering); "goldsmith" for "money-lender," 40, 1. 45.

18. A Latin elegy, "To the Girl who Married the False Rival" (*Poemata* 1610; V, 7, see Chapter 4, p. 71), addressed to the same girl must also have been written in 1609 or early 1610. Grotius repeatedly urged Heinsius to write Dutch verses to the girl (*Briefwisseling*, I, nos. 140 and 142).

19. *Den Bloemhof* (1608), no. 2, is a "Bruyloft-Liedt" signed D[aniel] H[einsius]; the poem for his own wedding in 1617 appeared first in the appendix to *Afbeelding van Minne . . .* (Leiden: H. van Westerhuysen, 1619), then was included in the 1622 and 1650 editions of the *Neder-duytsche Poemata*. On the epithalamium see L. Forster, *The Icy Fire* (Cambridge, England, 1969), pp. 94–115.

20. The names are omitted in *Den Bloemhof*. Burchgrave was Heinsius' maternal cousin who studied at Leiden from 1601 to 1603 and married there on February 18, 1603.

21. Bornemann, pp. 169–70.

22. At the end of the prefatory letter to his brother, who edited the poems, Grotius states: "You know about my little poem on Ostend which changeable fortune had ascribed to many a great author" (*Poemata collecta*, Leiden, 1617). Scaliger, when questioned about the poem, had pointed to Grotius; E. H. Bodkin, "The Minor Poetry of Hugo Grotius," *Transactions of the Grotius Society*, 13 (1928), p. 111.

23. O. Kluge, *Die Dichtung des Hugo Grotius* (Leiden, 1940), p. 36.

24. As early as 1604 Grotius wrote, but did not publish, *De iure praedae* (The Law of Booty), discovered and printed in 1868. This treatise contains *in nuce* the principles of his famous *De iure belli ac pacis*, a first codification of the laws governing war and peace which he wrote in 1625.

25. The Beggars' Songbook. *Geuzen*, from French *geux* (beggars), was first used derisively for the Protestants, then adopted by the leaders of the revolt against the Spanish.

26. See the detailed study by the editors of Heinsius' Bacchus and Christ hymns, J. D. P. Warners and L. Ph. Rank, *Bacchus. Lyrisch leesboek over de god Bacchus, met aantekeningen en vertalingen, tevens een illustratie van het translatio-imitatio-aemulatio-principe*. 2 vols. (Amsterdam 1968 and 1971); vol. 1 surveys the mythographers and scholars on Bacchus from the Middle Ages to the Renaissance; vol. 2 provides a chronological survey with selections from poetic writings on Bacchus from the Homeric Hymns to Nicolaas Heinsius' Bacchus poem.

27. Rank et al., *Bacchus en Christus*, pp. 99–104. All quotes of the Bacchus and Christ hymns are taken from this edition; page numbers will be used for prose, verse numbers for the poems. See also F. D. P. Warners, "Daniel Heinsius en Bacchus," *Hermeneus*, 25 (1953–54), pp. 9–17, 25–32, and 42–49.

28. The 1605 edition with a Latin translation contained a commentary by Heinsius; Sellin, Checklist 274.

29. Between 1548 and 1553 Ronsard wrote four poems to Bacchus. It is the learned "Hinne de Baccus" (publ. 1554) consisting of 286 alexandrine lines that served as a model for Heinsius. Ronsard's hymn was inspired above all by Marullus' hymns (publ. 1497). Heinsius, well acquainted with the Neo-Latin poetry, thus had before him not only this tradition, but also Ronsard's French hymn.

30. P. Albouy, *Mythes et mythologies dans la littérature française* (Paris, 1969), pp. 29–30.

31. L. 169; *Les Oeuvres de Pierre de Ronsard. Texte de 1587*, ed. I. Silver (Chicago, 1968), p. 219.

32. Texts and details about the tradition in Warners-Rank, *Bacchus. Lyrisch leesboek* (see n. 26), II, 13–70.

33. E.g., Van Es, *Letterkunde*, p. 21: "more and more enslaved to drinking." For a possible source, see Remonstrant attacks upon Heinsius after the Synod of Dort, Sellin, "The First Collection of Dutch Love Emblems," p. 339, n. 1.

34. G. A. Van Es. *Barokke Lyriek* (see n. 10) pp. 7–8; similar in *Letterkunde*, pp. 27–29.

35. Grotius rendered it into Latin verses 1625–27, *De veritate religionis christianae;* the influential work was translated into 12 languages.

36. P. Böckmann, "Der Lobgesang auf die Geburt Jesu Christi von Martin Opitz . . . ," *Archiv für Reformationsgeschichte*, 57 (1966), pp. 184–85. Opitz translated the Christ hymn (publ. 1621) and the Bacchus hymn (publ. 1622).

37. See Chapter 7, p. 136.

38. *De Dichter Revius* (Amsterdam, 1928), p. 78; see also *Protestantse Poëzie der 16de en 17de Eeuw*, ed. K. Heeroma (Amsterdam, 1940), I, xxii–xxiii. Van Es, *Letterkunde*, p. 31, sees it as an isolated work, not the beginning of Calvinist poetry.

39. Weevers, p. 84. Heinsius wrote a Dutch prefatory poem to Heyns' translation and to Wessel van den Boetseler's of 1622.

Chapter Three

1. On the nature of emblematic works, see P. M. Daly, "Trends and Problems in the Study of Emblematic Literature," *Mosaic*, 5 (1972), 53–68.

2. See my "Selected Bibliography" for descriptions of Heinsius' emblem books by R. Breugelmans, H. de la Fontaine Verwey, and M. Praz.

3. Reprinted with introductory note by C. N. Smith; the introduction needs revision after Breugelmans' research.

4. There is a splendid facsimile in *Pieter Corneliszoon Hooft. Alle de gedrukte werken 1611–1738. Deel 1: Emblemata amatoria 1611. Verspreide gedichten* (Amsterdam, 1972), pp. 1–144.

5. Facsimile reprint of the third edition of 1620, with an introduction by

H. de La Fontaine Verwey, see also Verwey's article on this collection in
Quaerendo, 8 (1978).

6. The poems by the Amsterdam burgher and poet Roemer Visscher
(1547–1620) had previously appeared in his *Brabbeling* (Chatter, 1614).
Roemer Visscher was also the author of the popular emblem book *Sinnepoppen* (Allegorical Pictures, 1614).

7. J. Landwehr's attempt to ascribe the work to Jacob de Vivere has
been refuted by Sellin, "The First Collection . . .," pp. 332–42; A. K. H.
Moerman, "Jacob de Vivere en Theocritus à Ganda," *Open*, 4 (1972), 623;
and by Breugelmans, p. 282.

8. R. Breugelmans, p. 283, convincingly interprets and dates a letter in
which Heinsius mentions the printing of the emblem book as having been
written in 1601. L. Forster corroborates this with a dated entry (Feb. 1602)
in a copy of *Quaeris quid sit amor* used as an *album amicorum* by a Swiss
student in Leiden, *Quaerendo*, 4 (1974), 335–36.

9. In the second edition of 1616, p. 82.

10. I. Q. van Regteren Altena, *Jacques de Gheyn. An Introduction to the
Study of His Drawings* (Amsterdam, 1935); disputed by Landwehr, *Emblem
Books*, p. xii.

11. "Quaeris quid sit Amor, quid amare, Cupidinis et quid Castra sequi?
chartam hanc inspice, doctus eris. Haec tibi delicias hortumque ostendit
Amorum:—Inspice; sculptori est ingeniosa manus."

12. The same artist also engraved a new set of plates for the original
emblem series; they are close copies of de Gheyn's, often reversed. In 1613
the two emblem series were also published with Latin texts only as
Emblemata amatoria nova . . . Auctore Theocrito à Ganda.

13. A popular children's game, the spinning top became a frequently
used symbol for life, as in Roemer Visscher's *Sinnepoppen* (1614), emblem
20, where the turning top designates the restlessness of life, a second idle
one shows rest symbolizing death.

14. See W. Stechow, "Homo bulla," *The Art Bulletin*, 20 (1938), 227.

15. In the *Nederduytsche Poemata* Cupid is stringing hearts for a
necklace; in the 1613 edition he is sewing hearts onto a garment.

16. See Sellin, "The First Collection . . .," p. 332.

17. See the edition by A. K. H. Moerman.

18. See E. de Jongh, *Zinne- en minnebeelden in de schilderkunst van de
zeventiende eeuw* (n.p. [1967]).

Chapter Four

1. Most representative collection of Neo-Latin poetry: *Delitiae* (The
Delights) by the Heidelberg philologist and librarian Janus Gruterus from
Antwerp (3 volumes for Italy, 1608; 2 volumes for France, 1609; 6 volumes
for Germany, 1612; 4 volumes for the Netherlands, 1614). The standard
history for Neo-Latin poetry of the Netherlands and Germany is still

G. Ellinger's. Though thorough and comprehensive, Ellinger evaluates the poetry according to individual expression and experience of the poet in question and disregards the specific qualities and aesthetic principles of this poetry. A revival of Neo-Latin studies is centered around the Louvain journal *Humanistica Lovaniensia*. See now also J. IJsewijn, *Introduction to Neo-Latin Studies*, Amsterdam, 1977.

2. See J. IJsewijn, "Diffusion et importance historique de la littérature néo-latine," *Arcadia*, 4 (1969), 179–98.

3. Grotius in a letter to Heinsius of May 13, 1608 (*Briefwisseling*, I, no. 132).

4. Meursius, p. 204.

5. "Iambi, partim morales, partim ad amicos, partim amicorum causa scripti," pp. 89–143.

6. "Amico Lectori," *Poemata*, 1613; p. [iy]. All quotes and references identify the edition with the year of publication; see the bibliography for a full citation of the poetry editions.

7. Though called 6th edition on the title page, it is only the 5th revised edition, possibly Gruter's sizable selection in his *Delitiae poetarum Belgicorum*, 1614, II, 895–1131, counted as 5th edition.

8. Ellinger, III, pp. 195ff, wants to see a development from the youthful lover to the sedate scholar interested in pomp and social prestige.

9. *Amores*, I, 1, 27–28. See G. Luck, *The Latin Love Elegy* (London, 1959), p. 11.

10. Eleg., III, 7. *Jean Second*, p. 174. The "uneven rhythm" refers to the elegiac couplet with its hexameter and pentameter:

Most dactyls (long-short-short) can be replaced by spondees (long-long). The hexameter can be completely dactylic with the last foot always a spondee, or a complete sequence of spondees, though these extremes are rare. The pentameter had always a strong dactylic element, and a middle caesura (pause). Schiller's famous distich—"In the hexameter rises the fountain's silvery column,/ In the pentameter aye falling in melody back" (Tennyson's translation)—visually captured the tripartite division of rise, retardation, and fall inherent in the elegiac couplet, the most melodious and versatile meter of antiquity. The scansion was, of course, quantitative, that is to say, determined by the length of the syllable, not by stress. But already for Greek and classical Latin both pitch and stress played a part in the metric. The stress dominant vernacular must have influenced the reading of Neo-Latin verses many of which were still written with an audience in mind.

11. *Joanni Secundi . . . Itineraria tria* (Leiden, 1618).

12. Except for some minor stylistic changes this programmatic poem remains in the same place throughout all editions, an indication of its fundamental importance for Heinsius.

13. "Rossa" may have been derived from Dutch "rossig" (ruddish,

sandy-colored), rather than from Latin "rosa," referring perhaps to the girl's reddish-blond hair.

14. Greek for "single book." Janus Secundus used the heading "Julia, monobiblos" for the first book of his elegies after the example of Propertius.

15. In 1602–03 Heinsius had toyed with the idea of going to France. He was to accompany Paul Choartus Buzanvallus, the French ambassador, who had presented him with a portrait of the French king; but Heinsius decided to stay in Leiden when he was awarded a professorship. In 1603 elegy I, 2, is addressed to Choartus, deploring his departure.

16. See Meertens, p. 70.

17. In 1613, p. 98, the line reads: "lex haec certaminis una est" (this is the only law of the struggle); the idea of the struggle (certamen) is more pointedly phrased.

18. Canzoniere, 134. See L. Keller, Übersetzung und Nachahmung im europäischen Petrarkismus (Stuttgart, 1974), pp. 348–72, for translations.

19. Jerôme Du Quesnoy the Elder (b. before 1570–1641) sculptured pieces for the palace (destroyed by fire in 1731) of the Duke of Brabant (Albert of Austria, 1559–1621 prince-sovereign of the Catholic Nether- lands). In 1605 he was paid by the ducal exchequer for four garden statues for the so-called labyrinth and in 1612 for statuary for the grotto. In 1619 the magistrate of Brussels commissioned the famous Manneken-Pis which probably was based on an earlier statue of the very motif that Heinsius describes in the poem (Allgemeines Lexikon d. bildenden Künstler, ed. U. Thieme, Leipzig, 1914, vol. 10, p. 191–94).

20. Only lines 45–50 have undergone revision: In 1610 love and friend- ship are praised, in 1613 (p. 84) a girl Hyella (Greek for "crystal clear") is mentioned.

21. St. Commager, The Odes of Horace. A Critical Study (Bloomington, Ind., 1967), p. 323.

22. See K. Garber, Der locus amoenus und der locus terribilis in der deutschen Schäfer- und Landlebendichtung des 17. Jahrhunderts (Köln, 1974), esp. pp. 85–111.

23. God in a Biblical metaphor is "fons vitae" (Ps. 36: 10); Ronsard's ode "A la Fontaine Bellerie" uses the hymnic address to the fountain. An epi- gram from the version of the Greek Anthology discovered ca. 1605 by Salmasius in Heidelberg (IX, 326) is the earliest classical model for the theme of the wanderer refreshing himself at the clear spring.

24. Several new recipients appear, e.g., Janus Rutgers (his later brother-in-law) or Johan Reigersberg (Grotius' brother-in-law). Except for I, 1, all poems to Scaliger have been incorporated into the separate cycle "Manes Scaligeri," pp. 129–32.

Chapter Five

1. The edition of 1621 contains: Three books of Silvae, Hipponax (reflective and invective poems in choliambic meter), three books of

elegies, Monobiblos, miscellaneous poetry, Greek poems, translations from the Greek, elegies of his youth, poetry addressed to Heinsius. See Chapter 4 for editions.

2. *Poemata*, 1621, p. 20; from the dedication to Dominicus Baudius of "Silvae II."

3. K. O. Conrady, "Die Erforschung der neulateinischen Literatur," *Euphorion*, 49 (1955), 437.

4. Meursius, p. 216. Published separately in 1602 (Sellin, Checklist 68), the poem appeared in *Poemata*, 1603, pp. 199–205. Dousa was born in Noordwijk (1545) where the family estate was.

5. "Iambs Written by Hugo Grotius into the Album of Heinsius," 1603, p. 228.

6. Heinsius' Latin poetry throughout this chapter is cited by year of edition and page number.

7. Published separately in 1617; Sellin, Checklist 79. Jacques Auguste de Thou (1553–1617), a friend of Scaliger's, served Henry III and Henry IV and worked as State Councillor for religious peace. From a rich library and notes begun by his father, he wrote the classic history of France of the sixteenth century, *Historia sui temporis* (1604–1608). In spite of his attempts to remain impartial the presentation of the religious wars caused an outcry among Catholics.

8. These "Manes" (lit.: souls of the deceased) were written in 1609 (for Scaliger), in 1606 (for Lipsius) and in 1604 (for Dousa) and included in the *Poemata* of 1610, pp. 271–81. A separate section in 1613 and 1617, the three cycles comprise Book III of the "Silvae" in 1621. There are many stylistic and thematic references to classical (esp. Statius, Ovid, Propertius) and Neo-Latin (esp. the Scaligers, Eobanus Hesse) commemorative poetry.

9. See S. F. Witstein, *Funeraire poëzie in de nederlandse renaissance* (Assen, 1969), pp. 98–131; and H. H. Krummacher, "Das barocke Epicedium," *Jahrbuch der deutschen Schillergesellschaft*, 18 (1974), esp. pp. 97–98.

10. Among other Renaissance poetics the various types of funeral poems are described in Julius C. Scaliger's *Poetices*, Book III, chap. 122, pp. 167ff. An "epitaph" can: a) be held, like a funeral oration, at a graveside and contains praise of extraordinary merits; b) be held at the anniversary of a death when there should no longer be manifestations of grief; or c) be the inscription for the tombstone, the meaning prevailing in English.

11. John Rooke, *Select Translations from the Works of Sannazarius, H. Grotius, Bapt. Amaltheus, D. Heinsius . . .* (London, 1725), p. 36.

12. J. v. Stackelberg, "Das Beinengleichnis," *Romanische Forschungen*, 68 (1956), esp. pp. 273–74; F. M. Rener, "Opitz' Sonett an die Bienen," *Europäische Tradition und deutscher Literaturbarock*, ed. G. Hoffmeister (Berne, 1973), pp. 67–84 (comparison with Secundus' "Basium XIX," Ronsard's "Aux mouches a miel," and Opitz).

13. *Poetices*, pp. 108–13; Book III, chap. 24. Recent research has ex-

plored rhetoric and the German Baroque; among numerous specialized studies W. Barner, *Barockrhetorik* (Tübingen, 1970) and K. O. Conrady, *Lateinische Dichtungstradition* (Bonn, 1962) are especially pertinent for Neo-Latin literature.

14. Heinsius had mentioned the *Greek Anthology* in his 1603 Theocritus edition; on his scholarly use of the *Greek Anthology*, see J. Hutton, *The Greek Anthology in France* (Ithaca, N.Y., 1946), pp. 255–59. The epigram may well be a reversal of Theocritus' epigram VII, an epitaph in which the dead father is said to live on through the son.

15. "Monobiblos" 5, since 1606. Reprinted with a translation, *Lateinische Gedichte deutscher Humanisten*, ed. H. C. Schnur (Stuttgart, 1967), pp. 188–97.

16. Still basic for the discussion of *imitatio* is H. Gmelin, "Das Prinzip der Imitatio in den romanischen Literaturen der Renaissance," *Romanische Forschungen*, 46 (1932), 83–359; Meter, pp. 77–182, traces Heinsius' development from a poet relying on his inspiration to a classical philologist and literary critic.

17. Bornemann, p. 198, rightly points to the role of classical philology as the mediator between the classical past and contemporary poetic and intellectual achievements.

Chapter Six

1. Unpaginated introduction to *De contemptu mortis lib. IV* (Leiden: Elzevier, 1621). Bound separately at first, the poem was appended to Heinsius' revised edition of his Latin poetry in the same year of 1621, issued again in 1622, and reprinted together with his poetry in 1666 by his son Nicolaas. A Dutch translation by Heinsius' cousin Jacobus Zevecotius appeared in Leiden in 1627. All quotes are from the 1621 edition, and page numbers are given in the text.

2. Pp. 155–67.

3. F. Van Ingen, *Vanitas und Memento Mori in der deutschen Barocklyrik* (Groningen, 1966), esp. pp. 301–46.

4. The English translation by Sir John Stradling, *Two bookes of constancie* (1594) was reedited by R. Kirk and C. M. Hall (New Brunswick, 1939); see also M. van de Bilt, *Lipsius' De constantia en Seneca* (Nijmegen, 1946), esp. pp. 23–47; J. L. Saunders, *Justus Lipsius. The Philosophy of Renaissance Stoicism*, (New York, 1955); and esp. G. Oestreich, "Justus Lipsius als Universalgelehrter zwischen Renaissance und Barock," in *Leiden University in the Seventeenth Century*, pp. 177–202.

5. See Chapter 5 above.

6. C. Bangs, *Arminius. A Study in the Dutch Reformation* (Nashville-New York, 1971), pp. 332–55.

7. A. Wang, *Der "miles christianus" im 16. und 17. Jahrhundert und seine mittelalterliche Tradition* (Berne, 1975).

8. Meursius, p. 202.

9. Tyrtaios. Passages of Book III follow in detail arguments from the Flemish humanist Thomas Vlas' *Oratio in Laudem belli* (1531), which had just been reprinted under the title "Belli encomium" in Caspar Dornau's *Amphitheatrum sapientiae* (Hanau, 1619). This volume also contained the first publication of Heinsius' popular encomium "Laus pediculi" and other poems; thus it is very likely that Heinsius had a copy.

10. W. C. Cunningham, *Martin Opitz. Poems of Consolation in Adversities of War* (Bonn, 1974). Another influence was Lipsius' *De constantia*.

11. See above Chapter 2, p. 54.

12. See Chapter 2, p. 51 and n. 34.

Chapter Seven

1. "Dedication to the Estates of Holland and West-Friesland," *Auriacus* (Leiden, 1602), p. [1]. All subsequent references to *Auriacus* are from this edition and given parenthetically in the text.

2. See J. Wille, "De Gereformeerden en het toneel tot ongeveer 1620," *Literairhistorische Opstellen* (Zwolle, 1962), pp. 59–142.

3. "Amico lectori." No details are known about the performance which took place in the city hall; Molhuysen, *Bronnen*, I, 407. D. J. H. ter Horst, "De 'Auriacus' van Daniel Heinsius," *De Gids*, 97 (1933), 205, assumes there were two performances.

4. Text and English translation in W. Kirkconnel, *The Celestial Cycle. The Theme of "Paradise Lost" in World Literature with Translations and Major Analogues* (Toronto, 1952), pp. 96–219; edition with Dutch translation: *Sacra in quibus Adamus exul*, vol. I. A. of *De Dichtwerken van Hugo Grotius*, ed. G. Kniper, L. Ph. Rank, and B. L. Meulenbroek (Assen, 1970).

5. The importance of the Latin school drama for the development of Dutch Golden Age drama was pointed out by J. A. Worp, *Geschiedenis van het drama en van het tooneel in Nederland* (Groningen, 1904), I, 239; presented again for consideration by W. A. P. Smit, "The Dutch Theatre in the Renaissance—A Problem and a Task for the Literary Historian," *Dutch Studies*, 1 (1974), esp. 45–48 (English adaptation of Smit's 1964 Dutch essay).

6. See Vermaseren, esp. pp. 31–41. A drama from the Catholic point of view entitled *Nassovius* (Paris, 1590) by an otherwise undistinguished French author remained unknown in the Netherlands. On social actuality, see N. C. H. Wijngaards, "De zgn. Orangestukken en hun publiek," *Handelingen van het Nederlands Filologencongres. Groningen*, 32 (1972 [1974]), 117–31.

7. In the printed text the epilogue (pp. 85–86) is set in a different type as is also an addition to Louise's speech in act 4, scene 2 (p. 65); subsequent

pagination has not been adjusted, another indication that the epilogue and addition were inserted later.

8. A comparative analysis of the plays by Van Duym and Heinsius can be found in *Het moordadich Stvck van Balthasar Gerards, begaen aen den Doorluchtighen Prince van Oraignen. 1584*, ed. L. F. A. Serrarens and N. C. H. Wijngaards (Zuthpen, 1976), pp. 19–50.

9. Vermaseren, p. 43, and Ter Horst, p. 200, by regarding the account merely as a ruse, overlook the dramatic impact of the description of the bloodbath, a familiar contemporary occurrence on both sides. Heinsius omits references to the Spanish, thus describing the horror of war regardless of the party.

10. These were probably neither sung nor accompanied by instruments, as was the case in some sixteenth century school dramas (e.g., Gnapheus' collected edition of 1552 contained notation for several plays). Heinsius' choral passages were rhythmical declamations, probably set apart from the dialogue by pitch and rhythm. See R. v. Liliencron, "Die Chorgesänge des lateinisch–deutschen Schuldramas," *Vierteljahrsschrift für Musikwissenschaf*, 6 (1890), 309–87.

11. See Vermaseren, p. 48.

12. See P. Stachel, *Seneca und das deutsche Renaissancedrama. Studien zur Literatur- und Stilgeschichte des 16. und 17. Jahrhunderts* (Berlin, 1907), pp. 142–50; J. A. Worp, *De invloed van Seneca's treurspelen op ons toneel* (Amsterdam, 1892), pp. 58–90, 291–93; and W. A. P. Smit, "État des recherches sur Sénèque et les dramaturges hollandais," *Les Tragédies de Sénèque*, ed. J. Jacquot (Paris, 1964), pp. 221–30.

13. These are the very features of French classical drama; Ch. Wanke, *Seneca, Lucan, Corneille. Studien zum Manierismus der römischen Kaiserzeit und der französischen Klassik*, Studia Romanica 6 (Heidelberg, 1964), p. 186.

14. Heinsius made numerous corrections and annotations in his copy (Leiden University Library, sig. 754. B.34). In a letter of April 19, 1610, Hooft asked Heinsius if he could write a dedicatory poem for the revised edition (see Ter Horst, "Auriacus . . . ," p. 207).

15. Stachel, *Seneca . . .* , p. 23, counts 66 such elaborate Homeric similes in Seneca, while the Greek tragedians usually use metaphors or short comparisons.

16. In a letter of March 3, 1608, Grotius mentions that he has seen a part of the Herod drama (Molhuysen, *Briefwisseling*, I, p. 98). In his preface to *Thamara* (1611) Honerdus remarked "What the critics are going to say about his [Heinsius'] Herod tragedy when it appears, I can presage from the fame of his *Auriacus*." Even if the work was mostly completed in 1611, for which there is no evidence, Heinsius did not publish it until 1632. Extensive revisions and additions may well have been made in the time prior to

1632. Meter, p. 400, assumes completion for 1608–1611 without giving a source.

17. Stachel (above note 12), p. 147–49.

18. Scaliger, *Poetices*, p. 323 A.

19. This defense of Euripides was in part directed against Heinsius' criticism of rhetorical excesses in Euripides in *De tragoediae constitutione* (chapter 17). Artistic collaboration, later competition, and rivalry seem to have spurred the dramatic production of Grotius and Heinsius: Grotius' *Adamus exul* (1601) was followed by Heinsius' *Auriacus* (1602). After *Christus patiens* (1608) appeared, Heinsius was busy with revising the *Auriacus*, writing parts of *Herodes*, editing Seneca's plays, and writing *De tragoediae constitutione* in 1611. The appearance of *Herodes* (1632) was followed by Grotius' *Sophompaneas* in 1634.

20. *Herodes infanticida. Tragoedia* (Leiden, 1632); all quotes cited in the text are from this edition. It was reprinted together with Heinsius' Latin poetry edited by his son Nicolaas in 1666 (Sellin, Checklist 16). Dominicus vander Stichel's Dutch play *De Moord der Onnoozelen*, 1639 (Sellin, Checklist 90, 91), is not a translation but a selective, free reworking of parts of Heinsius' drama.

21. *On Plot in Tragedy*, p. 34. K. Loukovitch, *L'Évolution de la tragédie religieuse classique en France* (Paris, 1933), p. 108, points to Aeschylus as model for the simple action.

22. See M. Heren, "Der bethlehemitische Kindermord in der deutschen Literatur des 17. Jahrhunderts," Diss. Vienna, 1960.

23. Herod's derangement is modeled on Seneca's *Hercules furens* who sees two suns (vv. 939–53), since Hippocrates had considered the visual distortion of heavenly bodies a sign of insanity. Hercules is also pursued by the Furies who delude him into believing his own fantasies as does Herod in the dream scene (4, 1).

24. Chronology in R. Lebègue, "L'*Herodes infanticida* en France," *Neophilologus*, 23 (1938), 388–94; for De Balzac's role best account is Youssef, pp. 117–164.

25. H. Gillot, *La querelle des anciens et des modernes* (1914; rpt. Paris, 1968).

26. This is thoroughly studied in B. Seidensticker, *Die Gesprächsverdichtung in den Tragödien Senecas* (Heidelberg, 1969).

27. *Johann Klaj. Redeoratorien*, ed. C. Wiedemann (Tübingen, 1965), pp. [129–90].

Chapter Eight

1. *Q. Horatii Flacci opera omnia; cum notis Danielis Heinsii. Accedit Horatii ad Pisones epistula, Aristotelis de poetis libellus; ordini suo nunc demum ab eodem restituta* (Leiden, 1610); Sellin, Checklist 236.

2. *Aristotelis de poetica liber. Daniel Heinsius recensuit, ordini suo restituit, Latine vertit, notas addidit* (Leiden, 1610); Sellin, Checklist 194.

3. *Aristotelis de poetica liber. Daniel Heinsius recensuit . . . Accedit eiusdem de tragica constitutione liber* (Leiden, 1611); Sellin, Checklist 196. Reprint: Hildesheim, New York: Olms, 1976.

4. *Dan. Heinsii de tragoediae constitutione* (Leiden, 1643); Sellin, Checklist 198. The very useful and close English translation of this work by P. R. Sellin and J. J. McManmon is entitled *On Plot in Tragedy*. See the discussion of the title in my review of this book (*Daphnis*, 4 [1975], 110–13); *constitutio* means "arrangement" or "what constitutes tragedy." When used by Heinsius in the text *constitutio rerum* (also: *dispositio actionis*) means "plot." Similarly, Heinsius inscribed his bilingual selections from Aristotle's *Poetics* "Aristotelis de Poetica, in quo de Tragoediae imprimis Constitutione agitur . . ." (1643), since he left out passages dealing with poetic subjects other than those pertaining to tragedy; G. J. Vossius had entitled his Aristotelian handbook on rhetoric, which Heinsius studied thoroughly for his Aristotelian scholarship, *Oratoriae institutiones* (1606).

5. See P. R. Sellin, "From *res* to *pathos*. The Leiden 'Ordo Aristotelis' and the Origins of Seventeenth Century Recovery of the Pathetic in Interpreting Aristotle's Poetics," *Ten Studies in Anglo-Dutch Relations*, ed. J. van Dorsten (London, 1974), pp. 72–93; and Meter, esp. pp. 287–300.

6. Note 3 above, "Notas," p. 186 (separate pagination).

7. Honerdus was influential in the politics of the Dutch Republic. He was nominated by Prince Maurice to the High Court of Holland, Zeeland, and West Friesland; prominent in the cause of the Counter-Remonstrants, he was appointed curator of the University of Leiden after the Synod of Dort, replacing a Remonstrant official. With Heinsius he shared literary interests (Latin poetry and tragedy) as well as political bonds. His *Thamara* was dedicated to Heinsius.

8. 1643, p. 1. All translations are from *On Plot in Tragedy* (above, note 4) and are cited in the text by page number.

9. M. Kommerell, *Lessing und Aristoteles* (Frankfurt, 1960), pp. 272–74, relegates Heinsius' catharsis to an "Abstumpfungslehre" (insensitivity training).

10. The Latin reads: "Terrorem in animo ac misericordiam componat, et parere rationi, ut oportet, duos hos affectus doceat," 1643, pp. 19–20.

11. Notably by Kern, p. 61, and Sellin, *Heinsius*, p. 127; Meter, p. 351, proposes that "the treatment of catharsis in Heinsius grows into an exposition of the various effects of tragedy upon the audience. Here he distinguishes a) a therapeutical, b) an esthetic and c) an ethical aspect." There is a response to this thesis in my review of Meter, *Daphnis*, 7 (1978).

12. Sellin, *Heinsius*, pp. 129–33.

13. *In librum Aristotelis de arte poetica explicationes* (1548); see

B. Weinberg, *A History of Literary Criticism in the Italian Renaissance* (Chicago, 1961), pp. 396–98.

14. "Utque non enarrando, sed per misericordiam et metum, similium perturbationum expiationem inducat," Latin translation of Aristotle's definition of catharsis in *Poetics*, chapter 6. Substitutions of key words in Latin, such as *horror, metus,* or *terror* for the Greek *phobos* (fear); *misericordia, commiseratio,* or *miseratio* for *eleos* (pity), *perturbatio* or *affectus* for *pathemata* (emotions); and *purgatio* or *expiatio* for *katharsis* are constantly employed by Heinsius without differentiation in meaning, probably for stylistic reasons.

15. R. Bray, *La formation de la doctrine classique en France* (Paris, 1957), pp. 39–48; P. R. Sellin, "Milton and Heinsius: Theoretical Homogeneity," *Medieval Epic to the "Epic Theatre" of Brecht,* ed. R. P. Armato and J. Spalek, University of Southern California Studies in Comparative Literature I, 1968, 125–34; and P. R. Sellin, "Le pathétique retrouvé: Racine's Catharsis Reconsidered," *Modern Philology,* 70 (1973), 199–215.

16. H. J. Schings, "Consolatio Tragoediae. Zur Theorie des barocken Trauerspiels," *Deutsche Dramentheorien,* ed. R. Grimm, I (Frankfurt, 1971), p. 10.

17. M. Zerbst, *Ein Vorläufer Lessings in der Aristotelesinterpretation,* Diss. Jena, 1887, esp. pp. 19–31; modified by M. Kommerell (above, note 9), p. 274.

18. Appearing in the 1612 edition of orations for the first time and not yet in the 1609 edition, this oration must have been written between 1609 and 1612.

19. Quoted from the last collected edition of Heinsius' orations edited by his son Nicolaas, *Orationum editio nova* (Amsterdam, 1657), pp. 273–74.

20. See, for example, W. Barner, *Barockrhetorik* (Tübingen, 1970), pp. 86–134; and P. Rusterholz, *Theatrum Vitae Humanae* (Berlin, 1970).

21. See note 19, above, p. 270 and 271.

22. A. A. Angillis, "Daniel Heins, Hoogleeraar en Dichter," *De Dietsche warande,* 6, (1864), p. 41.

23. *Cras credo hodie nihil* (I'll Believe You Tomorrow not Today).

24. M. Pattison, *Isaac Casaubon 1559–1614* (Oxford, 1892), p. 256; now refuted by Sellin, *Heinsius,* p. 78.

25. There is an unbiased view in Sellin, pp. 43–51.

26. O. Kluge, *Die Dichtung des Hugo Grotius* (Leiden, 1940), p. 15. Confused with his son Nicolaas, Heinsius is made the father of an illegitimate son in the last year of his life by H. Schnur, *Lateinische Gedichte deutscher Humanisten* (Stuttgart, 1967), p. 442.

27. For another perspective on Heinsius' supposed preoccupation with money, see Sellin, esp. pp. 52–63.

28. Because of his uncle's (Daniel de Burchgrave) service to Leicester; Meter, p. 23.

29. Smit, p. 51, interprets the portrait of Heinsius as exhibiting the passionate traits of his "southern blood" in conflict with his intellect and discipline. On Van Es on Heinsius as an alcoholic, see above Chapter 3, note 33.

30. L. v Müller, *Geschichte der klassischen Philologie in den Niederlanden* (Leipzig, 1869), p. 38; Heinsius' contribution to classical scholarship has not been studied; Meter, pp. 203–86, gives some fine observations.

31. John Dryden, *A Discourse concerning the Original and Progress of Satire* (1693), quoted from J. Brummack, "Zu Begriff und Theorie der Satire," *Deutsche Vierteljahrsschrift*, 45 (1971), esp. pp. *304–*11. Dryden used the slightly enlarged definition from the 1629 edition.

32. Meter, p. 607, concludes "a concise study of Heinsius' influence on Dutch tragedy in the seventeenth century is much to be desired." For Germany, Schönle treats Gryphius and Lohenstein, pp. 59–120.

33. *The Retrospective Review*, I (1820), p. 50.

34. Usually referred to as Renaissance poetry, Heinsius' works introduce features of the Baroque, though this term is sparingly used in Dutch literature in contrast to the continuing discussion in Germany on the Baroque documented in *Der literarische Barockbegriff*, ed. W. Barner (Darmstadt, 1975).

Selected Bibliography

PRIMARY SOURCES

(For Heinsius editions and the most complete listing to date see the "Short-Title Checklist" in P. Sellin, *Daniel Heinsius*, pp. 203–52, which contains 437 entries).

1. Poetry

Quaeris quid sit amor, quid amare, Cupidinis et quid castra sequi? [Amsterdam: Hans Matthijsz., ca. 1601]. First emblem book, introductory poem signed Theocritus à Ganda, i.e., D. Heinsius.
Emblemata amatoria: iam demum emendata. [Amsterdam: Hans Mathijsz., ca. 1607]. The *Quaeris* collection enlarged by two Dutch poems. There is a reprint of the 1608 edition with introductory note by C. N. Smith, Continental Emblem Books, no. 10. N. p.
Afbeeldingen van minne. Emblemata amatoria. Emblemes d'amour. Op een nieu oversien ende verbetert door Theocritum a Ganda. Leiden: Jacob Marcusz., 1613. Contains besides *Emblemata amatoria* "Het ambacht van Cupido" and two more Dutch poems.
Spiegel vande doorluchtige vrouwen. Amsterdam, 1606. In A. K. H. Moerman, *Daniel Heinsius zijn "spiegel" en spiegeling in de literatuurgeschiedschrijving.* Leiden: New Rhine Publ., 1974, pp. 1–35. Eight poems describing scenes of 'Famous Women in History.'
Nederduytsche Poemata. By een vergadert en uytgegeven door P. [etrus] *S.* [criverius]. Amsterdam: W. Janssen, 1616. There are two editions in 1616 with identical title pages; *Lof-sanck van Bacchus* is appended with a separate title. There is a reprint of the first edition with an introduction by B. Becker-Cantarino in Nachdrucke Deutscher Literatur des 17. Jahrhunderts, no. 32, Berne/Frankfurt, 1978.
Nederduytsche Poemata. Amsterdam: W. Janssen, 1618 [i.e., ca. 1621]. Third edition.

Lof-sanck van Iesus Christus . . . Ende zyne andere Nederduytse poemata.
   Amsterdam: W. Janssen, 1622. Christ hymn prefaced to *Ned. Poem.;*
   this edition reprinted in 1650.
Bacchus en Christus. Twee Lofzangen van Daniel Heinsius. Ed. L. Ph.
   Rank, J. D. P. Warners, F. L. Zwaan. Zwolle: W. E. J. Tjeenk Willink,
   1965. Edition with commentary of Bacchus and Christ hymns.
Elegiarum lib. III. Monobiblos, Sylvae. Leiden: Joannes Maire, 1603. First
   ed. of the elegies and other Latin poems.
Poematum nova editio auctior emendatiorque. Leiden: J. Maire, 1606. Sec-
   ond edition; enlarged.
Poematum editio tertia; ita aucta et emendata. Leiden: J. Maire, 1610.
   Enlarged third edition.
Poemata emendata . . . et aucta. Leiden: J. Orlers and J. Maire, 1613.
   Fourth enlarged edition.
Poemata, emendata nunc postremo et aucta. Editio sexta. Leiden: J. Maire,
   1617. I.e., fifth revised edition.
Poematum editio nova. Accedunt . . . libri De contemptu mortis. Leiden:
   Elzevier and J. Maire, 1621. Sixth revised edition, issued with *On
   Contempt of Death.*
Poemata auctiora. Editore Nicolao Heinsio. Leiden: F. Heger, 1640.
   Seventh edition by son Nicolaas Heinsius.
Poemata Latina et Graeca; editio . . . postrema, longe auctior. Amsterdam:
   J. Janssen, 1649. Eighth and final edition. Reprinted Amsterdam,
   1666.
De contemptu mortis lib. IV. Leiden: Elzevier, 1621. *On Contempt of
   Death.*

Drama

*Auriacus sive libertas saucia. Accedunt . . . Iambi partim morales, partim ad
   amicos, partim amicorum causa scriptos.* Leiden: A. Cloucquius, 1602.
   William, or Wounded Liberty and occasional poems.
Herodes infanticida. Leiden: Elzevier, 1632. *Herod, Child Murderer.*

2. Prose

*Epistola, qua dissertationi D. Balsaci ad Heroden Infanticidam, respon-
   detur.* Leiden: Elzevier, 1636. Epistle in response to De Balzac's criticism of the Herod drama.
*Aristoteles: De poetica liber. Daniel Heinsius rec., ordini suo restituit, Lat.
   vertit, notas add. Acc. "De tragoediae constitutione."* Reprint of the
   1611 edition. Hildesheim, New York: Olms, 1976 (Documenta
   semiotica Ser. 2: Litteraria). Edition of Aristotle's *Poetics,* containing a

newly arranged text, notes, a Latin translation, and the treatise *On Tragedy* by Heinsius.

De tragoediae constitutione. Leiden: Elzevier, 1643. Revised version of 1611 treatise *On Tragedy*.

On Plot in Tragedy. Tr. Paul R. Sellin and John J. MacManmon. The Renaissance Editions, no. 5. Northridge, Ca.: San Fernando Valley State College, 1971. Translation of *De tragoediae constitutione* (1643) with introduction and notes.

Quintus Horatius Flaccus. Accedunt nunc . . . de satyra Horatiana libri duo. Leiden: Elzevier, 1629. Enlarged version of 1610 essay (revised 1612) "On Horatian Satire," appended to this famous Elzevier Horace.

Orationum editio nova. . . . Accedunt dissertationes aliquot, cum nonnullis praefationibus. Amsterdam: Elzevier, 1657. Most complete edition of orations, with some essays and prefaces, collected by Nicolaas H. It is based on the editions of 1609, 1612, 1615, 1620, 1627, 1642, and 1652.

The Value of History. Tr. George W. Robinson. Cambridge, Mass.: Privately printed, 1943. Translation of *De praestantia ac dignitate historiae*, 1614.

Funeral Orations on the Death of Joseph Scaliger by Daniel Heinsius and Dominicus Baudius. Tr. George W. Robinson. Cambridge: Harvard University Press, 1917. Translation of *In obitum Josephi Scaligeri*, 1609.

3. Other Primary Sources

BALZAC, J. L. Guez de. "Dissertation sur une tragédie de Monsieur Heinsius intitulée Herodes Infanticida." *Les Oeuvres diverses*. Leiden: Elzevier, 1658. Pp. 110–52.

Briefwisseling van Hugo Grotius. Ed. P. C. Molhuysen. 2 vols. The Hague: M. Nijhof, 1928.

Den Bloem-hof van de Nederlantsche Ieught naar de drukken van 1608 en 1610. Ed. L. M. van Dis, Jac. Smit. Amsterdam/Antwerp: Wereld Bibliotheek, 1955.

GROTIUS, Hugo. *Poemata collecta*. Leiden: A. Cloucquius, 1617.

[Janus Secundus] *Jean Second. Les Baisers et l'épithalame suivis des odes et des élégies*. Ed. Maurice Rat. Paris: Garnier, 1967.

[Meursius, Johannes.] *Illustrium Hollandiae et Westfrisiae ordinum alma academia Leidensis*. Leiden: J. Marcus, 1614. Autobiographical vitae—according to preface to 1625 edition—of Leiden professors, Heinsius, pp. 200–208.

Martin Opitz Teutsche Poemata. Abdruck der Ausgabe von 1624. Ed. Georg Witkowski. Neudrucke deutscher Literaturwerke des XVI. und XVII. Jahrhunderts, nos. 189–92. Halle, 1902.

MOLHUYSEN, P. C. *Bronnen tot de geschiedenis der Leidsche universiteit,* vol. I. The Hague: M. Nijhof, 1913.

Illustriss. viri Josephi Scaligeri, . . . epistolae omnes quae reperiri potuerant. Ed. D. Heinsius. Leiden: Elzevier, 1627.

Julius Caesar Scaliger. Poetices libri septem. Faksimile-Neudruck der Ausgabe von Lyon 1561. Ed. August Buck. Stuttgart: F. Frommann, 1964.

Thronus Cupidinis. Facsimile-uitgave van de derde druk, 1620. Introduction by H. de la Fontaine Verwey. Amsterdam: Universiteits-Bibliotheek, 1968.

SECONDARY SOURCES

(Specialized bibliographies in U. Bornemann, pp. 322–35; J. H. Meter, pp. 615–24; A. K. H. Moerman, pp. IX–XVI; and P. R. Sellin, *On Plot in Tragedy,* pp. 167–69)

BORNEMANN, ULRICH. *Anlehnung und Abrenzung. Untersuchungen zur Rezeption der niederländischen Literatur in der deutschen Dichtungsreform des siebzehnten Jahrhunderts.* Assen/Amsterdam: van Gorcum, 1976. Excellent study of Dutch influence, especially Heinsius', on early seventeenth century German literature, makes all previous ones obsolete.

BREUGELMANS, R. "Quaeris quid sit amor? Ascription, Date of Publication and Printer of the Earliest Emblem Book to be Written in Dutch." *Quaerendo,* 3 (1973), 281–90. Identification of Heinsius' emblem books.

CONRADY, KARL OTTO. *Lateinische Dichtungstradition und deutsche Lyrik des 17. Jahrhunderts.* Bonn: Bouvier, 1962. Formal discussion of Neo-Latin poetry; some references to Heinsius' style, pp. 114–83.

ELLINGER, GEORG. *Geschichte der neulateinischen Lyrik in den Niederlanden.* Geschichte der neulateinischen Literatur Deutschlands im sechzehnten Jahrhundert, vol. 3, pt. 1. Berlin/Leipzig: de Gruyter, 1933. Still most valuable, informative survey of Neo-Latin poetry, but lacks documentation of quotations and editions.

FONTAINE VERWEY, H. DE LA. "Notes on the début of Daniel Heinsius as a Dutch poet." *Quaerendo,* 3 (1973), 291–308. History of the emblem editions and *Nederduytsche Poemata* until 1621.

HORST, D. J. H. TER. *Daniel Heinsius (1580–1655).* Diss. Leiden. Utrecht, 1934. Most detailed biography to date; subjective judgments and negative attitude towards Heinsius the man, poet, and scholar.

KERN, EDITH G. *The Influence of Heinsius and Vossius upon French Dramatic Theory.* Johns Hopkins Studies in Romance Literatures and Languages, vol. 26. Baltimore: The Johns Hopkins Press, 1949. First major study on Heinsius' and G. Vossius' influence on French classicism.

LANDWEHR, JOHN. "De Gentse liefdesembleemdichters en D. P. Pers: het raadsel Theocritus à Ganda." *Tijdschrift voor Nederlandse taal- en letterkunde,* 85 (1969), 105–20. Wrongly identifies Theocritus à Ganda as Jacob de Vivere.

————. *Emblem Books in the Low Countries. 1554–1949. A Bibliography.* Utrecht: Dekker and Gumbert, 1970. A bibliography of Dutch emblem books; corrections concerning Heinsius in Breugelmans' review, *Quaerendo,* 5 (1975), 265–68.

Leiden University in the Seventeenth Century. Ed. Th. H. Lunsingh Scheurleer et al. Leiden: University Press, Brill, 1975. Magnificently illustrated and edited commemorative volume for the 400th anniversary of Leiden University; pertinent for Heinsius: "The Study of the New Testament" by H. J. de Jonge; "Classical Philology" by J. H. Waszink; "The Library" by E. Hulshoff-Pol.

MEERTENS, P. H. "De Groot en Heinsius en hun zeeuwse vrienden," *Archief. Vroegere en latere mededelingen voornamelijk in betrekking tot Zeeland* (1949–50), pp. 53–99.

METER, J. H. *De literaire theorieën van Daniël Heinsius. Een onderzoek naar de klassieke en humanistische bronnen van De Tragoediae Constitutione.* Amsterdam: Hakkert, 1975. Detailed study of Heinsius' literary theories, especially concerning tragedy.

PRAZ, MARIO. *Studies in Seventeenth-Century Imagery.* 2nd edition. Rome: Ed. di Storia e Letteratura, 1964. This classic on emblem books contains a source study of Heinsius' emblem series, pp. 88–98.

SCHÖNLE, GUSTAV. *Deutsch-niederländische Beziehungen in der Literatur des 17. Jahrhunderts.* Leidse Germanistische en Anglistische reeks, no. 7. Leiden: University Press of Leiden, 1968. Valuable survey of Dutch-German relations in the seventeenth century.

SELLIN, PAUL R. *Daniel Heinsius and Stuart England.* Leiden/London: Sir Thomas Browne Institute, 1968. Best biography of Heinsius followed by a study of English criticism and Heinsius, and a checklist of his works.

————. "Le pathétique retrouvé: Racine's Catharsis Reconsidered." *Modern Philology,* 70 (1973), 199–215. Lucid examination of Racine's indebtedness to *De tragoediae constitutione.*

————. "The First Collection of Dutch Love Emblems. The Identity of Theocritus à Ganda." *Modern Language Review,* 66 (1971), 332–43. Convincingly refutes Landwehr; evaluates Heinsius' Dutch work.

SMIT, W. A. P. *De dichter Revius.* Diss. Leiden. Amsterdam, 1928. Survey of Heinsius' life and Dutch poetry, pp. 44–81.

VAN ES, G. A. et al. *De letterkunde van renaissance en barok in de zeventiende eeuw.* Part I. Geschiedenis van de letterkunde der Nederlan-

den, vol. 4. Brussels, 's Hertogenbosch: Teuling's and Standaard
Boekhandel, n.d. Most comprehensive of the standard histories of
Dutch literature for the seventeenth century, on Daniel Heinsius'
Dutch works, pp. 19–32.

VERMASEREN, B. A. "Humanistische drama's over de moord op de vader
des vaderlands." *Tijdschrift voor Nederlandse taal en letterkunde*, 58
(1951), 31–67.

VRIES,' A. G. C. DE. *De Nederlandsche emblemata. Geschiedenis en bib-
liographie tot de 18e eeuw*. Diss. Amsterdam: Ten Brink, 1899. Still
important for bibliography of Heinsius' emblem books and *Ned.
Poem*.

WEEVERS, THEODOOR. *Poetry of the Netherlands in its European Context
1170–1930*. London: The Athlone Press, 1960. On Heinsius, pp. 64–
101. Very readable account of Dutch poetry with sample texts, translation; Weever's previous specialized studies on Heinsius' and German
literature have been incorporated.

YOUSSEF, ZOBEIDAH. *Polémique et littérature chez Guez de Balzac*. Paris:
Nizet, 1972. Most detailed account of the Heinsius-De Balzac quarrel,
pp. 117–64.

Index

177